RECONSTRUCTING THE NATIONAL BANK CONTROVERSY

RECONSTRUCTING THE NATIONAL BANK CONTROVERSY

Politics and Law in the Early American Republic

ERIC LOMAZOFF

THE UNIVERSITY OF CHICAGO PRESS

CHICAGO AND LONDON

The University of Chicago Press, Chicago 60637
The University of Chicago Press, Ltd., London
© 2018 by The University of Chicago
Published 2018
Printed in the United States of America

27 26 25 24 23 22 21 20 19 18   1 2 3 4 5

ISBN-13: 978-0-226-57931-3 (cloth)
ISBN-13: 978-0-226-57945-0 (paper)
ISBN-13: 978-0-226-57959-7 (e-book)
DOI: https://doi.org/10.7208/chicago/9780226579597.001.0001

Library of Congress Cataloging-in-Publication Data

Names: Lomazoff, Eric, author.
Title: Reconstructing the national bank controversy : politics and law in the early
    American Republic / Eric Lomazoff.
Description: Chicago : The University of Chicago Press, 2018. | Includes
    bibliographical references and index.
Identifiers: LCCN 2018017410 | ISBN 9780226579313 (cloth : alk. paper) |
    ISBN 9780226579450 (pbk. : alk. paper) | ISBN 9780226579597 (e-book)
Subjects: LCSH: Bank of the United States (1791–1811)—History. | Bank of the
    United States (1816–1836)—History. | Constitutional history—United States. |
    Law—Political aspects—United States—History—19th century. | Banking law—
    United States—History—19th century.
Classification: LCC HG2529 .L66 2018 | DDC 346/.082—dc23
LC record available at https://lccn.loc.gov/2018017410

⊗ This paper meets the requirements of ANSI/NISO Z39.48-1992 (Permanence
of Paper).

TO MY DEAR KATE

CONTENTS

ACKNOWLEDGMENTS

This book has its origins in research conducted within the Department of Government at Harvard University. The scholars who so ably advised me there included two political scientists, Daniel Carpenter and Nancy Rosenblum, and one economic historian, Robert E. Wright. Each offered unstinting support for a project that lay somewhat outside his or her already-sizable intellectual wheelhouse, and I will always be grateful for these acts of generosity.

Over the years, a number of other scholars have read and commented on various versions of the arguments found here. For that I am grateful to Alan Gibson, Mark Graber, Peter A. Hall, Richard John, Sandy Levinson, Julie Novkov, Stephen Skowronek, Kathleen Thelen, Justin Wert, and Emily Zackin.

Support from a number of institutions facilitated the research and writing that led to this book. These include Harvard's Center for American Political Studies (where Lilia Halpern-Smith did yeoman's work), the Miller Center of Public Affairs at the University of Virginia (where Brian Balogh and Sid Milkis deserve special thanks), and the University of Oklahoma College of Arts and Sciences (which provided a Junior Faculty Summer Fellowship following my first year as a faculty member).

It is a privilege to teach, write, and serve at Villanova University. My colleagues in the Department of Political Science render working at Villanova a true pleasure as well. David Barrett and Catherine Warrick warrant special mention here, as they took the time to mentor a junior colleague during his first days at the university. While their mentorship continues, I cherish the fact that it has been supplemented by real friendship. Speaking of which: coffee in the department lounge in five minutes?

With respect to mentors and friends, I also need to acknowledge three fellow travelers in the world of American constitutionalism. Justin Wert is no Louis Brandeis, and I am surely no Felix Frankfurter, but I like to think that Brandeis's conception of Frankfurter as "half brother, half son" nicely captures my relationship to Justin; he has been helping me to navigate the world of public law (not to mention life generally) for close to twenty years now. While I probably would have encountered Emily Zackin at some point as a political scientist, our chance meeting at the 2010 Policy History Conference in Columbus offered me an early introduction to a very talented colleague and an even better friend. And long before the national bank controversy was on my radar, Will Harris taught me about the Constitution for the first time.

I owe a special debt of gratitude to Chuck Myers at the University of Chicago Press. The journey from submitted manuscript and peer review through contract and publication was, in my case, especially long and bumpy. More to the point, the ultimate completion of that journey owes much to Chuck's belief in (and support for) the project. For assistance between contract and publication, a number of other individuals working at or with the press—Holly Smith, Christine Schwab, Carol McGillivray, and Melinda Kennedy among them—are also deserving of my heartfelt thanks.

To write publicly about Kate McKinley is to invite private scandal, as she would surely prefer that most of the world know as little about her as possible. The small circle in which this monograph will probably travel should allay most of her concern. As for the rest, an opportunity to celebrate her leaves me eager to court domestic disaster. The gift of Kate's love has changed me forever, and it has made possible not simply this book but (far more importantly) the life we share beyond it. For me at least, the most important words in *Reconstructing the National Bank Controversy* are the four on the dedication page.

Eric Lomazoff
Bryn Mawr, Pennsylvania
January 2018

Getting the Ship out of the Bottle

The Conventional Wisdom

In 1791, Secretary of State Thomas Jefferson picked up where several members of Congress had left off, arguing to President George Washington that Congress could not charter a national bank under the Necessary and Proper Clause. In response, Treasury Secretary Alexander Hamilton offered the president a broader interpretation of congressional power under that provision. Washington proceeded to sign the bill that had inspired the dispute, and the Bank of the United States was born. In 1811, its charter expired.

In 1819, lawyers for the state of Maryland found themselves repeating Jefferson's argument, this time to the Supreme Court. Unsurprisingly, counsel for their opponent—a national bank chartered in 1816 and bearing the same name as its predecessor—echoed Hamilton's claims. Chief Justice John Marshall, writing for a unanimous Court in McCulloch v. Maryland, *affirmed the institution's legitimacy and offered a decidedly Hamiltonian take on the meaning of the so-called Sweeping Clause.*

In 1832, Congress passed legislation extending the life of the second Bank beyond 1836, when its charter was set to expire. President Andrew Jackson vetoed the bill and issued a lengthy message justifying his decision. After stressing that the Supreme Court's decision in McCulloch *did not preclude his own constitutional judgment, Jackson explained why he considered the Bank of the United States both "unnecessary" and "improper."*

Ask any scholar of American constitutionalism for a decent capsule summary of the national bank debate, and you will probably receive something quite close to the foregoing account. If he or she is inclined toward a pithier response, you will simply be told that the Bank served as the recurring touchstone for a two-sided debate over how to interpret the Necessary and Proper Clause.[1] Briefer still would be a claim that federal officials spent forty years arguing over the meaning of the word *necessary*.

On the assumption that nearly every response to your query would vary only with respect to length, we can draw two immediate conclusions. First, the Bank controversy is a kind of "set piece" in the constitutional history of the Early American Republic.[2] Every scholar tells some version of the same basic story. Second, the defining feature of that story is stability over time. The terms of the constitutional conflict never change, only the participants.

This is not a book about how the set piece emerged.[3] This is a book about why the set piece fails to capture the *full* Bank controversy. In fact, it does not even come close.

The traditional account is easy to engage with. It imbues at least a small portion of our constitutional history with a real sense of order. And, regardless of your own position on the meaning of the Necessary and Proper Clause, there are "good guys" to be found.

This book offers a far more robust account of the constitutional politics of national banking between 1791 and 1832. My account is harder to engage with, in part because it shows that the Coinage Clause of Article I, Section 8—Congress's power to "coin Money, regulate the Value thereof"— was as crucial to the constitutional action as the Sweeping Clause.[4] It draws belated attention to the less-than-orderly manner in which three forces—gradual change within the Bank itself, growing tensions over federal power among Republicans, and the endurance of monetary turmoil beyond the War of 1812—worked to reshape the constitutional debate during the early to mid-1810s. By the time John Marshall penned *McCulloch*, we had something close to an agreement between Republicans and Federalists that a national bank was constitutional, yet deep disagreement as to why that was so—precisely the sort of middle ground that can belie a clear distinction between good guys and bad guys.

To recast the Bank debate in this manner is also to powerfully reinforce (and, I will argue, refine) the proposition that our constitutional conflicts are routinely shaped as much by politics as by law. Institutional change, partisan infighting, and the economic consequences of war should strike readers as the everyday stuff of politics. These forces drove the development of our first major debate over the scope of federal power at least as much as the formal dimensions of the Constitution (for example, its failure to identify a supreme interpreter) or the absence of a shared legal definition for the word *necessary*. In that sense, this book renders the Bank controversy even more foundational to American constitutionalism than it already is.

FIRST CENTRAL ARGUMENT: THE
BANK DEBATE WAS DYNAMIC

Our standard narrative of the Bank debate, to borrow a metaphor recently employed by Pamela Brandwein, is akin to a "ship in a bottle"; it is a structure "so firmly established that it look[s] as though it always must have been just as it [is]."[5] My first central argument[6] is that this narrative needs to come out of its "bottle of validity."[7] The claims respecting Congress's power (or lack thereof) to charter the institution were constantly evolving between 1791 and 1832, and at no point during this period were they limited to one broad and one strict interpretation of the Necessary and Proper Clause.

The case for dispensing with our traditional account begins in 1791, when the opponents of Secretary Hamilton's national bank bill offered not one but several strict interpretations of the Sweeping Clause. Hamilton and others had claimed that the provision authorized Congress to enact any law that would contribute to, or be useful for, the exercise of an enumerated power. Because a national bank would facilitate the collection of taxes and the borrowing of money, their argument went, a law creating one was "necessary" for executing those Article I powers.

The bill's opponents uniformly rejected this broad interpretation. Agreement on what the Necessary and Proper Clause actually meant proved more elusive. All of them suggested, in language that varied slightly from person to person, that a law was not "necessary" unless the means chosen bore a very close relationship to the authorized end. The standard narrative treats every 1791 national bank opponent as making this claim and this claim *alone*. Several elected and unelected officials went further, however, arguing that Congress also had to lack viable alternatives for achieving the end in question. One member of the House even went so far as to supplement these two requirements with a third: Congress was restricted to the means typically employed by other governments in pursuit of a given end.

Our traditional account takes little notice of 1811, a year that saw both an extended congressional debate over the Bank's constitutionality and convergence among the institution's opponents on a particular interpretation of the Sweeping Clause. The Bank of the United States had received a twenty-year charter in 1791, and its directors petitioned Congress for an extension of the same as 1811 approached. The ensuing debate saw at least thirty-five federal lawmakers speak to the constitutional question.[8] The Bank's supporters continued to uniformly insist that because the institution contributed to the management of the federal government's fiscal affairs, it was "necessary" for executing one or more Article I powers. This time around, only a handful of their opponents offered up the stand-alone complaint that "necessary" means had to more or less directly achieve an end (rather than merely facilitate its achievement). By contrast, many more Bank critics tested the institution against both this requirement *and* the requirement that Congress lack alternative means for achieving the same end. These lawmakers concluded, almost to a man, that in 1811 a national bank met neither condition.

The standard Bank narrative also treats 1816 as a year of little constitutional import, despite the fact that federal lawmakers both revived the institution and managed to do so while saying nary a word about the Necessary and Proper Clause. The Bank of the United States shuttered its doors in March 1811 after Congress narrowly rejected a charter extension bill, but its death ultimately proved short-lived. In December 1815, Treasury Secretary Alexander J. Dallas proposed legislation to charter a new national bank. A bill to this effect was introduced in late February 1816 and became law less than two months later. Neither Secretary Dallas nor the lawmakers who shepherded the bill through Congress had suggested that it was "necessary" for collecting taxes or borrowing money. Instead, they argued that it exercised Congress's power to "coin Money, regulate the Value thereof." Whether this meant that the power to coin money was being directly exercised, or that a national bank was manifestly "necessary" for exercising the same, was never made clear. The result, however, was all too clear: Congress had chartered a national bank with recourse to the Coinage Clause and *without* a third round of debate over the meaning of the Sweeping Clause.

Because our traditional account ignores the fact that the national bank was rebuilt on novel constitutional ground in 1816, it naturally fails to recognize that the Supreme Court all but openly rejected the Coinage Clause argument in deciding McCulloch v. Maryland *(1819).* After the Bank of the United States challenged the constitutionality of Maryland's 1818 tax on it, John Marshall and his colleagues agreed to hear the dispute. In doing so, however, the Marshall Court also requested oral argument on a second (and logically prior) question: Was the Bank itself constitutional? In answering this question, counsel on both sides eschewed discussion of

Congress's recent reliance on the Coinage Clause, opting instead to revive older claims about the Bank's necessity (or lack thereof) for exercising other Article I powers. Marshall's ensuing opinion for the Court was also silent with respect to Congress's power to coin money. While his holding that Congress was empowered to charter the Bank may not have rested principally on the Necessary and Proper Clause,[9] the opinion nonetheless embraced a broad interpretation of the same. The chief justice's case for that interpretation included an assertion that the existence of alternative means for achieving an enumerated end could have "no possible influence" on the question of whether Congress's chosen means were "necessary."[10]

Our standard narrative stresses that President Jackson judged the Bank "unnecessary" in rejecting 1832 legislation to extend its charter but fails to acknowledge that his veto message explicitly addressed the Coinage Clause as an alternative anchor for the institution. The Court's decision in *McCulloch* hardly sounded the death knell for claims respecting Congress's power to coin money. After Jackson's first message to Congress (December 1829) questioned the Bank's constitutionality, a House committee offered mere recognition to the argument that the institution was "necessary" for collecting taxes and borrowing money but open support for the idea that it was valid under the Coinage Clause. When Congress considered a bill to extend the national bank's charter a few years later, the most frequent constitutional claim on behalf of the institution concerned the power to coin money. After passage of the bill, President Jackson justified his decision to veto it by suggesting both that he was free under *McCulloch* to evaluate the Bank's necessity and that Congress had overstepped (or, barring that, improperly delegated) its power under the Coinage Clause.

SECOND CENTRAL ARGUMENT: ORDINARY POLITICS DROVE MUCH OF THAT DYNAMISM

If the debate over a national bank was dynamic, then it makes sense to ask why that was the case. My second central argument is that much of the variation in constitutional interpretation that we observe between 1791 and 1832 is attributable to forces that have little to do with the Constitution or law more broadly: institutional change, ideological conflict, and economic stress.[11] As we will see, these three forces—sometimes alone and sometimes in combination—repeatedly reshaped the terms on which the Bank's constitutionality was contested. The influence of ordinary politics on constitutional argument during this period was hardly complete,

however. Those who participated in post-1816 debates over the Bank's constitutionality, for example, largely picked and chose from the smorgasbord
of arguments already in existence, and I will argue that their basic ability
to do so flowed from the Constitution itself.

To capture the effect of ordinary politics on the national bank debate,
we need to document where those three dimensions of the polity[12] stood
in early 1791 as well as how they changed over time and then trace the
manner in which those changes periodically led federal officials to prioritize, invent, discard, or merely select among certain claims about constitutional meaning.[13] This book both documents and traces, but the former
in particular will require—and I intend this as part description and part
disclaimer—that we sometimes go for lengthy stretches far from the Constitution or disputes over its meaning.

*Our baseline institutional, ideological, and economic conditions are
those under which the 1791 national bank debate took place.* The young
republic was at peace in February 1791, and prices for goods and services
were relatively stable.[14] American banking was still very much in its in-
fancy, as just three cities (Boston, Philadelphia, and Baltimore) played host
to banks authorized by their respective state governments and none of
those institutions had more than $2 million in capital.[15] The First Con-
gress was not yet formally organized along party lines, but both chambers were controlled by members who generally took a capacious view
of federal power and would subsequently affiliate with the Federalists.[16]
Given the ideological conditions in particular, it is hardly surprising that
Secretary Hamilton's proposal for a $10 million national bank to support
the federal government's fiscal operations was able to withstand a constitutional challenge in the House. As for the character of that challenge
(to recall, a number of strict interpretations of the Sweeping Clause were
offered in 1791), we need to remember that this debate represented the first
postratification opportunity for federal officials to float ideas respecting
the provision's meaning. As such, it makes sense that those who opposed
a national bank (and agonized to varying degrees about future exercises of
federal power) used the occasion to test out different conceptions of constitutional necessity.

*Altered ideological and institutional conditions led participants in the
Bank debate of 1811 to focus on the relevance of alternative means for
discerning constitutional necessity.* The years between 1791 and 1811 witnessed not simply the birth of the Republican party and its seizure of both
Congress and the presidency in the elections of 1800 but the subsequent ap-

pearance of serious divisions among its members over the legitimate scope of federal power.[17] Running parallel to these ideological developments was a slow but steady diminution of the national bank's industry dominance. While the Bank of the United States had but a handful of competitors upon birth and controlled roughly 70 percent of total industry capital, by 1811 the number of state banks had crossed the century mark and Hamilton's brainchild appeared less a financial leviathan and more the biggest fish in an increasingly crowded pond.[18] I demonstrate that these ideological and institutional changes bear primary responsibility for the fact that the 1811 debate over the Bank's constitutionality meaningfully departed from its 1791 predecessor. The constitutional critics in Congress now not only enjoyed strength in numbers but displayed newfound agreement on textual meaning: Because the Bank was not closely related to one or more enumerated powers, and a network of state banks could be employed to manage the federal government's fiscal affairs, the institution met *neither* requirement imposed by the Necessary and Proper Clause.

Those who revived a national bank in 1816 went where no constitutional interpreters had gone before—a journey that began with economic crisis and continued through both institutional change and ideological accommodation. After British forces climbed the Chesapeake Bay and assaulted the nation's capital in August 1814, most state banks located south and west of New England quickly suspended the payment of specie for their notes and checks.[19] The value of this paper quickly depreciated, and millions of Americans who used said paper were just as quickly introduced to price inflation.[20] Citizens cared less about the wartime onset of inflation, however, than its endurance beyond the Treaty of Ghent. When state banks proved unwilling to resume specie payments on their own, I will argue, Republicans in Congress looked to the past for a solution. There had been a *second* slow-moving change in the national bank between 1791 and 1811: The institution had developed the capacity to regulate its state-chartered peers, or force them to observe some proportion between their specie reserves and their lending.[21] The resulting hope among Republican lawmakers was that a revived Bank would bring the state institutions to heel. This scheme furnished no solution to their constitutional problem, however. In 1811, the party's deep divisions over federal power had been on full display. The war and its aftermath had reconciled many Republicans to a national bank, but not to federal power more broadly. Could the institution be revived *without* embracing a broad interpretation of the Sweeping Clause—that is, without seeming to sanction things such as fed-

eral support for internal improvements or a ban on slavery in federal territories? I demonstrate that leading party members cut this Gordian knot
by presenting their national bank bill in novel constitutional terms: as an
exercise of Congress's power to "coin Money, regulate the Value thereof."

While legal factors explain the Supreme Court's ability in McCulloch
*(1819) to opt for one understanding of the Bank's constitutionality over
another, the reason it chose the Necessary and Proper Clause remains unclear.* Three years after Congress revived the Bank of the United States
under the Coinage Clause, the Court asked anew whether the Constitution empowered federal lawmakers to charter the institution. Even if John
Marshall and his colleagues were to conclude (as they did) that the Bank
was constitutional, they were hardly obligated to do so for the reason
laid out by Congress. I will argue that two features of the Constitution—
Article VI's requirement that all federal judges (not to mention federal
lawmakers) be "bound by Oath or Affirmation" to support it and its failure to identify a supreme interpreter—are responsible for this fact. Taken
together, these features empowered the justices to reach their *own* conclusions with respect to the textual anchor for congressional activity. Law
can only reliably explain so much of *McCulloch*, however. It cannot, for
example, necessarily solve a mystery of judicial behavior that this book
introduces: *Why* did the Court discard Congress's understanding of the
Bank's constitutionality in favor of an understanding that partook (at least
in part) of Secretary Hamilton's 1791 reasoning?

*In 1832, a confluence of law and ideology led Congress to reassert the
national bank's constitutionality under the Coinage Clause, and this move
all but forced the institution's leading antagonist to author a veto message that engaged multiple claims respecting textual meaning.* Just as the
Constitution did not compel the Supreme Court (in deciding *McCulloch*)
to follow Congress's 1816 understanding of the Bank's constitutionality,
it did not compel members of a post-*McCulloch* Congress to follow the
Court's understanding of the same. The Democrats who controlled Congress in 1832 were, like many of the mid-1810s Republicans from whom
they descended,[22] wary of an active federal government but generally convinced of a national bank's importance. This ideological orientation, I argue, led them to eschew *McCulloch*'s reasoning and pass legislation for
extending the Bank's life on the same constitutional terms as their partisan ancestors had given that life in 1816. The behavior of congressional
Democrats left President Jackson in a bind. To veto the charter extension
as beyond the scope of federal power, he would need to address two very
different accounts of the Bank's constitutionality: one furnished by the

Court and a second by Congress itself. This is precisely what Jackson's veto message did.

THIRD CENTRAL ARGUMENT: THE BANK DEBATE REINFORCES AND REFINES THE ROLE OF ORDINARY POLITICS IN CONSTITUTIONAL DEVELOPMENT

This book is about more, however, than jettisoning our traditional account of the Bank debate in favor of a more dynamic constitutional conflict shaped in large part by ordinary politics. My third and final central argument is that this account of the national bank controversy works to both reinforce and refine the general proposition that such politics are important drivers of American constitutional development. With respect to reinforcement, the Bank debate was already foundational to American constitutionalism in that it was "the most important and sustained . . . controversy in the early republic over how strictly [federal power] should be construed."[23] This book *burnishes* that status by casting the means by which this controversy developed as a veritable sampling of the broader range of forces that would shape constitutional politics going forward and down to the present day. As for refinement, my account works to both sharpen our understanding of ideological conflict and economic stress as agents of constitutional development and offer slow-moving institutional change a place in that same category.

Consider, for example, my claim that ideological conflict among Republicans over the scope of federal power worked to reshape the Bank debate, especially between 1811 and 1816. Students of American constitutionalism have long been familiar with the notion that tension within "political regimes," or party coalitions with long-term control over the government's "basic commitments of ideology and interest,"[24] can drive constitutional development. The standard claim here is that regime leaders will encourage federal courts, which they have staffed with an eye to advancing the regime's "vision of constitutional governance,"[25] to act whenever pieces of that vision divide members to the point of inhibiting legislative and/or executive action.[26] My account of the Bank debate reaffirms the importance of intraparty conflict for constitutional development while denying that deference to the judiciary is the *only* option for divided regimes. They are also free to broker internal compromises on questions of constitutional governance, though federal courts (as *McCulloch* reveals) are not obliged to honor them.

This book offers similar confirmation for (and amendment to) the claim that economic forces have meaningfully shaped constitutional politics. On the one hand, three major flash points in American constitutional history—1787, the mid- to late 1860s, and 1937—already speak to the salience of these forces. State legislatures enjoyed almost "limitless power to embargo or slap fees on imports, exports, or vessels from other countries or states" in the 1780s, and the resulting slew of protectionist laws both helped to produce the Constitutional Convention and led to its delegates' call for federal power to "regulate Commerce with foreign Nations, and among the several States[.]"[27] The Civil War, which wrought enough constitutional change to qualify as a second founding,[28] sprang at least in part from Southern anxiety that the 1860 election of Abraham Lincoln (coupled with the rise of Republican majorities in both the House and Senate) posed an existential threat to slavery, the primary source of labor for its agricultural economy.[29] And the Supreme Court's early twentieth-century police powers jurisprudence, whether conceived as the expression of a free-market ideology or as a principled effort to weed out "class" legislation, was "complicated and ultimately derailed" by industrialization, or "the maturation of capitalist forms of production[.]"[30] Appreciation for the role of economic forces in shaping high-profile "constitutional moments,"[31] however, may blind us to the fact that these forces also drive more run-of-the-mill constitutional development. My account of the national bank's rebirth supplies an important corrective here by tying the appearance of the Coinage Clause argument in part to the price inflation that lingered beyond the February 1815 cessation of hostilities with Great Britain.

Far more novel is my suggestion that gradual change in an institution once subject to constitutional challenge can alter the terms of future debate over its status. The study of slow-moving institutional transformations sprang from a perception that students of comparative political economy were too preoccupied with a model of institutional change in which "long periods of . . . stasis" were separated by much shorter periods of "radical reorganization."[32] To my knowledge, no one has made the case that this scholarship is relevant for the study of American constitutionalism. I make that case here, drawing attention to slow-moving transformations in the Bank and (more importantly) their downstream effects on its constitutional politics. The institution underwent two gradual changes between 1791 and 1811—*drift* from its initial position of market dominance and *conversion* into a regulator of state banks[33]—and my estimate of their respective roles in shaping future iterations of the Bank debate is reflected in the fact that each receives chapter-length treatment.

For several decades now, students of American constitutionalism have been hammering away at the idea that important developments in our constitutional practice take place "outside the courts" or "law" more broadly defined.[34] My account of the Bank controversy fits squarely in this tradition, calling attention to the developmental import of institutions, ideology, and economics without denying the importance of law. By the same token, however, it also reminds us that general propositions respecting the influence of ordinary politics must remain open to both amendment and expansion. Divided regimes do not always punt the ball to courts; they sometimes call the constitutional version of an audible. Smaller waves of constitutional development, not simply tsunamis, hit our shores when economic energy is released. And when the object at the center of a constitutional controversy changes, we cannot act surprised when a future conversation about its status follows suit.

A BRIEF OVERVIEW

The organization of this book is somewhat irregular, and the device that opens a number of its chapters also warrants comment. Because changes in the Bank following its 1791 birth had such a significant effect on subsequent debates over its status, they must be documented *within* a broader retelling of its constitutional history. I have chosen to do this by recounting the 1791 debate (chapter 1), pausing to consider the institution's transformations over the following two decades (chapters 2 and 3), and then examining the constitutional effects of these and other forces between 1811 and 1832 (chapters 4 through 7). The procession here is thus chronological without being exclusively constitutional.

I opened this book with a vignette that captures our traditional account of the national bank debate. Vignettes, I hasten to add, also open every chapter save chapter 2, chapter 3, and the conclusion. Their purpose in these contexts is more specialized than it is here: confronting readers with the conventional wisdom respecting *a given round* of the national bank controversy. Their use is inspired by the chapter-opening vignettes in *A Monarchy Transformed*, Mark Kishlansky's chronicle of constitutional development in seventeenth-century Britain. That fact would be unimportant save Kishlansky's frank acknowledgment that the device would "not be to everyone's taste, especially those who already know the details."[35] I suspect that some readers of this book will feel precisely the same way about repeatedly encountering the conventional wisdom. Those with limited knowledge of constitutional history will benefit from the vignettes, however, as will anyone interested in appreciating time and again just how far our traditional account of the Bank debate deviates from the historical reality.

The details of my second central argument obviate the need for an extended outline of the chapters to follow. Chapter 1 reviews the opening act of the Bank's constitutional drama, a cross-branch debate set in the waning days of the First Congress (1789–1791). Chapter 2 offers the first of two sustained assaults on the traditional (if largely implicit) assumption that the Bank was an unchanging institution, describing its drift from industry dominance. Chapter 3 follows up by exploring the national bank's conversion from a purely fiscal instrument to one with both fiscal and monetary functions.

We begin to see the constitutional effects of these and other developments in chapter 4, which focuses on the Bank's ill-fated struggle to win a charter extension from the Eleventh Congress (1809–1811). Institutional death gives way to resurrection in chapter 5, an outcome facilitated by a constitutional compromise among members of the Fourteenth Congress (1815–1817). Members of the Supreme Court ignored their account of the Bank's constitutionality in *McCulloch v. Maryland* (1819) but still managed to offer the institution judicial validation, and I offer a reassessment of this landmark Supreme Court decision in chapter 6. We see competing legislative and judicial understandings of the Bank's status again in chapter 7, where I examine both the context and reasons for President Jackson's decision to veto the charter-extending legislation passed by the Twenty-Second Congress (1831–1833). I conclude the book by explaining how its more robust account of the national bank's affairs helps us to understand the constitutional basis for modern American monetary politics.

CHAPTER ONE

Varieties of Strict Interpretation

The Conventional Wisdom

Despite a constitutional challenge from James Madison and several other members of the House of Representatives—a challenge rooted in a strict interpretation of the Necessary and Proper Clause—that chamber passed, in early February 1791, "[a]n act to incorporate the subscribers to the Bank of the United States." Given the Senate's passage of the same bill nearly three weeks earlier, it soon landed on the desk of President George Washington. The president, per Article I, Section 7 of the Constitution, had ten days to sign the Bank bill, return it to Congress with his objections, or let it become law via inaction. Sundays were constitutionally excepted from this window, and Washington understood his signature or veto to be due by the close of congressional business on Friday, February 25.[1]

By the time Washington received the Bank bill, two additional documents were already in his possession: short memoranda from Attorney General Edmund Randolph. Both were authored on February 12, both expressed doubt about congressional power to charter the Bank, and both did so along the constitutional lines traced by Madison and his House colleagues. Secretary of State Thomas Jefferson's comparable constitutional qualms arrived in written form the following day. With his veto clock continuing to tick, on Wednesday, February 16, Washington forwarded the Randolph and Jefferson memoranda to Treasury Secretary Alexander Hamilton.[2]

Accompanying these memoranda was nothing less than an essay prompt for Hamilton and a fast-approaching due date. "[T]he Secretary of State and the Attorney General dispute the constitutionality of the act," wrote Washington. "[B]efore I express any opinion of my own, I give you an opportunity of examining and answering the objections contained in the enclosed papers." The opinions of Jefferson and Randolph having been "submitted in writing," those of Hamilton were now required.[3]

On Monday, February 21—five days after receiving his prompt and mere days before Washington's decision was due—Hamilton wrote the president with apologies, promises, and justifications befitting the modern undergraduate. Writing about himself in the third person, the Treasury secretary requested the president's "indulgence for not having yet finished his reasons on a certain point. He has been ever since sedulously engaged in it, but finds it impossible to complete before Tuesday evening, or Wednesday morning early. He is anxious to give the point a thorough examination."[4]

Unsurprisingly, the president saw nothing from his Treasury secretary on Tuesday night. The evening at 79 Third Street in Philadelphia was an especially long one, stretching well into Wednesday morning. Hamilton, of course, was laboring against a Friday constitutional deadline that offered neither sympathy nor the possibility of extension—nor much time for Washington to read and effectively grade his work. Accordingly, Eliza Hamilton "sat up all night" with her husband to help him defend a broad interpretation of the Necessary and Proper Clause. She copied out his writing—nearly 13,000 words, or enough to fill almost forty double-spaced pages in modern academic formatting—and had it ready for early-morning delivery. The note accompanying Hamilton's submission captures the essence of the Early American Republic's great all-nighter: "The Secretary of the Treasury presents his respects to the President, and sends him the opinion required, which occupied him the greatest part of last night."[5] *Two days later, Alexander Hamilton received the only written feedback he desired: Washington's signature on the Bank bill.*

The foregoing account of the national bank's 1791 journey from bill to law is far from novel. Though I supplied the ornamentation of academic life,[6] a basic confrontation between strict and broad interpretations of the Necessary and Proper Clause is the constitutional core of an early Bank narrative widely shared among legal scholars, political scientists, and historians.[7] The strict/broad dichotomy, however, ultimately obscures far more than it reveals.[8]

A careful rereading of the 1791 debates (in both Congress and the executive branch) reveals a surprising fact about the first iteration of the national bank controversy. Those who opposed the proposal for a Bank of the United States on constitutional grounds actually staked out a *variety* of positions respecting the meaning of the Sweeping Clause. That is to say, far from participating in an echo chamber that effectively recirculated a single strict interpretation of the provision, these elected and appointed officials invoked—sometimes alone, sometimes in combination—three different standards of constitutional necessity. I will refer to these as the *functional, federal,* and *frequency* standards.

When combinations of these three standards are considered along-side single-prong arguments, it becomes apparent that the six men who spoke and wrote against a national bank's constitutionality in 1791 (House members James Jackson, James Madison, Michael Jenifer Stone, and William Branch Giles, along with Attorney General Edmund Randolph and Secretary of State Thomas Jefferson) actually offered three distinct interpretations of the Necessary and Proper Clause. In short, far from wielding a single interpretive weapon, the national bank's opponents seemed inclined to throw everything but the kitchen sink at it.

This variation in constitutional argumentation has gone almost entirely unappreciated, and documenting it is the principal objective of this chapter.[9] While recognition of constitutional history's fine details is valuable in its own right, I have a second, forward-looking purpose in mind. A detailed accounting of the 1791 arguments will serve as a crucial (if partial) prologue to chapter 4, where I review the constitutional debate of 1811. That debate was anything but a simple rerun of its 1791 edition. It was far longer (more than thirty members of Congress gave floor speeches addressing the constitutional question), was conducted not against a clean slate but in the shadow of its predecessor, and saw most recharter opponents—all of whom were members of the Republican party, which formed not long after the 1791 debate—line up behind a single interpretation of the Sweeping Clause. This chapter, then, is designed to both record fine details and facilitate a later comparison between the constitutional debates of 1791 and 1811.

IMPROVING PUBLIC CREDIT AND FINANCIAL ADMINISTRATION

The federal government that first opened its doors in the spring of 1789 was hardly the picture of short- or long-term fiscal health. With respect to the former, though bills for basic operational expenses were entirely predictable, members of the First Congress spent their early days in office debating questions of procedure (e.g., how to address the president[10]) rather than procuring necessary revenue. In fact, it was not until July 1789 that Congress first flexed its most prominent new constitutional muscle: the power to lay and collect taxes. Two revenue bills were passed that month and signed by President Washington—the Tariff Act and the Tonnage Act[11]—but their initial yields were more trickles than streams. On September 13—just his third day in office as Treasury secretary—Alexander Hamilton had to ask the Philadelphia-based Bank of North America for a short-term loan to fund the federal government.[12]

Meeting basic expenses with new revenue, however, would solve only *part* of the new government's fiscal problem. Long-unpaid debts from the Revolutionary War totaled roughly $79 million at face value, with $54 million owed by the United States and the balance by the thirteen states.[13] The total figure, moreover, said little "about the actual market value of the debt," since holders and potential purchasers had little knowledge of when interest on these securities (let alone the principal) would be paid.[14] Primary and secondary sources estimate the market value of many forms of Revolutionary War debt in the mid- to late 1780s at somewhere between ten and twenty cents on the dollar.[15]

As Hamilton would write in early 1790, "immutable principles of moral obligation" compelled the federal government to repay those who had supported the war effort.[16] However, there was also an important instrumental reason to service (and ultimately repay) these debts: protection of the federal government's ability to borrow in the future.[17] As any modern American will attest, one way to raise an individual credit score (and keep it elevated) is to consistently make payments on outstanding debt. Conversely, the road to poor credit—and its most natural consequence, difficulty in borrowing—lay in irregular debt payments (or none at all). In 1789, the aforementioned war debts left the new federal government with poor credit; though not technically bankrupt, it was certainly not in a position to borrow at favorable rates of interest.[18]

Wholly cognizant of the distressed state of public credit, the House (in late September 1789) directed the new Treasury secretary to "prepare a plan" for its improvement and deliver that plan at the next session of Congress.[19] Hamilton's resulting *Report on Public Credit* (January 9, 1790) offered three core suggestions for placing the federal government in a position to borrow—when borrowing became necessary—"upon good terms." First, the unpaid war debts of the states should be "assumed" by the federal government. Second, provision should be made for the "funding" of all unpaid debts (i.e., the payment of regular interest on them). Finally, Hamilton counseled that only *current* holders of public securities should receive interest payments; Congress should not pay (or "discriminate" in favor of) war veterans or other creditors who had previously sold their continental or state securities at some fraction of their face value.[20]

Debate over Hamilton's proposals commenced in Congress the following month and continued (off and on) until his scheme was effectively adopted in late July and became law in early August.[21] This short, outcome-oriented summary hardly does justice to the federal government's first great experience with fiscal politics. However, the frequently technical debate over debt funding—which ultimately (and famously) became intertwined with the question of where to locate the permanent national capital—has been aptly reviewed elsewhere.[22] For my purposes, only the primary effect of Hamilton's proposed-and-enacted scheme is relevant: a manifest improvement in the public's credit. The price of public securities had already doubled over the course of 1789 (probably in anticipation of a congressional funding plan), and by November 1790, a federal bond paying 6 percent interest—the principal security created by the debt-funding legislation—was trading at roughly 70 percent of face value in Boston, New York, and Philadelphia.[23]

Seventy percent, however, was hardly satisfying to Alexander Hamilton. In fact, to a man who would later characterize the market price of a government's bonds as "the thermometre of its credit[,]" this figure still suggested far-from-perfect health.[24] How, then, could the remaining gap between market and par value be closed? The secretary organized his thoughts, put them on paper, and (on December 13) submitted to Congress his *Second Report on the Further Provision Necessary for Establishing Public Credit*.[25]

Hamilton's submission, however, traditionally goes by a very different name: *Report on a National Bank*.[26] This invites an obvious question: How would the chartering of a national bank help to raise the market price of federal bonds? Otherwise put—and to borrow Hamilton's own language—how would a national bank "be of the greatest utility in the operations connected with the support of the Public Credit[?]"[27] His answer lay in a specific feature of institutional design: the composition of the bank's capital.

The *Report on a National Bank* called for an institution with $10 million in capital; that sum would consist of "Twenty five thousand shares, each share being four hundred Dollars[.]" The federal government would purchase five thousand of these shares for $2 million, leaving the remainder for individuals, private institutions, and other "[b]odies politic[.]" More importantly, Hamilton's plan did not call for these investors to purchase their shares exclusively with gold and silver coin; while one-quarter of each share ($100) would need to be paid in specie, federal bonds paying 6 percent interest "could be tendered at par value" for the remainder.[28]

One clear purpose of the proposed purchase rule—certainly the one most connected with the public credit—was to stimulate demand for (and thus raise the price of) 6 percent federal bonds; Hamilton wrote that it would "in all probability . . . accelerate" a rise in securities prices "to [their] proper point" (i.e., par value).[29] As it turned out, the mere *prospect* of this purchase rule was sufficient to further restore public credit; the 6 percent bond was trading at 70 (percent of par value) in Philadelphia on December 9, but rose to 75 by December 15 (two days after Hamilton's report was submitted to Congress). By Christmas Day, it was trading at 90.[30]

In at least one respect, then, Hamilton's bank was designed to serve as a fiscal auxiliary to the federal government: It would (by virtue of its capital) place the government in a position to borrow on more advantageous terms.[31] However, the Treasury secretary was also clear that *additional* fiscal benefits would flow from its establishment.[32] In this vein, he called the bank "an Institution of primary importance to the prosperous administration of the Finances[.]"[33]

The aids to public finance invoked by this remark—the bank's ability to (1) circulate a convenient medium for tax payments, (2) make periodic loans based on the Treasury's needs, (3) serve as a safe depository for federal revenue, and (4) complete basic transactions for the government (e.g., routine payments to bondholders and employees)—tend to be emphasized in chronicles of the institution's birth (at least relative to its effect on public credit).[34] This is hardly surprising, given that two of these four functions were integral to the 1791 constitutional debate. To that subject I now turn.

THREE STANDARDS OF NECESSITY

With the core propositions of Hamilton's *Report on a National Bank* now sketched out, readers should either revisit the vignette that opens this chapter or simply consult this abridged version of the ensuing constitutional drama:

> *The House considered a bank bill based on Hamilton's report. Madison challenged its constitutionality, strictly reading the Necessary and Proper Clause. The bill nonetheless passed the House and (having already passed the Senate) headed to the president's desk. Jefferson,*

advising the president in writing, echoed Madison's concerns. Hamil-
ton rebutted them both, broadly construing the same Article I provi-
sion. President Washington said nothing but signed the bill.

Given the ubiquity of this account—in either its skeletal or fleshed-out forms—a new rendering of the events from February 1791 is only warranted if something significant remains unsaid.[35] This, I contend, is principally the case; several colorful strands of constitutional thought have gone unappreciated in the midst of scholarly preoccupation with the broader fabric of the 1791 dispute. More to the point, a closer look at the arguments offered in Congress and the executive branch reveals that the national bank's constitutional foes were united in their conclusion but not in their reasoning.

What remains to be said with respect to the 1791 constitutional debate is best communicated not through a stepwise recitation of the traditional account interspersed with novel elements, but rather through a topic-based reorganization and expansion of the existing historical material. In simpler terms, what follows is less an expanded chronology of intra- and interbranch debate and more a catalog of the various ways in which national bank opponents conceptualized constitutional necessity. This cataloging effort, I need hardly add, takes all claims about the meaning of the Necessary and Proper Clause at face value; my aim here is simply to document the variation in antibank constitutional arguments, not investigate its causes.[36]

Because the following analysis applies some fairly unfamiliar terms to some fairly familiar material, working definitions for those terms are essential. In particular, the three aforementioned standards of constitutional necessity—*functional, federal,* and *frequency*—require some preliminary discussion. Each offers a distinct conception of the requisite relationship between the means selected by Congress and the constitutional end.

Functional necessity is concerned with the contribution offered by the selected means toward the achievement of the Article I prerogative. Moreover, that contribution is evaluated without the slightest regard for external institutions.[37] The national bank, of course, offers a concrete way to think about this standard. At issue is the contribution made by a national bank toward the achievement of a valid congressional object (e.g., borrowing money). A loose or broad reading of this standard would suggest that *any* facilitation of borrowing, however minor, is enough to render the bank functionally "necessary." A bill creating an institution that might lend to Congress in the future would pass muster here. By contrast, a strict

or narrow reading of functional necessity would require that a bank substantially contribute to (if not directly achieve) borrowing by Congress. In
this vein, debate over the functional standard might be crudely reduced to
the question of whether means that indirectly achieve an Article I prerogative (or only those that directly do the same) are valid under the Necessary
and Proper Clause.

The stand-alone value of a chosen means for achieving an Article I objective stands in sharp contrast to the *federal* standard of necessity, which
assesses the relative value of substitute means. In short, if there are one
or more viable alternatives to congressional action, resort to the selected
means is not "necessary."[38] Accordingly, this second standard is (by definition) concerned with the surrounding institutional landscape. Returning to the national bank (vis-à-vis borrowing as a federal objective), the
constitutionality of Hamilton's proposal would hang on the question of
whether other institutions (e.g., state-chartered banks) could adequately
service congressional requests to borrow money. I need only add (by way
of comparison with the functional standard) that because there is no loose
reading of federal necessity, bank supporters in 1791 were disposed to reject it outright.

The *frequency*-based standard of necessity is concerned with comparing the selected means with the means typically used to achieve the end in
question. Under this standard, the external environment is neither wholly
irrelevant to the question of necessity nor represents a potential source of
alternatives to federal action; it instead furnishes crucial evidence of how
other governments have pursued the same objective. If it is "customary
for governments to execute [the relevant power] in that manner," then the
chosen means is "necessary."[39] As for the question of whether chartering
a bank represented a customary public approach to borrowing money, the
national bank's friends and foes disagreed. That fact underscores the reality that the frequency standard is neither intrinsically strict nor permissive (as the functional standard is) of divergent understandings; everything
here hinges on an assessment of past and present governmental practice.

The bank's constitutional foes deployed these three standards in their
floor speeches and memoranda, though typically not as isolated interpretive weapons. As suggested earlier, most offered interpretations of the
Necessary and Proper Clause that required satisfaction of two (or even
all three) of these standards.[40] Obviously, an interpretation that calls for
multiple criteria to be met simultaneously is stricter with respect to the
exercise of federal power than an interpretation that imposes only a single
condition for action.

THREE INTERPRETATIONS OF THE SWEEPING CLAUSE

The constitutional fire that consumed American politics for the better part of February 1791 began with rather inconspicuous sparks on the first day of that month. Representative James Jackson of Georgia, speaking to the bill recently taken up by the House—"An act to incorporate the subscribers to the Bank of the United States"—urged, essentially out of the blue, "the unconstitutionality of the plan[.]"[41] What followed this pithy suggestion was hardly a disquisition on matters constitutional; Jackson merely read a few unspecified passages from *The Federalist* in support of his position.[42] This performance apparently left the next speaker—Hamilton friend and bill supporter John Laurance of New York—inspired to do little more than claim that Congress had the power to borrow money and "a right to create a capital by which they may, with greater facility, carry the powers of borrowing, on any emergency, into effect." Laurance's ensuing commentary was actually more tangential to this claim than supportive of it; he noted that (1) the Continental Congress had chartered a bank in 1781, and (2) the new Congress surely possessed *at least* the powers of its predecessor.[43]

For a few moments, at least, members of the House conspicuously ignored the chasm that had just yawned in American constitutionalism. Since Jackson and Laurance had technically spoken on a motion (from William L. Smith of South Carolina) to send the bank bill back to committee, several members proceeded to offer short and unmemorable speeches on that narrow question. One of the last to speak was John Vining of Delaware. Perhaps sensing that the motion to recommit would fail and that more could (and very soon would) be said on the merits of the constitutional question, he tried to frame that impending discussion by staking out a middle ground. Confessing that "he was not perfectly satisfied as to the constitutional point[,]" Vining "hoped gentlemen would state their objections, that those who are satisfied on the point, may offer their reasons."[44] The motion to recommit then formally failed (23–34), and the House moved on to other business.[45] The following day, when debate on final passage commenced, James Madison both realized Vining's hope and nurtured the sparks generated by James Jackson and John Laurance into a full-blown conflagration.

In a debate spanning three weeks and two branches of the federal government (I use Madison's February 2 speech on the House floor and Hamilton's February 23 memorandum to the president as end points), the bill's constitutional critics and apologists seemed to agree on just two points. First, there was no *explicit* authorization for the bank in the Constitution. Charter opponents either made this point directly in their speeches and writings or clearly operated from this premise, and several supporters of the bill—including Elias Boudinot of New Jersey—conceded that "the power [to charter a bank] was not contained in express words[.]"[46] Second, *if* Congress had the authority to charter the bank, it was supplied by the Necessary and Proper Clause. To this end, charter advocates presented the institution as a means "necessary" for the effective exercise of one or more Article I powers; those cited in debate included the powers to lay and collect taxes, borrow money, and regulate interstate commerce.[47]

The bank's constitutional foes, of course, all rejected the Necessary and Proper Clause as a textual anchor for the institution. However, the rationale for this rejection was hardly uniform among the bill's detractors. In fact, the accumulated evidence suggests that those who agonized over the linchpin of Hamilton's public credit program struggled mightily to coalesce around—let alone operationalize—a more restrictive vision of federal power. In short, the six charter opponents who commented at length on the constitutional question offered three different understandings of the Sweeping Clause. Just as importantly, these interpretations *varied* in their strictness. One required satisfaction of (1) the functional standard alone, albeit a narrow version of that standard. Another, offered by several bank critics, demanded that (2) both the functional and the federal standards be met. Finally, an especially demanding interpretation of the Necessary and Proper Clause—one might even call it the most strict—would not sanction the bank bill unless (3) *all three* standards were met.

An antibank constitutional argument rooted in the functional standard alone—which I suspect will prove the most familiar to readers—was advanced by William Branch Giles of Virginia. Giles understood that the bill's supporters also construed constitutional necessity in terms of this standard, but were pressing for a permissive reading of it; they would characterize as "necessary" any means "which Congress may judge to be *useful*" for the effective exercise of a congressional power.[48] They would sanction a national bank, Giles concluded, because "it will tend to give a facility to the collection" of federal taxes. Giles, of course, could accede to neither this reading of the functional standard nor its consequence for the bank's constitutionality. By contrast, he insisted on a more "intimate connexion" between the means selected by Congress and the enumerated power to be exercised.[49] In order to be "necessary," Giles argued, the mean's contribution to achieving a constitutionally valid end had to be such that "the end could not be produced" without it.[50] By this reading of the functional standard, a national bank was unconstitutional; it was not integral (to redeploy Giles's example) to the collection of taxes.

Giles's interpretation found implicit support in the form of Attorney General Edmund Randolph's first memorandum to President Washington, submitted on February 12. In this highly organized and frequently technical piece—one certainly befitting his role as legal adviser to the executive branch[51]—Randolph reviewed and rejected claims that the bank was constitutional because it would "facilitate" the collection of taxes, the borrowing of money, the regulation of interstate commerce, and/or the regulation of national property.[52] Otherwise put, he—like Giles—embraced the requirement of functional necessity but rejected a lax understanding of it. By contrast, Randolph would only validate (under the banner of "Necessary and Proper") means that enjoyed a closer relationship with the enumerated end: "To be necessary is to be incidental, or, in other words, may be denominated the *natural* means of executing a power."[53]

A more demanding interpretation of the Necessary and Proper Clause —one that rendered satisfaction of the functional standard necessary but *insufficient* to achieve constitutionality—was advanced by several participants in the 1791 debate. For these men—James Jackson and James Madison in the House, and Thomas Jefferson in the executive branch—action under the Sweeping Clause could only be sustained if Congress (1) selected means that offered significant assistance in achieving a legitimate objective *and* (2) had no other workable options for achieving it.

Madison's February 2 speech offers an especially apt example of this interpretation at work. About midway through this lengthy oration—the House heard nothing else respecting the bank bill that day—Madison pointedly rejected (like Giles and Randolph above) his opponents' lax reading of the functional standard; against claims that "any means could be used, which . . . might be conceived to be conducive to the successful" exercise of federal powers, he argued that only "direct and incidental" means were available to Congress. This led to a memorable warning from the man who three years earlier had characterized federal powers as "few and defined": Endorse the more permissive reading of functional necessity, and lawmakers exercising these limited powers would nonetheless be able to "reach every object of legislation, every object within the whole compass of political economy."[54]

Had Madison's constitutional argument gone no further, it would represent little more than a restatement of the Giles/Randolph claim. However, the House's most prominent member proceeded to tighten the constitutional screws on the bank bill. Madison argued that the national bank's "uses to the Government"—at least with respect to borrowing—"could be supplied by keeping taxes a little in advance; by loans from individuals; [and] by the *other banks*" in the United States.[55] In other words, because loans could be provided by state-chartered banks—in February 1791, these consisted of the Massachusetts Bank, the Bank of North America, and the Bank of Maryland—a national bank "could not . . . be called necessary to the Government[.]"[56] Here, Madison was invoking not a national bank's stand-alone value—the contribution it would make, when considered in isolation, toward the objective of borrowing money—but its value relative to other institutions. By this account, the bank could not meet the federal standard of necessity.

The logic of Madison's interpretation deserves closer scrutiny. Its underlying premise is reasonably clear: To be "necessary," the means selected by Congress must satisfy both the functional standard and the federal standard.[57] On the merits, Madison saw neither as satisfied. On the one hand, he was explicit in suggesting (as already noted) that the bank could not meet the functional standard. In that sense, it effectively failed the threshold inquiry of a two-prong test. On the other hand, Madison's argument about state banks seems to imply that even if a national bank could meet the functional standard, it would *still* be unconstitutional; the federal standard would not be satisfied.

Madison's thoughts on the meaning of the word *necessary* were echoed by James Jackson. Seizing an opportunity to flesh out his bare-bones constitutional claim from February 1, Jackson rose two days later to reject the interpretive "latitude contended for" by bank advocates, namely their permissive understanding of functional necessity. Absent an obligation to select means that did more than merely facilitate the exercise of enumerated powers, Jackson warned, the federal government would "soon be in possession of all possible powers."[58] The bank's failure to satisfy a more restrictive reading of the functional standard was not, however, the only red flag sent up by Jackson. Alluding to Hamilton's aforementioned September 1789 decision to borrow money from the state-chartered Bank of North America,[59] Jackson found the Treasury's behavior on that occasion sufficient to "shew [sic] that there is no necessity of instituting any new bank, those already established having been found sufficient for the purpose."[60] Like Madison, then, Jackson saw failure to meet the federal standard as doubling the bank's constitutional woes.

On the off chance that President Washington had failed to follow the House proceedings with great care, thus rendering him unfamiliar with the interpretation offered by Madison and Jackson, Thomas Jefferson's February 15 memorandum was designed to acquaint the nation's chief executive with their two-prong argument. The secretary of state acknowledged but immediately rejected the reading of functional necessity pressed by charter advocates: "It has been much urged, that a bank will give great facility, or convenience, in the collection of taxes. Suppose this were true, yet the constitution allows only the means which are 'necessary,' not those which are merely convenient for effecting the enumerated powers."[61] Having implied that a stricter version of the functional standard applied (and could not be met), Jefferson then made it clear that the bank bill suffered from a *second* constitutional shortcoming. "Besides," he added, "the existing banks will, without a doubt, enter into arrangements [with the Treasury] for lending their agency . . . [t]his expedient alone suffices to prevent the existence of that *necessity*, which may justify the assumption of a non enumerated power as a means for carrying into effect an enumerated one."[62]

The foregoing material suggests that the three men traditionally associated with strict interpretation in 1791—Madison, Randolph, and Jefferson—did not evaluate the national bank's constitutionality in precisely the same way. In particular, there is considerable daylight between Randolph and his colleagues with respect to the meaning of the word *necessary*. However, the most *demanding* interpretation of the Necessary and Proper Clause in 1791 actually belonged to the relatively anonymous Michael Jenifer Stone of Maryland, who spent just a single term in the House; he left office less than a week after President Washington signed the bank bill. For Stone, constitutional necessity entailed the simultaneous satisfaction of all three standards; Congress had to (1) select means that substantially contributed to the effective exercise of its power, (2) lack viable alternatives, and (3) be acting in a manner consistent with the behavior of other governments exercising the same power.

Given the attention offered to the first two interpretations, much of Stone's argument on behalf of a three-prong test of constitutional necessity will sound familiar. For one thing, his discussion of functional necessity was effectively completed by way of a footnote. With respect to the principal argument of bank advocates—that mere facilitation of the exercise of express powers was enough to satisfy the functional standard—Stone noted that the "spirit of the constitution, in this respect, had been well explained by Mr Madison, and he should not recapitulate." In addition, Stone found the national bank wanting in terms of federal necessity, albeit prospectively: "I say there is no necessity, there is no occasion, for

this bank. The States will institute banks, which will answer every purpose." Finally, with respect to Stone's *further* tightening of the constitutional screws, he asked sarcastically on the House floor whether creating
a bank was the "known and usual means" of borrowing money, especially
since the proposed charter did not require that loans be made to the federal
government.[63] Stone failed to elaborate on this point, leaving rhetorical de-
rision to stand in for domestic and international empirics. It is probably
fair to say, in short, that Stone considered a national bank less "necessary"
than any of his fellow charter opponents.[64]

Two points require further comment. First, far from presenting (as the
traditional 1791 narrative suggests) a united front of opposition, the bank's
constitutional foes pointedly failed to coalesce around a single strict interpretation of the Necessary and Proper Clause. At the end of the day, the
only thing they seemed to share (apart from a conviction that the bank
was unconstitutional) was a belief that means must satisfy a demanding
version of the functional standard; all three antibank interpretations of
the Sweeping Clause included this requirement.[65] Second, the distinction between the Giles/Randolph interpretation (functional necessity
alone) and the Madison/Jackson/Jefferson interpretation (functional and
federal necessity) is especially important. Not only does the latter offer
an inherently stricter test of constitutionality than the former—and thus
clear evidence of interpretive variation among bank opponents—but *both*
interpretations would assume roles in the 1811 recharter debate. While a
few Republican opponents of recharter would continue to press the Giles/
Randolph line of argument, most of their fellow partisans would embrace
the two-prong definition of constitutional necessity.

REBUTTING THE CONSTITUTIONAL CRITICS

The organization of the previous section—a progressive review of one-,
two-, and three-prong tests of constitutional necessity—might encourage a misleading understanding of how an internally divided set of bank
opponents waged their constitutional assault. More to the point, it con-
jures the image of a strengthening campaign: Giles and Randolph using
standard weapons to fire the first shots; Madison, Jackson, and Jefferson providing important supplementary artillery; Stone adding one final
weapon to the arsenal. As already noted, however, the foregoing review
was *not* chronological; bank opponents simply did not open their constitutional campaign by invoking a narrow reading of the functional standard alone and then gradually build toward a three-prong interpretation

of the Sweeping Clause. By sharp contrast, their assault could be readily characterized as haphazard. At one point, three consecutive national bank critics who spoke on the House floor—Jackson on February 3, Stone on February 5, and Giles on February 7—invoked three different interpretations of the Necessary and Proper Clause. Moreover, the memoranda that President Washington received between February 12 and 15 from members of his cabinet—Randolph and Jefferson—offered different definitions of constitutional necessity. In short, bank defenders probably had little sense (at any given moment) of which interpretation would be offered next.

This might seem like a trivial point, but it appears to have colored efforts by national bank supporters to rebut the arguments of their opponents. Faced with what amounted to a moving target, the bank's five principal constitutional defenders—Fisher Ames, Theodore Sedgwick, Elias Boudinot, and Elbridge Gerry in the House, coupled with Alexander Hamilton in the executive branch—spent less time addressing specific interpretations of the Necessary and Proper Clause (for example, Stone's ultrarestrictive three-prong argument) and more time scrutinizing the individual standards of necessity deployed by their opponents. The functional standard was embraced in the abstract by charter advocates, but a laxer version of it was urged. The same could not be said for the federal standard, which was cast as a veritable nonissue by two bank supporters and dismissed outright by Hamilton. Finally, the institution's apologists declined to explicitly embrace the frequency standard as a requirement for constitutional necessity, but nonetheless contended that a national bank could meet that standard.

I have alluded to the probank perspective on functional necessity so frequently in this chapter that only a concise statement of its principles seems required. In short, charter advocates accepted the standard but complained that their opponents were demanding an unduly significant contribution toward enumerated ends from selected means. Sedgwick offered a backward-looking critique here, suggesting that his opponents' reading of functional necessity would "prove, perhaps, that all the laws which had [previously] been passed, were unconstitutional." Such an understanding, he concluded, was "infinitely too narrow and limited."[66] The alternate rendering of functional necessity was fleshed out by Hamilton, whose memorandum to the president famously suggested that Congress may—by virtue of the Sweeping Clause—employ any means that is "needful, requisite, incidental, useful, or conducive to" the execution of a specified power.[67] This liberal understanding of functional necessity, conceded Boudinot, would effectively leave the choice of means "to the discretion of those in whom the trust is reposed"—namely members of Congress.

The first two bank advocates to address the federal standard of necessity—Fisher Ames and Theodore Sedgwick—actually did not immediately dismiss it. Ames, for example, observed that the federal government was obliged to pay quarterly interest on its debt, and to do so at one location in every state. The bulk of federal revenue, however—the yield of the Tariff and Tonnage Acts—was collected in a few major port cities. Absent the ability to quickly "transport [this] revenue from one end of the continent to the other[,]" short-term loans would be required. "This imposes," said Ames, "an absolute necessity upon the Government to make use of a bank"—and a branched one at that. At this point, he noted, bank detractors would invoke the federal standard: "[Their] answer is, that the State banks will supply this aid." Ames felt less threatened by this invocation and more inclined to hoist such constitutional critics on their own petard: "This [standard] is risking a good deal to the argument against the bank . . . [t]en of the States have no banks[.]"[68] Sedgwick was of a very similar mind on this point; he asked whether the bank critics pressing the federal standard were "serious in their observations": "Do they believe the capitals of the present banks adequate to the exigencies of the nation?"[69] Otherwise put, three state banks hardly represented—for the purpose of ensuring timely interest payments throughout the Union—a viable alternative to a national bank. This take on the federal standard should ultimately be construed less as an implicit endorsement of its relevance for establishing constitutional necessity and more as a simple claim that the national bank could (if needed) meet that standard.[70]

The federal standard's treatment at the hands of Ames and Sedgwick looks forgiving when compared with that of Alexander Hamilton. The Treasury secretary wrote that some constitutional critics (including Thomas Jefferson) had gone so far in their "restrictive interpretation of the word, as even to make the case of necessity . . . depend on casual and temporary circumstances." By "casual and temporary circumstances," Hamilton meant state decisions to charter and dissolve banks. The constitutionality of the national bank, he continued, must be "the same to-day as to-morrow"; its status could not vary in accordance with the number of state-chartered banks in existence. Here, Hamilton was perhaps anticipating—and preemptively rejecting—a constitutional argument that federal necessity might very well be satisfied in a nation with just three state banks but could be compromised as the number of state institutions multiplied. His blanket rejection of this standard implied that its champions were poor constitutional thinkers: "All the arguments, therefore, against the constitutionality of the bill, derived from the . . . existence of certain State banks . . . must not only be rejected as fallacious, but must be viewed as demonstrative that there is a radical source of error in the reasoning."[71]

What Ames and Sedgwick did with respect to the federal standard—find the national bank in compliance with it *without* embracing the same as a formal requirement of constitutional necessity—was repeated by Hamilton for the frequency standard. To be clear, it was Sedgwick himself—speaking on February 3—who was responsible for its role in the 1791 debate; he argued on that occasion that "whenever a power is delegated for express purposes, all the *known and usual* means for the attainment of the objects expressed, are conceded also."[72] Michael Jenifer Stone was explicitly responding to this comment when he sarcastically asked whether chartering a bank was the "known and usual means" of borrowing money.[73] Hamilton subsequently tried to come to Sedgwick's rescue on this point, twice referring (near the conclusion of his memorandum) to a bank as a "usual" means for administering a government's finances.[74] As with Ames and Sedgwick above, Hamilton's commentary should be construed less as a concession that means must (as a constitutional matter) track customary ways of achieving specific ends and more as a simple claim that the national bank could meet this standard.

These varied rebuttals to bank opponents aside, the positive account of constitutional necessity offered by charter supporters—that is, their preferred interpretation of the Necessary and Proper Clause—consisted of nothing more than a permissive understanding of the functional standard. Means that facilitated (or were conducive to) the exercise of enumerated powers were "necessary" within the meaning of Article I, Section 8. Though some supporters (as noted above) suggested that other standards of necessity *could* be satisfied, not one argued that the means selected by Congress should face anything beyond a forgiving single-prong test. This was unquestionably—to borrow Elbridge Gerry's phrase—a "liberal interpretation" of federal power.[75]

CONCLUSION

Not only was a loose reading of the functional standard the favored interpretation of national bank advocates in 1791, but it was also the interpretation that ultimately prevailed. To be clear, despite the significant attention bestowed in this chapter on the constitutional arguments of charter opponents, they were badly outnumbered in the House of Representatives and lost again (despite ostensibly commanding a majority) in the executive branch. With respect to the former, "An act to incorporate the subscribers to the Bank of the United States" passed that chamber on February 8 by a vote of 39 to 20.[76] In the latter, President George Washington silently sided with Hamilton over Randolph and Jefferson in signing the bank bill on February 25. The traditional 1791 narrative certainly does not err, then, in acknowledging the ultimate triumph of a broad interpretation of the Sweeping Clause.

It would be a mistake to end here by simply acknowledging the national bank's establishment despite the variety of strict positions staked out against its constitutionality. Doing so would, I think, create the false impression that my effort to document the variation was simply an exercise in combating traditional (and reductionist) thinking about the 1791 debate. It is meant to be more than that. The period following the first debate over a national bank saw the establishment of the "First Party System," which pitted Federalists against Republicans.[77] The latter seized lasting control of Congress and the presidency following the election of 1800,[78] giving rise to what some have called the Jeffersonian (and I will call the Republican) regime.[79] As a number of scholars have noted, a fault line began to form within this regime during the first decade of the nineteenth century; Republicans were increasingly divided between an "Old" wing that held an unrelenting animus toward questionable exercises of federal power and a moderate or nationalist wing more comfortable with the same.[80]

This emerging schism was reflected in debate in the Eleventh Congress (1809–1811) over a bill to extend the national bank's soon-to-expire charter. While the Federalist minority proved broadly supportive of the recharter bill, Republicans were deeply divided. Some party members embraced the legislation, but most objected on both constitutional and policy grounds. Among the Bank's constitutional critics, however, there was disagreement about why the institution fell short. That disagreement was reflected in the *recurrence* of single- and multiprong reasoning about constitutional necessity. It was not simply the case, however—as I discuss in chapter 4— that "Old" antibank Republicans systematically embraced a stricter understanding of the Necessary and Proper Clause than their moderate antibank peers. The interpretive lineup was more complex than that, a fact owing much to the slow but steady multiplication of state-chartered banks between 1791 and 1811. To that development I now turn.

CHAPTER TWO

"Banco Mania" and Institutional Drift

I n the course of reviewing Alexander Hamilton's proposals for enhanc-
ing public credit in the previous chapter, I did little more than gloss
over one particular feature of his *Report on a National Bank* (and ultimately, the charter granted to the Bank of the United States): the setting
of the institution's capital at $10 million. This may no longer be such a
princely sum—members of the United States Supreme Court, after all,
now suggest in the midst of oral argument that $3.5 million is not "a heck
of a lot of money"—but $10 million was a staggering figure in the Early
American Republic.[1] Not only would this sum have easily rendered an individual the richest American of his or her day—John Jacob Astor was considered "wealthy" in 1799 with a net worth of roughly $100,000[2]—but it
was enough (at least in 1791) to dominate an entire *industry*. Counting the
five state-chartered institutions then operating—whose combined capital
was $4.6 million—the $10 million Bank of the United States closed the
calendar year 1791 controlling over two-thirds of the nation's chartered
banking capital.[3]

Almost twenty years later, with the Bank's charter about to expire, the
institutional landscape looked very different indeed. As 1792 began, five
out of the fourteen states had chartered a single bank within their bor-
ders; by early 1811, each of the seventeen states contained at least one
state-chartered institution, and a bank was also operating in the Louisiana Territory.[4] In fact, sometime during the previous calendar year, the nation's hundredth state bank had commenced its operations.[5] Perhaps more
importantly, the period between 1791 and 1811 saw the national bank's
dominance of its industry significantly compromised, if not altogether destroyed. The Bank's $10 million in capital—good for over 68 percent of the
industry total in late 1791—accounted for roughly 15 percent by early 1811.[6]

Otherwise put, the national bank was gradually transformed from a towering structure on a relatively barren field to merely the tallest single edifice on an increasingly crowded surface.

Students of comparative political economy might describe the Bank's slow transformation here as an instance of institutional *drift*. As Wolfgang Streeck and Kathleen Thelen have recently argued, institutions "[d]o not survive by standing still . . . to remain what they are they need to be reset and refocused, or sometimes more fundamentally recalibrated and renegotiated." Should this maintenance operation—Streeck and Thelen label it "tending"—be ignored, the "scope, meaning, and function" of an institution may be gradually altered via change in external conditions.[7] To capture the intrinsic paradox here more directly, a formally "static" institution may nonetheless "change" due to evolution in the surrounding environment. With respect to the Bank of the United States, its capital remained fixed between 1791 and 1811; to request a capital increase from Congress would have been to invite a new round of debate over the constitutional question.[8] This institutional stasis, coupled with the proliferation of state-chartered banks, gradually eroded the national bank's dominance of its industry.

Tracing this development, with particular attention to the broad causes of state bank multiplication, is my principal task here. To be clear, the events to be reviewed in this chapter have enjoyed better coverage historically than their constitutional counterparts from chapter 1; the expansion of commercial banking in the opening years of the Early American Republic has been well chronicled by economic historians.[9] This review, however, is not an end in its own right, but rather a means for bringing certain institutional facts within the ambit of scholarship on American constitutionalism. As chapter 4 will demonstrate, those who participated in the recharter debate of 1811 were uniformly familiar with (and willing to recognize) the twentyfold increase in state banks over the preceding twenty years. More importantly, the proliferation of state-chartered institutions led 1811 Bank opponents to cluster (as their 1791 counterparts had not) around an interpretation of the Necessary and Proper Clause that considered the existence of viable alternatives to congressional action. In different and somewhat starker terms, if this chapter (and the next) delves deeper into institutional affairs than is typical of scholarship in public law, that is because (1) those affairs significantly informed future iterations of the constitutional debate over the Bank, and (2) the linkages between things institutional and constitutional have heretofore gone unappreciated.

This chapter opens with a summary of the national bank's affairs between July and November 1791, a brief period that nonetheless captures both the frenzied summer market for its stock and the studied fall decision by its board of directors to establish branches in several coastal cities. I draw attention to the Bank here less because the institution must perpetually be kept in view and more because these early days help to illuminate two causes of state bank proliferation. First, shares of bank stock were seen during the 1791–1811 period as promising investment vehicles; the "scripomania" associated with the initial sale of the national bank's stock reveals this all too well. To charter a new institution, then, was to create additional options for private and public profit seekers. Second, local communities sought state-chartered banks in response to the national bank's decision to open offices outside its Philadelphia headquarters. To be clear, the granting of a state charter offered no obvious signal to the national bank; some states created local institutions to entice the Bank to open a branch in that community, while others did the same to *repel* the Bank's presence in that city. Ensuing sections of the chapter offer examples of both causes at work in state bank formation between 1791 and 1811, in addition to evidence of institutional generation driven by a third factor: the collective search for solutions to credit access problems in particular markets. A number of early state banks were chartered, in short, either because local credit-granting institutions were virtually nonexistent or because existing facilities catered (or were perceived as catering) only to certain portions of the public.

SCRIPOMANIA AND THE BRANCH QUESTION

After President Washington signed the national bank bill in late February 1791, attention quickly turned to the task of organizing the Bank of the United States. Though organizing can encompass a wide range of institutional activities, I have just two in mind here: (1) the initial sale of the Bank's stock and (2) the election and early decisions of its first board of directors. The former has never wanted for scholarly attention; the public offering of Bank stock initiated an asset price bubble that inflated and burst within six weeks.[10] More importantly for my purposes, that bubble taught many early Americans—rightly or wrongly—to seek their fortunes in the buying and selling of bank stock. The latter, by contrast, has never attracted sustained interest[11] but is integral to the story of state bank proliferation—not to mention the Bank's subsequent development as a regulatory force vis-à-vis those institutions (the subject of chapter 3). Both facets of the Bank's organization are treated below.

TABLE 2.1 Payment schedule for one share in the National Bank

	Amount due	
Date	Specie	Federal bonds
July 4, 1791	$25	—
January 1, 1792	$25	$75
July 1, 1792	$25	$75
January 1, 1793	$25	$75
July 1, 1793	—	$75
	Total: $100	Total: $300

Source: Cowen, Origins and Economic Impact, 37.
Note: This schedule captures both the public credit-enhancing purchase rule discussed in chapter 1 and the fact that both types of capital (specie and federal bonds)
were gradually collected.

Americans flocked to five major commercial centers along the eastern
seaboard on July 4, 1791—the nation's fifteenth birthday—for the opportunity to purchase stock in the Bank of the United States.[12] For twenty-five
dollars in specie, an individual could purchase a transferable certificate—a
"scrip"—that entitled its bearer to make four semiannual payments to acquire the Bank share in full (see table 2.1).

In other words, a down payment just north of 6 percent would secure
the right to purchase the share; that right could subsequently be exercised
or sold (conceivably at a premium). Across these five sites, the subscription
books were filled with impressive speed, in times ranging from just fifteen
minutes to approximately three hours.[13]

The initial sale of Bank scrips should not be confused with the secondary market that immediately developed for these certificates. On the
expectation that the national bank would generate substantial dividends
for its shareholders—an expectation rooted in the performance of institutions like the Bank of North America[14]—the scrips quickly began to trade
at prices far above twenty-five dollars. In fact, within a month "the price
of scrip in New York had skyrocketed *tenfold* in the Coffee Houses[,] from
$25 to $250[.]"[15] Given the $375 still due for acquisition of the full share, an
investor who offered $250 for scrip was setting the market value for Bank
stock at $625. Publications in at least three cities—Boston, New York, and
Philadelphia—began making references to "scripomania" or "scriptoma-
nia."[16] The summer market for scrip—which today might be described
as "frothy"—peaked in mid-August, with prices briefly reaching $325 (or

$700 for the full share) in Philadelphia before retreating to the $130–$170 range for the rest of the year.[17]

If Thomas Jefferson had assumed the role of calm constitutional critic back in February 1791, then scripomania quickly added the part of agitated moral critic to his résumé. As Stanley Elkins and Eric McKitrick have written, the speculative scenes were "all that was finally needed to goad [him] into shudders of loathing."[18] A July 24 letter to Edmund Pendleton—then chief justice of Virginia—made passing reference to the "delirium of speculation" that had swept the country, but that was mere warm-up for Jefferson's protracted August jeremiad.[19]

In letters to several correspondents—all penned between August 23 and 30, or just after the scrip bubble had popped—Jefferson agonized over the individual and collective consequences of recent events. In his eyes, the first victim of scripomania was individual industriousness. Jefferson wrote David Humphreys—the new US minister to Portugal—on August 23 to complain that a "spirit of gambling in the public paper has lately seized too many of our citizens . . . [m]any are ruined by it; but I fear that ruin will be no more a correction in this case than in common gaming."[20] Writing to Edward Rutledge two days later, Jefferson was clear on what an individual sacrificed when scrip trading was prioritized, even temporarily: "The taylor [sic] who has made thousands in one day, tho' he lost them the next, can never again be content with the slow and moderate earnings of his needle."[21]

Jefferson's letters also characterized the broader American economy as a victim of scripomania. His logic here was aggregative in nature: The nation's productivity might not be significantly affected if a few citizens were poached from their regular work, but hundreds or even thousands across multiple sites was a very different story. In this vein, Jefferson's August 25 letter to Rutledge inquired about the latter's thoughts respecting "scrip-pomany" before volunteering more of his own: "Ships are lying idle at the wharfs, buildings are stopped, capitals withdrawn from commerce, arts and agriculture, to be employed in gambling, and the tide of public prosperity almost unparalleled in any country, is arrested in its course, and suppressed by the rage for getting rich quick in a day."[22] He called Gouverneur Morris's attention to the same effect a few days later: "[T]he abundance of paper has produced a spirit of gambling . . . which has laid up our ships at the wharves as too slow instruments of profit[.]"[23] While Jefferson's anguished observations help to paint a fuller portrait of scripomania, they also offer a partial explanation for the pursuit of state bank charters in 1792 and beyond; the summer of 1791 led many Americans to view bank stock—possibly through long-term dividends on full shares, but more likely through short-term scrip trading—as the path to wealth.

In late October, roughly two months after the peak in the Bank scrip market and two months before a $100 payment on the full share was due, shareholders elected the institution's first board of directors. That election yielded a board that was heavily weighted toward the major commercial centers, with twenty of the twenty-five seats falling to men from Boston, New York, and Philadelphia. After Oliver Wolcott Jr.—then one of Hamilton's subordinates at the Treasury Department and later his successor as Treasury secretary—declined the board's invitation to serve as Bank president, the honor fell to Bank of North America president Thomas Willing.[24]

A flurry of activity followed Willing's election, including the full board's establishment (and filling) of various salaried positions in the Bank and the stockholders' determination of institutional bylaws and regulations.[25] The bylaws (as adopted on October 31) included a clear admonition to the Bank's elected leadership: "It is the sense of the stockholders of the Bank of the United States, that the president and directors should turn their immediate attention to the establishment of offices of discount and deposit at such places in the United States as the interest and safety of the institution will permit."[26] In simpler terms, the principal instructed its agent to create branches of the national bank.

The stockholders' instruction here deserves greater scrutiny, if for no other reason than its clear departure from Alexander Hamilton's preferences. The *Report on a National Bank* had briefly treated the subject of branches, with Hamilton recognizing that the "situation of the United States"—namely, its vast geographic scope—"naturally inspires a wish, that the form of the institution could admit of a plurality" of them. He had reservations, however, not the least of which was a concern that limited domestic expertise in bank management would erode prospects for the "safe and orderly administration" of these offices.[27] Given that commercial banking was still relatively novel in late 1790—the pioneering Bank of North America was less than a decade old—the thought of entrusting inexperienced employees far from Philadelphia with authority that (if misused) could "hazard serious disorder" for the institution as a whole was hardly inspiring to Hamilton.[28] This express concern notwithstanding, the Treasury secretary conceded that the branch question could be left to the discretion of the national bank's board.[29]

Economic historians have stressed that Hamilton's two-paragraph discussion of branches failed to offer a comprehensive account of his opposition to them. Two additional explanations have been offered: (1) a desire to prioritize the Treasury Department's fiscal needs and (2) concern over the feasibility of hosting multiple banks in a single city. With respect to the former, Hamilton is thought to have favored a concentration of the national bank's resources in order to render them available for use by the federal government. As Edwin Perkins has noted, organization along these lines would have emulated the Bank of England, which lent to some private parties near London but "remained principally an institution oriented toward serving the needs of the Exchequer."[30]

The other imputed source of Hamilton's opposition is ultimately rooted in uncertainty. In 1784, there had been an effort to charter a rival to the Bank of North America in Philadelphia. The push aroused concerns over the "feasibility of [hosting] two or more commercial banks . . . in a single market." More specifically, no one knew if two banks issuing convertible currency (i.e., paper redeemable on demand in gold and silver) could exist without one eventually being drained of its specie. When the organizers of the rival institution halted their efforts to secure a charter from the Pennsylvania General Assembly in lieu of joining an enlarged Bank of North America, it meant that no answer would be forthcoming on this question. Because this state of affairs—one city, one bank—still held six years later, Hamilton "may have retained some lingering doubts" about establishing branches in cities already home to state banks.[31] At least one city would play host to multiple banks—the Bank of the United States and the Bank of North America would both operate in Philadelphia—but a concentrated national institution could have limited that experiment to a single site.

Hamilton's reservations—real and ascribed—aside, the Bank's board of directors chose to follow the stockholders' October 31 instruction; eight days later, it ordered the creation of branches in Boston, New York, Baltimore, and Charleston.[32] Three points bear consideration with respect to the board's final decision. First, however much Hamilton favored a unitary institution—and however much the Bank's directors might have agreed with him substantively—they were simply not in a position (mere days removed from their election) to flaunt the stockholders' instruction. Plenty of non-Philadelphians owned shares in the Bank, and this crowd was "adamant in their determination" to share the institution's benefits with their localities.[33]

The board's behavior also powerfully affirms the idea that institutions, once created, invariably take on a life independent of their creators.[34] Hamilton, writing to Bank of New York cashier William Seton several weeks after the decision to establish branches, clarified his role (or rather, nonrole) in that development: "[T]he whole affair of branches was begun, continued and ended; not only without my participation but against my judgment. When I say against my judgment, you will not understand that my opinion was given and overruled, for I never was consulted, but that the steps taken were contrary to my private opinion of the course which ought to have been pursued."[35] Despite, then, the board's early reputation—"many considered [it Hamilton's] tool"—the Bank's directors from the start not only "remained singularly independent of Treasury dictation," but wholly willing to act without consulting the Treasury at all.[36] In short, the Bank operated essentially from birth as an integral but *independent* auxiliary of the federal government.

Finally, the decision to establish branches—like the public's preoccupation with bank stock in the wake of scripomania—represents a piece of the state bank proliferation puzzle. The Bank of the United States, of course, was not limited to four branches; further expansion was possible (and ultimately did occur). Whether this prospect was promising or perilous often depended on the community in question. For locales preoccupied with the potential benefits of a Bank office, the acquisition of a state bank could signal that the city was prominent enough to warrant consideration as a future branch site. By contrast, for communities wary of federal power (and a Bank branch as a symbol of that power), the opening of a state-chartered institution could signal the city's desire to be dropped from any list of potential expansion sites.

SERVING MAMMON

There is ample evidence to suggest that profit seeking, especially in the immediate wake of scripomania, motivated both successful and unsuccessful efforts to secure state bank charters between 1791 and 1811.[37] Given Jefferson's prediction (in the Humphreys and Rutledge letters) that individuals once infected with the scrip bug would never be the same, he was probably not surprised to learn that the personal bankruptcies associated with the collapse of the 1791 scrip bubble failed to curb Americans' newfound appetite for bank stock (and its perceived benefits). Moreover, that hunger was hardly restricted to citizens; a few state governments chartered banks in order to invest in them and thus reap the rewards of stock ownership.

Though no legislative action ultimately came of them, the postscripomania clamor for state bank charters is nicely captured by events in New York City in mid-January 1792. The city's January 16 newspapers

included advertisements for an institution called the Million Bank of the
State of New York, which would consist of two thousand shares priced
at $500 apiece. At ten o'clock that morning, interested parties gathered
at Corre's Hotel and—like their Bank of the United States peers seven
months earlier—purchased the right to buy full shares in this institution.
Demand for Million Bank scrip that day far exceeded supply, and unsurprisingly, the next morning's papers included offers to sell those certificates at a heavy premium; one offered "Rights in the Million bank for
cash 92 dolls."[38]

Not only did a strong secondary market quickly emerge for Million
Bank scrip, but two other Manhattan-based bank projects immediately
sprang up. On January 18, a subscription was opened—and promptly
filled—for the Tammany Bank. Consisting of four thousand shares priced
at $500 each, it could have been called—technically speaking—the *two*
million bank. The following morning, Corre's Hotel again played host
to an open subscription book, this time for individuals who had been
excluded from the Million Bank; this third venture was called the Merchants' Bank.[39] Joseph Stancliffe Davis, who authored the first modern
chronicle of these events, wrote that "[t]he promotion of these new banks,
it seems fair to conclude, was in the main a speculative device."[40] In the
midst of these frantic organizing efforts, one observer offered words that
reproduced Jefferson's lament from the previous August: "[t]he merchant,
the lawyer, the physician and the mechanic, appear to be equally striv-
ing to accumulate large fortunes" through the buying and selling of bank
scrip.[41]

Perhaps anticipating that the state legislature would refuse to charter
three new banks in a city that would soon be home to two—the Bank of
New York and the New York branch of the Bank of the United States—
the organizers of these enterprises eventually joined forces and pursued a
single charter from that body for a $1.8 million bank. This relatively mea-
sured step notwithstanding, New Yorker James Watson—writing to Representative Jeremiah Watson of Connecticut near the end of the month—emphasized (yet ultimately waved his hands at) the delirium of the previous
two weeks: "I shall not tire you with a description of the Banco Mania in
this place."[42]

At the end of the day, however, it was all for naught. In mid-March,
with the request for a bank charter before the state legislature, the Panic
of 1792 began—arguably the first "stock market crash" in American history.[43] The story of that crisis—including Hamilton's efforts on behalf of
the Treasury Department to stem it—has been told many times over;[44] my

interest in it is restricted to its dampening effect on this particular charter effort. In short, the project's champions were informed that a charter for a Manhattan-based bank was not forthcoming.[45] Despite this conclusion, the lead-up remains instructive; the manic activity of early 1792 affirms that many citizens of the Early American Republic "recognized the powerful wealth-generating possibilities of the [bank] corporation."[46]

The legislature's reluctance to sanction more banking in New York City did not, however, spell doom for comparable ventures elsewhere in the state. In early February, just as "bank mania" had subsided near the meeting of the Hudson and East Rivers, it started to swell upstate.[47] Joel Munsell, author of the first history of the Bank of Albany, wrote that "[a] great many projects were on foot in the year 1792[,]" and the "capitalists" in that city wanted in on the action. If this description of the bank organizers failed to clarify their motive, Munsell's next observation was designed to rectify that failure; he noted that there was (at that time) "but one bank in the State, the Bank of New York, the stock of which was *50 per cent above par.*"[48] Accordingly, on February 3, this group proposed the Albany Bank, a relatively small institution—its capital would be just $75,000—composed of five hundred shares priced at $150 apiece. When fifteen-dollar scrips in the venture were offered for sale, they were gone within three hours.[49] In a development that may no longer seem surprising, the price for Albany Bank scrip doubled within twenty-four hours and at one point reached $115 (or $250 on the full share—a $100 premium on face value).[50] In late March 1792, *despite* the panic that had recently engulfed lower Manhattan, the state legislature granted a charter to (what became known as) the Bank of Albany.[51]

Of course, the Empire State was hardly the only site of profit-oriented efforts to get state banks up and running. In Connecticut, for example, the Union Bank of New London represented a partial "product of the 'banco-mania' precipitated by the chartering of the Bank of the United States in 1791."[52] In mid-February 1792, a group of prospective investors familiar with (1) the previous summer's scripomania, (2) the recent banking craze in New York City, and—as Chester McArthur Destler has emphasized—(3) the sizable dividends then being paid to Massachusetts Bank stockholders, met to plan a "[b]ank for the purpose of discount and deposite [sic] at New London."[53] The result was an institution with $100,000 in capital, or one thousand shares priced at $100 each; the shares set aside for New London residents—the remainder were to be sold in nearby Norwich—were subscribed within a few hours. Later that spring, the state's General Assembly passed a bill to incorporate the Union Bank of New London.[54]

State governments, no less than individuals, sought to "profit" from the creation and operation of state banks. I place that word in quotation marks because the point was less to line the state's coffers and more to reduce the burden on taxpayers. In other words, if a state purchased stock in—and received dividends from—a bank that it chartered, it could keep state taxes lower than they would otherwise be.[55] The birth of the Bank of Pennsylvania in 1793 furnishes an excellent—but surely not the only—example of this.[56] As one banking historian has put it, the commonwealth "made some overtures to the Bank of North America" in 1793 "with a view to participating in its business and profits."[57] Upon being rebuffed, it chartered the Bank of Pennsylvania for the express purpose of "promot[ing] the regular, permanent and successful operation of the finances of this State."[58] The crucial charter provision instructed the governor to subscribe $1 million on behalf of the commonwealth—a full third of the institution's capital. Moreover, the scheme worked; stock dividends proceeded to generate a tenth of the commonwealth's revenue between 1791 and 1795.[59]

BROADENING ACCESS

Whereas the previous section focused on charter drives rooted in the interests of would-be stockholders (or those who would indirectly engage in *lending*), this section focuses on institution-building efforts on behalf of prospective customers (or those who would engage in *borrowing*). Otherwise put, state banks were generated between 1791 and 1811 in response to real or perceived difficulties in gaining access to credit. Sometimes, especially early in the period under study, those difficulties were broadly felt in a particular community. For example, in cities or towns without a bank, few could secure the funds necessary to underwrite their business ventures. In situations of this sort, a state bank offered a promising vehicle for alleviating those conditions. As banks multiplied, however, credit access became a more specialized problem. A number of existing institutions faced complaints that their lending favored specific customers: friends and business associates of bank directors or fellow partisans of the same. In these circumstances, charter drives were designed to level—or at least reduce the imbalance in—the playing field for underserved groups.

The chartering of North Carolina's Bank of Cape Fear in 1804 furnishes an example of state legislative activity grounded in community-wide credit access issues. At that time, North Carolina was the *only* state among the original thirteen to lack a chartered bank. By comparison, its neighbors to the north and the south—Virginia and South Carolina—each

boasted multiple state banks *and* a branch of the national bank.[60] The
need for "adequate banking facilities to underwrite and promote trade"
was especially acute in Wilmington, the state's main port. When the need
became "too apparent to ignore" in 1804, the North Carolina legislature
responded by chartering the Bank of Cape Fear in that city. Mindful that
many of the state's citizens were unfamiliar with—and possibly harbored
prejudice against—commercial banks, the new institution's directors
sought to build public support by quickly publishing an explanation of
banking's benefits.[61]

That year also witnessed the memorably inelegant arrival of chartered
banking to the newly acquired Louisiana Territory. Because the 1791
charter for the Bank of the United States only authorized the opening of
branches in *states*, Congress needed to independently sanction the opening of a branch in New Orleans. This was accomplished in March 1804; in
signing the bill into law, President Jefferson approved the extension of an
institution he had openly opposed thirteen years earlier. By this time, however, William C. C. Claiborne—the territorial governor of Louisiana—had
yielded (*without* informing the Jefferson administration) to intense local
pressure for credit facilities and authorized the Louisiana Bank. Writing
to Secretary of State James Madison, Claiborne explained that the "Citizens of New Orleans [had] exercised uncommon solicitude for [a] Bank";
they had submitted "a Petition to me on the Subject . . . Signed I believe
by almost every respectable man in the City and its Vicinity."[62] Though
Secretary of the Treasury Albert Gallatin grumbled to the president that
Claiborne's behavior would likely "defeat the establishment of a branch
bank" in New Orleans, that turned out not to be the case; a branch was
opened the following year.[63] Governor Claiborne was able to escape with
only a written censure from Gallatin, and the Louisiana Bank ultimately
survived with a capital of $300,000.[64] Though the Louisiana Bank techni-
cally received its charter from a territorial governor (as opposed to a state
legislature), its birth still underscores the role played by broad credit access problems in early bank proliferation.

When existing institutions—including several banks already mentioned in this chapter—acquired reputations (rightly or wrongly) for dis-
criminatory lending, those adversely affected would sometimes seek relief
through the chartering of friendlier facilities. Historian Naomi Lamoreaux has documented one form of discrimination from this period: "insider lending," which privileged loan applications from both stockholders
and those with personal or business ties to bank directors.[65] For those out-

side this privileged circle, application denials were "bitter pill[s]" that often left them with a desire to secure more agreeable fare.[66]

In Boston, for example, there were suspicions "inside and outside the state legislature" by the early 1790s that a small group of wealthy individuals controlled the Massachusetts Bank and managed it for the benefit of themselves and a select few others. At the very least, the institution's own books from this period confirm that stockholders—many of whom were identified as "merchants" or "capitalists" more broadly—received a healthy share of the bank's loans, and most of the remaining borrowers were other "opulent Merchants of extensive business and credit."[67] When the commonwealth chartered the Union Bank of Boston in June 1792, its desire to involve and serve relative "outsiders" was manifest: Shares were priced between four and eight dollars—those figures are not misprints—and 20 percent of the institution's funds were reserved for small to medium-sized loans "wherein the Directors [would] wholly and exclusively regard the agricultural interest."[68]

New charters were also pursued by those who suffered from partisan discrimination in lending. To be clear, the difference between network-based and partisan discrimination could be a matter of perception. On the one hand, for example, the behavior of the directors at both the Bank of New York and the New York branch of the Bank of the United States appeared consistent with insider lending; throughout the 1790s, both boards made loans "primarily to their friends, relatives, and business associates."[69] On the other hand, these boards were also predominantly Federalist, and Republicans in Manhattan began to perceive—and editorialize about—a "system of exclusion" in which the "benefit of those institutions was chiefly confined to the adherents of one political sect."[70] Consequently, some urban Republicans began to think of a chartered bank controlled by their own party as a valuable tool for serving existing supporters—and even cultivating new ones: "If the Republicans had in their hands such a financial weapon as the [Federalists] possessed, what power would be added to their campaigns! They could give loans and discounts to good Republicans, attract wavering Federalists to their side, and even assist the property-less man to qualify as a voter."[71]

A memorable—some might say infamous—response to this sentiment in 1799 ultimately gave Republicans in lower Manhattan the institution they were looking for. Aaron Burr—former member of the US Senate, current member of the New York General Assembly, and future vice president of the United States—was convinced that the Bank of New York in particular had been "used to patronise and encourage business men who were Federalists, and to cramp and embarrass those who held republican principles."[72] However, the path to a more accommodating institution for fellow Republicans was effectively blocked by Federalist control of the New York legislature. Without an obvious way forward, Burr opted for deception.

His ruse was a suggestion that New York charter a private water company in Manhattan; it would be helpful for fighting fires, cleaning dirty streets, and—most importantly—supplying the city's residents with fresh water. Yellow fever was a perennial summer scourge in the Early American Republic, and the summer of 1798 had been no exception; nearly two thousand city residents died. More to the point, exposure to yellow fever was often attributed to the use of water from swamps and ponds, where disease-carrying mosquitos congregated. The proposed company, Burr and other project supporters reasoned, could draw citizens away from those hazardous sites and toward fresh water piped in from the Bronx River.[73] Just before the state legislature approved the charter bill in late March 1799, Burr advanced his "clandestine Republican cause" by quietly inserting a provision that permitted the water company to "employ all such surplus capital as may belong or accrue to the said company in the purchase of public or other stock or in *any other monied transactions or operations*."[74] Thus was born the Manhattan Company—later Chase Manhattan, and today JPMorgan Chase—an institution that spent far more time supplying loans to city Republicans than fresh water to all New Yorkers.

ATTRACTING AND REPELLING THE NATIONAL BANK

While the material interests of lenders (profit) and borrowers (credit access) dominate the story of state bank proliferation between 1791 and 1811, no account of this development would be complete without recognition that the Bank of the United States—and more specifically, its authority to open branches—also induced some state legislative activity. Local communities understandably viewed the Bank's expansion through the prism of their own economic or ideological interests, and several secured state bank charters as (in their eyes) interest-advancing responses to that expansion. For economically underdeveloped communities—at least relative to the four cities that were granted branches in late 1791—a state bank represented a means to two related ends: commercial prosperity in its own right and the resulting prominence necessary to acquire a future Bank office. By contrast, for communities with an animus toward federal power generally—and its physical presence more specifically—a state bank charter represented a signaling device. Their intended message to the Bank's directors was simple: The services of a branch are neither needed nor wanted here.

John Brown, a prominent merchant in Providence and one of the founders (in 1764) of a local institution of higher education that today bears his family name, badly wanted a branch of the new national bank for his city. In fact, Brown began scheming to obtain a branch in June 1791, a full five months *before* the decision to open them was formally made. The core problem, John explained to his brother Moses, was that Providence in 1791 was hardly a magnet for economic activity: "[W]ithout a spring to promote our young men in business here they must and will continue to go to such places as will aid them with the means of business; and in short all our wealth . . . must be transferred to other states, who by their banks promote all the valuable arts of mankind."[75]

According to Howard Kemble Stokes, an early student of Rhode Island banking, John Brown had a solution in mind. If Brown and others could succeed in getting the Rhode Island legislature to charter a bank in Providence, that institution might generate the economic growth necessary for national bank officials "to think the town entitled to a branch."[76] Efforts to take this first step proved successful; the Providence Bank was chartered in October 1791, in time to inform the early November deliberations of the national bank board. The second step, however, was never taken during the 1791–1811 period; Providence secured neither one of the first four branches nor one of the subsequent four: Norfolk (1800), Washington, DC (1802), Savannah (1802), and the aforementioned New Orleans (1805).[77]

A generation later, a second banking historian—Joseph Stancliffe Davis—argued that John Brown had a very different understanding of the relationship between chartering a state bank and obtaining a national bank branch for Providence. Davis pointed to evidence that Brown went to Philadelphia in October 1791—after the Providence Bank had secured its charter but before the branching decision was made—"to have the [state] bank *made* a branch of the national bank."[78] In other words, Brown's goal was to immediately *convert* the Providence Bank, not supplement it. His ultimate understanding need not be clarified here, because both the Stokes and Davis accounts render the Providence Bank an instrument for bringing the national institution—sooner or later—to Rhode Island.

In sharp contrast, consider the events that led to the November 1792 chartering of the Bank of Alexandria. In late 1791, a number of Federalist merchants in that Virginia town commenced a campaign to win a national bank branch. They began by petitioning the Bank's board of direc-

tors through their congressman, Richard Bland Lee. If their memorial was
meant to inform the board's initial discussion of branches, it was functionally dead on arrival; Lee was not able to forward their petition until ten
days *after* the first four branches had been named.[79] A few days after Lee
passed along their memorial, they appealed directly to Alexander Hamilton, seemingly ignorant of the Treasury chief's hostility to branches.[80]
Around the same time, Federalist merchants in Norfolk and Richmond
sent similar petitions to Philadelphia; the intrastate, intraparty scrum for
a Bank branch was officially on.[81] About seven months later, Hamilton—
now apparently reconciled to branches—solicited a site recommendation
from William Heth, a federal collector of customs in Virginia.[82]

Thomas Jefferson considered the Bank of the United States to be unconstitutional and loathed both the individual and collective effects of
speculative trading in its stock, but he was positively aghast at the prospect of Federalist "bank-mongers" invading his native soil. Moreover, he
believed that any Virginia branch of the Bank would serve mercantile interests almost exclusively. Accordingly, upon learning in early July 1792
that the Bank's board had "nearly settled" upon Richmond as its preferred
branch site, Jefferson asked James Madison if a "counter-bank might be
set up to befriend the agricultural man."[83] Governor Henry Lee III—the
"Light Horse Harry" of Revolutionary War fame—also wanted a state
bank in Richmond, but his reasoning was altogether different from Jefferson's. In mid-September, the governor wrote that "one way is left to pre-
serve the state from this undue operation, & that is to establish a bank
under the auspices of the C[ommon]wealth—This might easily be done
& would counter-act if not defeat the plan contemplated."[84] Lee's goal, in
short, was less to offer the proposed Richmond branch a state-chartered
peer and more to prevent its establishment in the first place.

For reasons that remain unclear, but probably owe something to the
project's frosty reception outside Federalist circles, the national bank can-
celed its plans to open a Richmond branch.[85] That decision left the Virginia General Assembly with calls from multiple cities for bank charters
and an opportunity to reinforce its opposition to the national bank by
granting one or more of those requests.[86] It promptly seized that opportunity, chartering banks in both Alexandria and Richmond by the end of
1792.[87] While the Bank of Alexandria was quickly up and running, Richmond's authorized venture never got off the ground; subscriptions to the
bank were insufficient to sustain it. As such, despite representing the first
choice of the Bank board in Philadelphia and one favorite (not to mention

the home) of the state legislature, Richmond went *without* a chartered bank until 1804.[88]

CONCLUSION

This chapter opened with several basic empirical claims. First, state banks multiplied during the period between 1791 and 1811. Second, there were several economic and ideological reasons for this proliferation. Finally, this period of institutional creation gradually undermined the national bank's dominance of the American banking industry. For the most part, I have prioritized the second of these claims, offering examples of how lenders, borrowers, and partisans all maneuvered (at different times and in different places) to win charters for state banks. I want to close this chapter by expanding a bit on the third claim—by appreciating, in other words, how state bank growth slowly altered the national bank's position in the broader industry.

One simple way to capture the effect of state bank multiplication[89] on the Bank of the United States is to consider the national institution's $10 million in capital—again, a constant between 1791 and 1811—as a changing percentage of the American banking industry. I did this—ever so briefly—at the start of the chapter, contrasting the Bank's position soon after its 1791 birth (68 percent of total industry capital) with the same as its 1811 battle to survive loomed (15 percent). Table 2.2 captures the intervening period at three-year intervals; it reveals that the Bank's market share

TABLE 2.2 The National Bank's declining market share, 1791–1811

End of calendar year	Number of state banks	Combined capital of state banks (in $ millions)	Resulting market share of the National Bank (%)
1792	12	6.31	61.3
1795	20	13.47	42.6
1798	22	14.17	41.4
1801	32	19.17	34.3
1804	64	31.17	24.3
1807	83	43.43	18.7
1810	102	56.19	15.1

Source: Fenstermaker, *Development of American Commercial Banking*, 13.

Note: The National Bank's market share is calculated by dividing $10 million into the combined state bank capital plus $10 million.

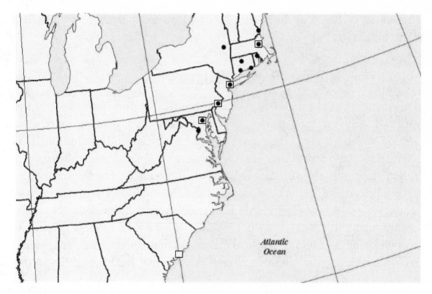

Fig. 2.1. Commercial banks in the United States, 1792. Black circles are state banks; white squares are Bank of the United States branches. Source: Generated from Fenstermaker, *Development of American Commercial Banking*, app. A. Figure first published in "Turning (Into) 'The Great Regulating Wheel': The Conversion of the Bank of the United States, 1791–1811," *Studies in American Political Development* 26, no. 1 (April 2012): 1–23. Copyright © 2012 Cambridge University Press; reprinted with permission.

dipped below 50 percent within a few years of commencing operations and (with the exception of the 1795–1798 period) declined steadily throughout the period.[90]

An alternative approach here—and one far more relevant for the 1811 constitutional debate, as I preview below—is to capture and compare bona fide snapshots of the American banking landscape. To map chartered banks near the beginning and end of the 1791–1811 period—both (1) the Bank of the United States and its branches, and (2) state-sanctioned institutions—is to capture significant change in the number and geographic spread of industry members. Figures 2.1 and 2.2 offer those snapshots.[91]

These figures help bring two developments into sharp relief. First, though state banking in the South was virtually nonexistent at the close of 1792—only the newly chartered Bank of Alexandria could legitimately claim that mantle—its presence by the end of 1811 was unmistakable. Though most state banks continued to be located in New England and along the New York–Philadelphia–Baltimore corridor, many southern cities—and even a handful of western towns—now hosted local institu-

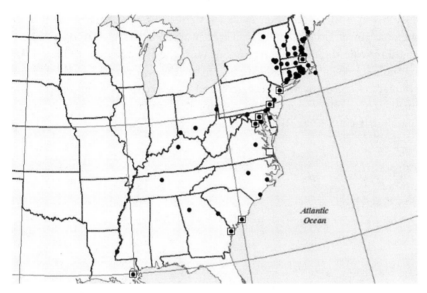

Fig. 2.2. Commercial banks in the United States, 1811. Black circles are state banks; white squares are Bank of the United States branches. Source: Generated from Fenstermaker, *Development of American Commercial Banking*, app. A. Figure first published in "Turning (Into) 'The Great Regulating Wheel': The Conversion of the Bank of the United States, 1791–1811," *Studies in American Political Development* 26, no. 1 (April 2012): 1–23. Copyright © 2012 Cambridge University Press; reprinted with permission.

tions. Second, as 1792 ended, a bare majority of states—eight out of fifteen—played host to institutions chartered by their respective legislatures. Almost twenty years later, each of the seventeen states in the Union housed a bank of its own creation (and some many more than that).

The latter development in particular would have both political and constitutional consequences as the expiration of the Bank's twenty-year charter approached (March 1811) and the Eleventh Congress (1809–1811) began consideration of a recharter bill. Politically, the new institutional landscape rendered the hundred-plus state banks a powerful—and nationwide—interest group; they pressured members of Congress to both (1) deny the Bank of the United States a charter extension and then (2) distribute the (profitable) deposits of the federal government among them.[92] Many (but surely not all) members of the Republican party that dominated the Eleventh Congress responded to this sizable and dispersed population of institutions by gravitating toward one of the antibank constitutional claims offered by their partisan forebears in 1791. The national bank, in their eyes, could not be anchored to the Necessary and Proper Clause not

only because the institution lacked a significant relationship to an enumerated power but *also* because a subset of the existing state institutions
could provide the federal government with the same fiscal services. That
is, the national bank could satisfy neither the functional *nor* the federal
standard of constitutional necessity (and it needed to do both). Their arguments to this effect, and the constitutional rejoinders of both pro-recharter
Republicans and Federalists, are the subject of chapter 4.

CHAPTER THREE

"The Great Regulating Wheel" and Institutional Conversion

The First Bank . . . endeavored to restrict state bank credit expansion when it appeared inordinate, by gathering bank notes and tendering them for specie.

—Alan Greenspan, 1996 speech to the American Enterprise Institute

The first twenty years of the national bank's life were remembered in the early nineteenth century—and are remembered today—more for the bank's unexpected activity than for the workmanlike performance of its expected functions. Between 1791 and 1811, the Bank of the United States delivered on all the fiscal promises made by Alexander Hamilton in his *Report on a National Bank*: It helped raise the market price of federal debt to (and above) par value, lent money to the federal government, served as a safe depository for the Treasury's revenue, facilitated collection of that revenue through the circulation of a paper currency, and made routine payments from public funds to various creditors (e.g., debt holders and federal employees). Its performance was hardly surprising to early federal lawmakers, because the fiscal utility of a national bank had not been a point of disagreement in February 1791.

What surprised those legislators—not to mention many of their constituents—was the Bank's slow but real emergence in the mid-1790s as an institution with *monetary* power: the capacity to control the "community's stock of money."[1] In the context of early American federalism, this meant regulating the supply of credit available from state-chartered banks. The lawmakers' sense of surprise is rooted in the fact that control of state institutions by the Bank of the United States formed no part of the 1791 debate, either in Congress or in the executive branch. As Bray Hammond wrote in his Pulitzer Prize–winning *Banks and Politics in America*, it was a development that "[n]either Alexander Hamilton nor any one else had foreseen[.]"[2]

Just as the development chronicled in chapter 2—the national bank's slow loss of industry dominance in the wake of state bank proliferation—was readily identified with a species of gradual institutional change, the transformation outlined above can be recognized as consistent with a member of that genus. Here, the Bank's gradual recognition (and deliberate exercise) of its regulatory power offers an example of institutional *conversion*. Institutions founded to solve a certain problem or set of problems, as Wolfgang Streeck and Kathleen Thelen note, may be subsequently "redirected to new goals, functions, or purposes." This may represent (1) a deployment of existing resources to meet an emergent problem or (2) the product of "changes in power relations": new institutional stewardship followed by a turn toward novel ports.[3] The terminology for this type of slow-moving change can be deceptive. In the case of the Bank of the United States, the emergence of its monetary function did not so much "convert" the institution in the colloquial sense of the term as *supplement* its existing fiscal functions; none of the responsibilities discussed by Hamilton were abrogated once the institution began to operate as a "watchdog over state banks and the economy."[4]

The Bank's conversion from simple fiscal auxiliary to instrument of both fiscal and monetary policy has received some attention from economic historians, but these treatments pale—in both breadth and depth—in comparison with scholarship on state bank proliferation. Some work does little more than mention the Bank's regulatory function in passing, employing language that may create the false impression that it was a feature of institutional operations from day one. Representative of this tradition is the claim from William J. Shultz and M. R. Cain that the national bank "[t]hrough its branch organization . . . to some extent controlled the newly-created state banks throughout the country."[5] Most who have treated the subject, by contrast, explicitly identify the Bank's monetary role as an *unexpected* post-1791 development and then briefly explain its method of controlling state institutions. Emblematic of the former is Stephen Mihm's recent observation that the "First Bank of the United States exercised a growing measure of control over the bank notes [that state] institutions issued, though this happened more by accident than design."[6] The latter is aptly represented by Edwin J. Perkins's suggestion that the Bank "regularly accumulated a substantial quantity of bank notes issued by state institutions. By presenting those bank notes routinely for conversion into specie, the national bank kept sufficient pressure on the reserves of state banks to prevent them from making an excessive volume of loans and [thus] imprudently expanding the volume of currency in circulation."[7] Even the most detailed of the available treatments, however—which employ some primary source material to both confirm the Bank's functional evolution and explain the regulatory mechanism[8]—are still quite limited; they fail to offer a comprehensive account of the Bank's transformation into what its first president, Thomas Willing, called the "great regulating wheel of all the Commercial Banks in the United States[.]"[9]

The primary goal of this chapter, simply put, is to provide an account of the Bank's conversion that is both wide and deep. This requires a survey of (1) the collection of then extant political conditions (ranging from formal institutions to administrative decisions) that made this slow-moving change possible, (2) the deliberate behavior of Bank officials that made it a reality, and (3) its reception among a diverse group of public and private actors in the Early American Republic. As with chapter 2's review of state bank growth, this account of the Bank's functional enhancement between 1791 and 1811 is not offered simply for its own sake; the point is to lay a foundation for the claim that this institutional development is relevant for the study of American constitutional politics.

As chapter 5 will make clear, this particular expansion of the institution's functions was not lost on members of the Republican party, who continued to control the elected branches during and after the War of 1812. The monetary turmoil that commenced during (but extended beyond) that conflict, which included the suspension of specie payments by many state banks, convinced many party members that a revived regulator for these institutions was in the nation's best interest. There was a problem, however: Republicans in late 1815 and early 1816 were just as divided over the meaning of the Necessary and Proper Clause as they had been in early 1811; the regime was split between a moderate and an "Old" wing. Collectively desirous of a national bank, but also collectively unwilling to embrace an expansive conception of federal power, party members leveraged the institution's functional evolution into a creative solution to their dilemma. Instead of launching another round of debate over the Sweeping Clause, prominent Republicans eschewed the provision entirely; their postwar bank bill was presented as an exercise of Congress's power under the Coinage Clause. They argued that the power to "coin Money, regulate the Value thereof," which had (to that point) never been invoked as a potential anchor for a national bank, had been intended as a kind of congressional carte blanche with respect to monetary affairs. Insofar as a revived Bank of the United States would facilitate the circulation of Congress's chosen money—gold and silver coin—the institution was valid under that provision.

I open this chapter by enumerating four conditions that placed the national bank in a position to develop monetary power: basic constitutional structures, policy choices at both the federal and the state level, and early Treasury Department rules respecting tax collection. Collectively, these led—across a number of sites—to the Bank's regular accumulation of large quantities of state bank notes. I then review the activity of institutional elites—in this case, members of the Bank's board of directors—that yielded (in October 1795) the first clear instance of "positive monetary control" over state banks.[10] While the Bank of the United States was routinely capable of redeeming state bank notes, thus draining those institutions of their specie reserves and effectively forcing reductions in their lending, it was not free to do so arbitrarily; politically, an institution with a time-limited federal charter could not afford to needlessly antagonize state banks. Accordingly, its officers elected to deploy their resources if (and only if) excessive lending by one or more institutions was thought to pose a threat to the broader banking system. Finally, I offer a brief discussion of the uneven manner in which this expansion of the Bank's functions was received. For example, many who were formally associated with the institution and its monetary activity openly defended its conversion; a board member at the Boston branch suggested in 1807 that regulation of state banks was "our best claim to praise," an admirable sacrifice of profit for the sake of maintaining system-wide order.[11] By the same token, those with ties to local economic institutions often cast the same development in a much harsher light; on the eve of the 1811 recharter debate, one prominent national bank critic wrote of the institution's "inordinate power of crushing all the other banks."[12]

ADVANTAGE, BANK OF THE UNITED STATES

The national bank's post-1791 development of monetary power—which altered the course of both its normal and its constitutional politics—was rooted in four background conditions. The first three of these—federalism, state authority to charter banking institutions, and national bank discretion to establish branches outside its Philadelphia headquarters—have either been implicit in the foregoing chapters or explored at some length. Nevertheless, further discussion of these conditions is required to fully appreciate both the institutional landscape taking shape in the early to mid-1790s—one marked by multisite interaction between the national bank and state banks—and the resulting need for (and development of) procedures to settle debts between these institutions. More often than not, the Bank of the United States emerged as the creditor in these settlements; its collection of a state bank's paper (i.e., notes and checks) exceeded that institution's collection of its paper. The fourth condition—Treasury Department acceptance of state bank paper for tax collection purposes—has wholly escaped discussion thus far. Because the Treasury deposited most of its revenue in the national bank, its collection policy only enhanced the institution's tendency to emerge as the creditor of state-chartered banks. That strong tendency, in short, was the rock on which the Bank's regulatory function would be built.

Federalism, state chartering authority, and the Bank's discretion to establish branches have not only been present in prior chapters, but they are sufficiently intertwined to justify joint treatment here. Simply put, regular contact between the national bank and its state-chartered counterparts across multiple cities—namely, their acceptance of each other's paper—represents the starting point for the conversion story. I detail the specifics of this interaction below, but the unvarnished proposition invites two preliminary observations. First, since state authority to charter banks under the US Constitution was never in dispute, the conclusion reached in February 1791—that Congress also possessed authority to charter a bank—rendered bank incorporation a *concurrent* power in American federalism. Consequently, though the landscape of the Early American Republic was increasingly populated with physically and functionally similar institutions—I include Bank branches in this imagery—each individual facility was technically sanctioned by one of two distinct "systems of authority."[13]

The second observation essentially follows from the first. Not long after the November 1791 decision to establish branches was made, the Bank of the United States found itself operating in four locations—Boston, New York, Philadelphia, and Baltimore—that hosted (and/or lay in close proximity to) state-chartered banks.[14] By 1805, with the opening of the New Orleans branch, that number had climbed to nine. Between its Philadelphia headquarters and its satellite locations, then, the national bank routinely interacted with nearly every state-chartered institution in the United States. Because those contacts ultimately led to the Bank's emergence as a regulatory instrument, the gradual transformation furnishes powerful evidence in support of Karen Orren and Stephen Skowronek's oft-repeated claim that "intercurrence" guides political development over time; distinct institutional patterns move "alongside one another" and collide in ways that mutually "reshape[] and distinguish[]" each other.[15]

In this particular case, the collision of interest was between patterns of federal and state authority.

A more embellished account of early interbank relations—or federal-state relations in one public policy realm—should begin with James O. Wettereau's observation that as 1791 drew to a close, "each of the existing State banks, except that of Providence, would soon face the competition of the mammouth [sic] National Bank or one of its branches."[16] While the Bank's main office would operate near the Bank of North America, the newly authorized branches in Boston, New York, and Baltimore would open their doors within walking distance of the Massachusetts Bank, the Bank of New York, and the Bank of Maryland, respectively. Moreover, it was clear from the start that each of these institutions would accept the paper of its neighbor at face value. For example, a customer of the Bank branch in Boston could hand over $100 in Massachusetts Bank notes and receive a $100 credit to his account. The premise here was that since the Boston branch could demand (and receive) $100 in gold or silver coin from the Massachusetts Bank for that paper, it could treat the notes as the equivalent of specie.

These four pairs of institutions would collectively answer a question that had lingered in American banking since 1784: Could multiple banks coexist in one city? More specifically, if two banks accepted each other's paper, would one emerge as the persistent creditor and ruin the debtor with constant demands for specie?[17] Jonathan Mason, a member of the Massachusetts House who was about to begin his appointment as a director of the Bank's new Boston branch, anticipated the impending bilateral contest (if not an answer to the coexistence question) in a December 1791 letter to Andrew Craigie: "The capital of [the Boston] branch ought to be attended to—unless it is as respectable as possible, the Mass[achusetts] Bank will control & check us instead of our commanding them."[18] Time would reveal that multiple banks could survive in a single setting, with the help of debt settlement protocols and despite the state banks' tendency toward indebtedness to the Bank of the United States.

Two procedures were established in 1792 for dealing with interbank debts: account balances and note exchanges. With respect to the former, the directors of the Massachusetts Bank opened an account with the Boston branch of the national bank in mid-June; into that account they deposited the branch-issued notes and checks currently in their possession. In effect, this provided the state bank with a balance for paying any debts subsequently owed to the Boston branch.[19] As for the latter, by the end of the calendar year, the two Boston banks had begun to mimic the institutional pairings in New York and Philadelphia: They were regularly exchanging bank-issued paper. In early February, the directors of the Bank of North America had approved a daily exchange of deposited notes and checks with the national bank's main office. Similarly, by late July, the Bank of New York cashier, William Seton, could report to Alexander Hamilton that his institution received the notes of the New York branch "indiscriminately with our own, & I believe they do the same—we make large interchanges now & then[.]"[20] Accordingly, the directors of the Massachusetts Bank were hardly acting in an unorthodox manner when, in late December, they "decided to send each week to the [Boston] branch of the Bank of the United States . . . all their [accumulated] notes" and to demand their own paper or specie in return.[21]

After these exchanges were conducted, the Bank of the United States frequently found itself in possession of excess state bank paper; this rendered it the creditor of those institutions. In this vein, Bray Hammond observed that "[f]rom time to time" the main office or a branch of the national bank would be "a greater debtor to some local banks than creditor; but this was exceptional."[22] The question, of course, is *how*—how the Bank found itself, on a regular basis, in such an advantageous position vis-à-vis state institutions. One crucial factor in this equation is also the fourth background condition for the Bank's gradual transformation into a regulatory force: its near-constant receipt of state bank paper from the "single largest transactor in the economy"—the federal government.[23] In short, the Treasury Department's tax collectors accepted the notes and checks of state banks, and usually proceeded to deposit that paper in the nearest office of the national bank.[24]

Much might be said respecting the Treasury's tax collection policy and its effect on interbank relations, but at least two related points warrant attention. The first offers a kind of analytic baseline: The importance of federal deposits for establishing and maintaining the Bank's advantageous position has long been appreciated. This has been true in work authored for both scholarly and popular audiences. For example, in *Money: Whence It Came, Where It Went*—a book written in the 1970s with a broad readership in mind—John Kenneth Galbraith noted that "the Bank of the United States was a privileged competitor [of state banks]. It had the deposits of the federal government."[25] More recently, and for a much narrower audience, J. Lawrence Broz claimed that "[b]ecause the First Bank was the [federal] government's fiscal agent, it received [on deposit] the notes of state banks in payment of taxes. This made it constantly the creditor of the state banks[.]"[26]

The second point of interest represents a partial challenge to the analytic baseline. Scholars have generally operated on the premise that Treasury Department officials received the paper of all state banks for the duration of the 1791–1811 period. The starting points here are two fall 1789 decisions by Alexander Hamilton, on behalf of the Treasury, to begin accepting the notes and checks of the two existing state-chartered banks: the Bank of North America and the Massachusetts Bank.[27] The unspoken understanding seems to be that this privilege (1) was extended to new state banks as they commenced operations and (2) continued down through the national bank's formal closure in early 1811. This understanding, to be clear, continues to permeate scholarly treatment of interbank relations in the 1791–1811 period. However, the implicit consensus here should not be confused with unanimity. More specifically, the late Stuart Bruchey—a prolific student of American economic history—argued that Hamilton's Treasury Department gradually *discontinued* the acceptance of state bank paper, moving to the exclusive receipt of national bank paper between early 1792 and mid-1793.[28] If Bruchey is correct, then the Bank's routine creditor status was a function of factors other than Treasury policy.

Bruchey's claim—couched in a 1970 footnote—has never garnered a response. While the evidence on this question is not especially plentiful, there is enough to carve out a middle ground between the traditional understanding of Treasury policy and Bruchey's competing account. For one thing, even the modified tax collection rules circulated by Hamilton in 1792 and 1793 did not foreclose the receipt of *all* state bank paper; the Treasury "continued to permit payment of duties in notes of various State institutions as well, at least those [banks] located in towns or cities where there was no office of the Bank of the United States."[29] In other words, the nonacceptance policy was never a universal one. At most, it limited the Bank's incoming stock of state bank paper to that issued by certain institutions.

The modified tax collection policy was not only limited in scope, but evidence suggests that it was also limited in duration. One potential end point is supplied by a November 1808 letter from Treasury Secretary Albert Gallatin to David Lenox, Thomas Willing's successor as president of the national bank.[30] Responding to recent complaints that the Baltimore branch of the Bank had made "unusually large & particularly draining" demands for specie from local institutions, Gallatin reminded Lenox that "[t]he large amount of public deposits necessarily gives a more than usual preponderance to the Bank of the United States over other Banks. No use of this ought certainly to be made to their injury or beyond what is necessary for the safety of the Bank of the United States."[31] This letter strongly implies—to invoke a second source—that deposits of federal revenue enabled the Baltimore branch "to make such large calls on the different Banks in [the] City."[32] In other words, federal tax collectors in Baltimore—and presumably other cities with Bank offices—had begun reaccepting state bank paper no later than October 1808.

Gallatin's letter suggests that the Treasury Department's nonacceptance of some state bank paper may have lasted up to fifteen years (1793–1808). An October 1802 letter to Gallatin from President Thomas Jefferson, however, effectively shortens that interval to no more—and possibly far less—than nine years. That fall, Jefferson was pondering a proposal to forgo the near-exclusive deposit of federal revenue in the national bank in favor of a "judicious distribution of [it]" among numerous institutions. In soliciting Gallatin's advice on the proposal, the president suggested that adoption of this alternative deposit scheme would deny the Bank of the United States the means to "swallow up the [other banks] and monopolize the whole banking business of the United States."[33] Jefferson's exaggerated account of the Bank's effect on state institutions notwithstanding, his comments imply that no later than October 1802, state bank paper was again *generally* receivable for purposes of federal tax payments. It is possible, of course—even likely—that Treasury policy reverted to its pre-1793 form well in advance of the president's letter. As such, late 1802 simply operates as an outer bound in time.

The upshot of this discussion is that early Treasury Department policy was a crucial (but slightly less than uniform) facilitator of the national bank's routine creditor status vis-à-vis state banks. The paper of many local institutions was always receivable for federal tax purposes, and that of the remaining banks for much of the 1791–1811 period. The big question, of course, is what the Bank of the United States *did* with its creditor status—how it responded to this "strategic position."[34] The reaction of national bank officials, which reflected both their sensitivity to political reality and their concern for economic stability, would transform their institution from the inside.

"THE GREAT REGULATING WHEEL" EMERGES

In one sense, the national bank's response to its creditor status seems unexceptional. The institution's leadership consciously eschewed an aggressive, sustained, and multisite campaign to drain state banks of their specie via redemptions of accumulated notes and checks. The Bank of the

United States, in other words, declined to behave like a ruthless competitor of its state-chartered peers. Instead, the institution elected to utilize its stockpile of state bank paper on an as-needed basis; specie would only be demanded if the Bank board concluded that one or more local institutions had engaged in excessive lending. In short, the national bank behaved like—not to mention regarded itself as—the "guardian of the [overall] 'System of Bank Credit.'"[35]

From another angle, however, the course pursued by the Bank's board *was* extraordinary; it reflected a sense of institutional purpose that seems to have bordered on hubris. The logic here is as follows: Any vigorous and protracted institutional effort across major commercial centers to limit state bank lending (and thus profitability) would have been politically suicidal for the Bank of the United States. It would have earned the institution the enmity of state bank officers and stockholders nationwide, and virtually guaranteed the organized opposition of that crowd to any future charter extension for the Bank. That being said, *any* redemptions of state bank paper—even demands limited to certain times or places—were bound to antagonize local economic interests to some degree. As such, it would have been safer—at least politically—for the national bank to avoid any and all activity that might have been construed as oppressive toward state banks. Simply put, the Bank could have consciously refrained from presenting state bank paper for redemption into specie; the notes and checks could have been held or even recirculated. However, as economist Richard H. Timberlake has pointed out, for the national bank "to have been in this strategic position and then to have adopted an attitude of 'no policy' would have denied the utility of human management and the very human notion that positive intervention could make a good thing work better."[36] Despite the inherent political risk, then, the Bank's leadership ultimately resolved to demand specie from local institutions only for well-defined purposes: to remedy and prevent excess credit creation.

It is unclear when precisely the Bank's board of directors determined on this course, which aimed to utilize the institution's advantageous position without exploiting it. However, there is strong evidence to suggest that the policy was in place no later than October 1795. That month, the Philadelphia board prepared a memorandum for circulation to the branches in Boston, New York, Baltimore, and Charleston. Invoking the "recent Institution of so many Banks"—a development chronicled in the previous chapter—the national bank's leaders expressed anxiety over the growing and (to their minds) "injurious Surplusage of circulating Credit."[37] Otherwise put, because banks circulated paper equal to some multiple of their specie holdings, a spurt of state institution building could quickly grow (and perhaps *over*grow) the aggregate money supply. After reiterating its conclusion that the existing supply of credit was "overexpanded," the board volunteered that this state of affairs left local institutions vulnerable both individually and as a group: "the Derangement of any one [bank], would create an Alarm & a serious Crisis, which would deeply injure the reputation of all."[38] In modern parlance, the national bank's leadership was concerned that a run on one state institution could lead to contagion.

The October 1795 memorandum not only offered the board's diagnosis of monetary disease but prescribed a *self-administered* remedy for it.[39] That is to say, having reached the conclusion "that extensive Credits [had] been too incautiously granted[,]" the Bank of the United States took it upon *itself* to "vary[] the system & essentially reduc[e]" those credits.[40] Not only would the institution reduce its own lending, but it would effectively force the hands of state banks by draining their specie reserves.

The broader import of this declaration warrants some reinforcement. In the first place, the memorandum clearly articulated an institutional objective—regulation of the overall supply of credit—that is the essence of monetary power. Second, that objective—effective oversight of the nascent "American banking system"[41]—was wholly unconnected with the institution's 1791 founding. Going forward, the Bank of the United States would not simply provide a range of fiscal services to the federal government; it would also monitor the lending of state banks and respond to self-detected anomalies in credit creation. Finally, the institution's monetary "policy" can be inferred from the board's memorandum: If a specific institution or the banking system as a whole was considered within acceptable bounds for lending, the Bank would forgo the redemption of accumulated state bank paper; it would hold or recirculate those notes and checks. If, however, the national bank "felt that credit restraint was called for," it would redeem the portion of that paper required to achieve the desired reduction in state bank lending.[42]

This account of the Bank's conversion, however, still needs to withstand a modicum of scrutiny. Earlier, I cited Streeck and Thelen's claim that this particular species of gradual but transformative institutional change typically represents an outgrowth of (1) new problems or (2) new institutional leadership. It is reasonably clear that the Bank's emergence as a monetary force did *not* result from personnel changes. For one thing, there are simply no claims to this effect in primary or secondary sources. For another, Thomas Willing served continuously as president of the national bank between 1791 and 1807, which covers the period of conversion. Finally, while the position of cashier—the institution's lead day-to-day officer—did experience turnover just prior to October 1795 (John Kean resigned due to "an infirm state of health" and was replaced by George Simpson[43]), the new incumbent was a bona fide "company man" with long experience in a subordinate position (first teller) and no manifest disposition to pursue institutional goals at odds with those of his predecessor.[44]

This leaves, of course, novel challenges as a foundation for the Bank's conversion. On the one hand, the October 1795 memorandum certainly appears to reflect this particular image of slow but significant institutional change; the board both identified an emergent monetary problem and directed resources toward its resolution. On the other hand, the likely authenticity of the board's claim respecting excess credit creation should be assessed. While an analytic temptation to simply take the directors at their word is understandable, it is possible that Bank officials (1) found themselves in a commanding position vis-à-vis state banks, (2) understood the political futility of exploiting that position, and thus (3) rhetorically constructed a problem in need of a solution (so as to justify at least modest use of their resources). In much simpler terms, the board might have fabricated the 1795 "Surplusage of circulating Credit."

The available evidence suggests that the Bank's monetary turn reflected genuine (and well-founded) concerns about aggregate credit creation in the mid-1790s, not a contrived distress designed to legitimate periodic specie demands on state banks. Change in consumer prices provides one window into these concerns. Citizens in the Early American Republic experienced modest price inflation during the first four years following ratification of the Constitution, but the following two years—1794 and 1795—were especially taxing on their wallets (table 3.1).[45]

TABLE 3.1 Consumer price index for all items, 1789–1795

Year	David-Solar index (1860 = 100)
1789	106
1790	110
1791	113
1792	115
1793	119
1794	132
1795	151

Source: Lindert and Sutch, "Consumer Price Indexes, for All Items: 1774–2003."

A 27 percent rise in consumer prices over a two-year period, however, is hardly the only evidence of genuine trouble in (and concern over) the nation's monetary affairs. Even individuals associated with state banks during this period acknowledged that something was not quite right. William Constable, a member of the board of directors at the Bank of New York, informed William Rogers in July 1795—a few months before the national bank resolved to restrict state bank lending—that "the Engagements which People have entered into are so far beyond their means & the currency & circulation of the country are so short of representing the Amount of Payments that I am really at a loss to conjecture how the business is carried on[.]"[46] All told, both objective economic indicators and commentary from those with direct ties to local credit creation suggest that the "problem" to which the Bank of the United States responded in late 1795 was, in fact, a real one.

The regulatory mission announced by the national bank, of course, endured beyond this particular "time of distress."[47] One example of a subsequent effort to act as a "restraining force on state banks"—this time limited to the institutions of a single city—comes from the turn of the century.[48] In January 1800, the Philadelphia board established a "permanent Regulation" for the Baltimore branch—a rule designed to "govern [the office's] Conduct" with state-chartered banks in that city. The directors ordered the Baltimore office to redeem the notes and checks of local banks "whenever a Balance due to the office shall exceed a certain Amount." Moreover, the board's order was not for internal circulation only; Baltimore's banks were to be informed, the point being to "place the Debtor [institutions] on their Guard, & prepare them to meet the Exigency of the Demand."[49] The Bank of the United States was signaling, in other words, that the city's banks would be subjected to a lending limit going forward—a limit effectively tied to their level of indebtedness.

REGULATOR'S RECEPTION

The historical reality of the national bank's mid-1790s conversion is reinforced by evidence that the transformation spurred critical commentary well into the early nineteenth century. The Bank's functional enhancement was received, of course, both in and out of doors—that is, within extant banking institutions and among the broader public (and their elected representatives). At least three general aspects of this reception are worthy of acknowledgment. First, and unsurprisingly, analyses of the Bank's turn toward the regulation of state institutions appear to have spiked during the short period between late 1810 and early 1811, as members of the Eleventh Congress (1809–1811) prepared to debate a charter extension bill; the 1791 charter was set to expire on March 4, 1811. Second, assessments of the national bank's development were decidedly mixed; where one commentator saw unexpected but valuable service to the American public, another saw an instrument for the oppression of state-chartered institutions. Finally, and here quite surprisingly, a natural assumption respecting the attitude of state banks toward this institutional development—that they would be uniformly antagonistic—is actually upset by at least one pro-recharter memorial sent to the US Senate in early 1811.

Those who owned and operated the Bank of the United States, of course, tried to present its conversion in the best possible light. The most authoritative expression of this sentiment came in December 1810, when Bank president David Lenox—writing on behalf of the institution's stockholders—formally "solicited the renewal of [his institution's] charter" from Congress.[50] Not only did Lenox acknowledge and champion the national bank's monetary function—he observed that physically dispersed branches had enabled it to act "as the general guardian of commercial credit" in the United States—but this discussion *preceded* a defense of the institution rooted in its steady performance of various fiscal functions. Implicitly, then, Lenox was also treating the Bank's ability to "foster[] and protect[] the banking institutions of the States" as its most important public function.[51]

The notion that the national bank's monetary role had quickly eclipsed its fiscal counterparts in terms of importance had been put somewhat more starkly a few years earlier. George Cabot, a US senator from Massachusetts between 1791 and 1796 and a board member at the Boston branch of the Bank between 1805 and 1811, recounted complaints about the institution's conduct in an 1807 letter to House member Josiah Quincy. In response to them, Cabot assured the future Boston mayor and Harvard University president that

> You know every particular of our Banks so well that it must seem superfluous for me to state many facts or opinions relating to them. Yet I cannot forbear to remark that *what is alledged* [sic] *as a most culpable part of our conduct we have consider'd as our best claim to praise.*—We are charged with doing injury to other Banks by draining them of their specie and retaining it by the limitation of our discounts. Now is there any man who does not see that there is a sacrifice of our profit to the public safety?—if every Bank were to efface its credit in the unbounded

manner that some do or to the extent that most of them do, the community wou'd . . . be inundated with a flood of paper.[52]

Not only did Cabot vindicate the national bank's regulatory role, but his
"best claim to praise" language explicitly prioritized that function relative
to others performed by the institution. Moreover, Cabot's lead-in remark
on this point—a reference to claims of institutional culpability—hinted at
less approving perspectives on the Bank's conversion.

Those perspectives appeared in, among other places, newspaper editorials and pamphlets. An example of the former comes from the Philadelphia-
based *Aurora General Advertiser*, an openly partisan paper that provided
(in Thomas Jefferson's words) "incalculable services to republicanism
through all its struggles with the federalists[.]"[53] William Duane, editor
of the *Aurora* between 1798 and 1822, authored a series of articles on the
impending Bank recharter fight between Christmas Day 1810 and January 7, 1811.[54] While Duane's avowed purpose was to offer "A Review of
Certain Pamphlets on Banking"—pamphlets that spoke to the recharter
question—each of the articles was manifestly colored by his animus toward the Bank of the United States. On the whole, in fact, Duane appears
less as a detached surveyor of the scene and more as an independent (and
quite partial) commentator on the recharter question. The first article in
Duane's series spoke unfavorably of the national bank's monetary power,
suggesting that "as soon as the United States bank ceases, [the] danger [to
state institutions] ceases with it."[55] A few weeks later, in the midst of a
separate series devoted to the Bank, Duane would again criticize the "conduct of [the institution] toward the banks in this city [i.e., Philadelphia]
and elsewhere."[56] In neither case, to be clear, did Duane explain his aver-
sion to the national bank's regulatory conduct in any detail. For him, the
mere existence of an institution with the capacity to menace state banks
appears to have been problematic.

A number of pamphlets also placed a less than approving gloss on the
Bank's conversion, among them Jesse Atwater's *Considerations on the Approaching Dissolution of the United States Bank*. Organized into twelve
sections that cumulatively run to just twenty-two pages, Atwater's 1810
tract opened by calling attention—via all-capital print—to the Bank's
reliance on foreign capital: "OF THE STOCK OF 10 MILLIONS FOREIGNERS
OWN TWO THIRDS." One implication of this fact, as Atwater observed a
few lines later, was that foreigners would ultimately receive two-thirds of
any profits resulting from the institution's possession of federal deposits.[57]
Two points warrant mention here. First, Atwater's two-part solution to

this purported problem was all but stated explicitly: (1) Deny the Bank of the United States a charter extension and (2) redirect federal deposits (and the profits flowing from them) to institutions principally owned by Americans (i.e., state-chartered banks).[58] Second, federal deposits were implicitly at issue later in the same section, where Atwater made passing reference to the Bank's "inordinate power of crushing all the other banks."[59] It is not surprising, of course, that a recharter critic would choose to harp less on the institution's actual (and moderate) behavior toward state banks and more on its potential to threaten their very existence.

Not every pamphleteer who touched on the national bank's rise to monetary prominence greeted the development with scorn. Erick Bollmann, who has been characterized as "the most prolific American writer on banking of his time," announced his support for a charter extension in a blandly named 1810 pamphlet, *Paragraphs on Banks*.[60] Bollmann's defense of the Bank rested in part on its regulatory activity; he emphasized that while Congress possessed "no power to suppress the many banks already in existence . . . renewing the charter of [the Bank] of the United States . . . [may] prevent their increase, and *control their conduct*."[61] Bollmann's implicit constitutional claim here—that Congress *was* empowered to regulate state banks—would be effectively taken up (and pointedly rejected) by Senator Henry Clay of Kentucky in the 1811 recharter debate.

A slightly more provocative defense of the Bank's conversion—but one component of a broader argument on behalf of extending its charter—was offered in Mathew Carey's self-published 1811 pamphlet, *Letters to Dr. Adam Seybert*. In the fifth of his nine letters to Seybert, a Philadelphia-based representative in the Eleventh Congress, Carey—like Erick Bollmann, a prolific commentator on the antebellum American economy[62]—implicitly invoked the national bank's regulation of state-chartered institutions. In essence, Carey reversed the spin of Jesse Atwater's argument by pointing out that the Bank of the United States had been in a position to crush local banks, but had clearly *declined* that opportunity; he wrote that the institution's early years were "precisely the time to secure" its influence over state counterparts "and their 'entire subservience to its views.' If there was any likelihood of the Bank of the United States ever swallowing up the other [b]anks, as Aaron's rod swallowed up those of the Egyptian magicians, as is now prophesied, to terrify us, that was certainly the golden opportunity."[63] Implicit here, of course, was both recognition and approval of the more modest regulatory path actually chosen by the national bank.

Perhaps the most surprising take on the national bank's monetary function belongs to the Bank of New York, whose president in early 1811—Matthew Clarkeson—authored a memorial on behalf of the institution's board urging Congress to renew the Bank's charter.[64] Since the Bank of New York began operations as an unincorporated institution in 1784, seven years prior to the national bank's creation, its directors had "witnessed, from the very commencement of the branch bank in [their] city," the conduct of that office. They could now conclude, Clarkeson wrote, that the New York branch routinely acted "with prudence, as it respected the public; with great liberality as it respected *other institutions*."[65] This statement offered, if not express approval of the national bank's regulatory efforts, a sign that the banking community in Manhattan did not uniformly view its monetary activity as oppressive.

CONCLUSION

This chapter, like the one that precedes it, explores a gradual but transformative change in the Bank of the United States between 1791 and 1811. Conceived by Alexander Hamilton as a fiscal instrument—an institution that would contribute in various ways to the "prosperous administration of the Finances"[66]—the national bank gradually took on monetary responsibilities as well; the same apparatus that facilitated both the influx and outflow of federal revenue and periodic borrowing by the federal government was consciously turned toward the regulation of state bank lending. For many who watched this transformation unfold, especially its own officers, the Bank's ostensible conversion meaningfully expanded the range of services it could offer to the American public.

This particular formulation of the Bank's early affairs—the effective expansion of its public service portfolio from purely fiscal duties to a combination of fiscal and monetary functions—also speaks to a question that I have avoided in this chapter: Was the Bank of the United States a "central bank"? I answer this question at some length elsewhere,[67] but offer only a summary claim here because the answer has no bearing on the Bank's constitutional history (or the import of that history for American constitutionalism more generally). In short, the question is wholly anachronistic; the term considerably *postdates* the 1811 demise of the institution,[68] so the national bank's documented activity cannot (with fairness) be evaluated against a prescribed set of central bank functions.[69] By contrast, a simple claim that the Bank was designed for "fiscal" service but later took on a "regulatory" or monetary role is entirely free of anachronism; rooted in the language employed by public and private actors in talking about the institution, it respects the economic concepts available between 1791 and 1811.

Just as the slow-moving change reviewed in chapter 2—the national bank's drift from industry dominance—would have downstream consequences in Congress, so, too, would the conversion chronicled here. While the political and constitutional fallout from the proliferation of state-chartered banks—events that I take up in the next chapter—was largely confined to the early 1811 recharter battle, that associated with the institution's assumption of a monetary role colored both the 1811 congressional debates that led to its death *and* the 1816 proceedings that produced its rebirth.

The Bank's conversion had greater political than constitutional salience in 1811, as members of the Eleventh Congress verbally jousted over the costs to federalism—and the benefits to the public—of state bank regulation. By 1816, however, the past transformation of the national bank was inspiring more novel constitutional thinking than real political squabbling. As chapter 5 details, monetary turmoil came during—and continued after—the War of 1812. In that troubled postwar environment, Republicans largely coalesced around a policy solution: the revival of a defunct institution—the Bank of the United States—long associated with monetary stability. Republicans, however, were deeply ambivalent about reviving the institution under the Necessary and Proper Clause; the issue here was less the Bank itself (which again, most party members now wanted) and more the range of future federal activity that would be implicitly sanctioned by anchoring it to that provision. Eager to secure a national bank's monetary services *without* asking the party's more conservative members to accept an expansive understanding of federal power (and courting a deeper intraregime schism in the process), leading moderate Republicans tried to leverage the institution's past conversion into a narrow argument in support of its constitutionality. They anchored the 1816 national bank bill to a provision never before associated with the institution: Congress's Article I, Section 8 power to "coin Money, regulate the Value thereof."

CHAPTER FOUR

More Than a Constitutional Rerun

The Conventional Wisdom

The twenty-year charter of the Bank of the United States—secured in late February 1791—was set to expire in early March 1811. Saddled with the knowledge of when it would die, the institution spent its last days doing what any self-loving creature would: laboring tirelessly to find the elixir vitae, the waters that would restore it from old age to youth.[1] The national bank's stockholders petitioned Congress in December 1810 for an extension of their charter.[2] Several weeks later, in January 1811, members of the outgoing Eleventh Congress (1809–1811) began consideration of a recharter bill. Though James Madison—one of the institution's most prominent foes in 1791 as a member of the House of Representatives—now sat in the White House, he never got the chance to openly embrace, alter, or simply abandon his old constitutional position. The recharter bill was defeated by one vote in the House on January 24 (65–64) and met a similar fate in the Senate on February 20, when Republican vice president George Clinton's vote to effectively table it broke a 17–17 tie.[3]

Federalists in the Eleventh Congress had been uniformly in favor of extending the Bank's charter and found themselves allied with a subset of Republicans who had no constitutional objection to the institution and were loath to part with its numerous public benefits. In both the House and the Senate, however, the Republican majority proved large enough—albeit barely—to handle these defections from its ranks.

Two things appear to have united those who offered floor speeches in the 1811 congressional debate. First, nearly everyone proved willing to discuss the constitutional question; only a handful of substantive addresses failed to touch on this subject. Second, no one said anything

new on the question. The advocates of recharter stressed that the na-
tional bank was constitutional under the broad interpretation of the
Necessary and Proper Clause effectively embraced in 1791. For their
part, the Republican opponents of recharter simply recycled the con-
stitutional claim that their partisan forerunners had pressed in 1791:
a strict interpretation of the Sweeping Clause. For these Bank critics,
the 1791 outcome represented a constitutional mistake, and the 1811
recharter debate offered an opportunity to correct it.

It is somewhat misleading to suggest that the preceding paragraphs offer
the "conventional wisdom" surrounding the Bank's affairs in 1811. A
number of scholars who purport to treat much or all of the constitutional
drama surrounding the institution between 1791 and 1832 actually offer
no attention to the 1811 episode. That is, they treat this round of congressional debate over the meaning of the Necessary and Proper Clause as if
it never occurred. The fact of the Bank's demise is often mentioned—and
sometimes briefly attributed to the Republican majority in the Eleventh
Congress—but the constitutional dimension of the debate that led to its
death is omitted entirely.[4] The sin here, of course, is not the retelling of a
faulty story but rather the absence of a story at all—the implication that
nothing of constitutional import took place in 1811.

Setting aside those guilty of sins of omission, however, still leaves
the scholars with sins of commission. In short, the traditional narrative
outlined above suffers from two related flaws.[5] First, it perpetuates the
false notion that national bank opponents in 1791 offered a single strict
interpretation of the Necessary and Proper Clause. As I suggested in chapter 1, there was significant variation in the antibank constitutional arguments that year. Second, the standard account is correspondingly blind
to the fact that two of those arguments reappeared in the 1811 debate. In
other words, the variation present in the 1791 proceedings was *reproduced*
twenty years later. Some recharter opponents continued to argue that a
national bank need only (but could not) satisfy a demanding version of the
functional standard, while others pressed anew the claim that constitutional necessity was only established if both the functional and the federal standards were met. Ironically, then, there is some unintended truth
in the traditional claim that nothing new was said on the constitutional
question in 1811.

Even if the constitutional claims offered in 1811 sounded much like
those offered two decades earlier, they were presented in a very different
ideological and institutional context. For example, while proto-Federalists

controlled Congress (and arguably the presidency[6]) in 1791, the so-called Revolution of 1800 ushered in long-term Republican dominance in the political branches.[7] As it turns out, this development did not spell automatic doom for the national bank's recharter prospects. During Thomas Jefferson's two terms as president (1801–1809), fault lines began to develop in the new Republican regime.[8] The scope of federal power represented one (but surely not the only) source of internal division,[9] with party members increasingly split between a conservative or "Old" wing firmly committed to the restraining logic of enumerated powers and a more moderate or "nationalist" wing that "had never been opposed to a strong national government *per se*" and thus viewed the party's electoral ascent less as an invitation to roll back the Federalist economic program of the 1790s and more as an opportunity to halt (or at least exercise control over) its expansion.[10]

Given what we know about national politics in early 1811—that the Republican regime was divided between Old and moderate elements with respect to federal power and that the party's recharter opponents were divided between one- and two-prong tests of necessity—it is relatively easy to generate a working assumption about the relationship between ideology and Republican constitutional thinking about the Bank. We would expect some moderates to have no constitutional truck with the institution—that is, to see it as satisfying a permissive version of the functional standard— and others to complain that it could not satisfy a restrictive version of that same single-prong test. We would also expect members of the regime's conservative or Old wing, consistent with their animus toward federal power, to embrace the more demanding two-prong understanding of constitutional necessity.

The working assumption simply does not square with the evidence, however. While some nationalists in the Republican party did conclude that Congress was empowered to charter and maintain a national bank, the remaining moderates who spoke to the constitutional question all insisted that both the functional and the federal standards of necessity had to be satisfied (but could not be). In fact, given that a number of Old Republicans applied this same test to the Bank of the United States (and similarly found it wanting), it appears that the opponents of recharter largely *clustered* around the two-prong argument first proposed by James Madison and Thomas Jefferson in 1791. What explains this apparent preference among moderate Republican recharter opponents for such an exacting test of constitutionality?

In short, an altered institutional landscape. As detailed in chapter 2, the First Congress debated the national bank bill at a moment when just three state-chartered institutions dotted the eastern seaboard. Twenty years later, when the Eleventh Congress debated a charter extension bill, over one hundred state banks peppered not simply coastal cities but the American mainland as far west as the Mississippi River.[11] While most moderate Republican lawmakers entertained no serious constitutional scruples about the Bank of the United States, several were invested in—or had constituents who were invested in—these state-chartered institutions. If the national bank were to be eliminated, state banks would both profit (because the federal government's money would need to be deposited *somewhere*) and escape the regulator of their activities. As such, some of these moderates (as I argue below) insisted on an especially restrictive understanding of constitutional necessity. In their eyes, the Bank failed to meet not only the functional standard but the federal one as well; a network of state-chartered institutions could provide its fiscal services to the federal government. At the end of the day, to recognize that state bank growth between 1791 and 1811 led to intraregime convergence on a particular antibank claim—and numerous floor statements verify the influence of that institutional development—is also to acknowledge that the 1811 battle was something more than a constitutional rerun of 1791.

This chapter offers the 1811 constitutional debate the kind of assessment usually reserved for its 1791 predecessor (not to mention its 1819 and 1832 successors). After offering a summary account of the growing tensions within the Republican coalition, I turn to the details of the debate itself. Eschewing (as I did in chapter 1) a blow-by-blow account of the action, I instead labor to distinguish between two groups of Republicans with constitutional opposition to the recharter bill: (1) a small cohort that wished to impose a test for necessity that was moderately more difficult to pass than that which prevailed in 1791, and (2) a much larger (but more ideologically diverse) cohort that sought to make the building or maintenance of federal institutions all but impossible. I then pivot to the constitutional arguments of recharter advocates, Federalist and Republican alike. In the course of defending a permissive reading of the Sweeping Clause, they launched a sophisticated—and, as I explain below, intellectually dishonest—assault on those recharter opponents who pressed for the two-prong test of necessity. I close by addressing the minimal effect of the Bank's recent emergence as a regulatory institution on the constitutional debate. While members of the Eleventh Congress were hardly shy about discussing this development, only one spoke to its constitutional implications.

WE ARE ALL REPUBLICANS . . . MORE OR LESS

Students of American politics and political history have frequently observed that a minority party, long united by its opposition to the majority,
will find that internal cohesion difficult to maintain after finally seizing
the reins of power.[12] In short, as William F. Connelly Jr. has noted, "[b]eing
in the majority is tougher than playing minority opposition."[13] Connelly
was referring to the infighting among congressional Democrats that began
shortly after they won control of both the House and the Senate in the
2006 midterm elections. The same has been said of Republicans following
the 1994 midterms, which saw them seize control of Congress for the first
time since the early 1950s; Connelly and John J. Pitney Jr. have written
that "swift action on the Contract [with America]" in the 104th Congress
"left a misleading impression of unity . . . [o]nce they voted on the Contract, [Republicans] start[ed] squabbling again."[14]

A similar conclusion has been reached with respect to the Republican
party of Thomas Jefferson's day. Throughout the 1790s, as Richard E. Ellis
has written, Republicans "had been an opposition party, united . . . by a
common enmity to Federalist policies." After the party's triumph in the
1800 elections, however, the absence of any "common ideal" among members became readily apparent; marching under the Republican banner was
a collection of groups "holding conflicting . . . attitudes toward the way
the government should be administered."[15] Along these lines, Noble Cunningham has observed that Republicans after 1800 "enjoyed a strong majority in Congress and in the country as a whole" but nevertheless found
"party discipline and unity difficult to maintain."[16] For his part, William
Nisbet Chambers made a distinction between the "utopian hopes of the
Republicans as an opposition party and the harsh realities of power."[17]

President Jefferson's March 1801 inaugural address, which included
his oft-cited effort at interparty conciliation ("We are all Republicans, we
are all Federalists"), also announced the principles that would guide his
administration.[18] The new president pledged to prioritize, among other
things, both "[t]he support of the state governments in all their rights
as the most competent administrations for our domestic concerns" and
"economy in public expense" coupled with "[t]he honest payment of our
debts[.]"[19] Republican John Randolph of Roanoke, who served Virginia in
the House of Representatives on and off between 1799 and 1833, invoked
those same principles in early 1813 when reflecting on what had brought
his party to power; he cited both "jealousy of the State governments

towards the General Government" and "a loathing of public debt, taxes, and excises[.]"[20]

Though these two principles hardly exhaust the party's functional platform from 1800, they are helpful for measuring the cohesiveness of the new Republican regime between 1801 and 1811. On the one hand, the coalition acted quickly (and with minimal internal rancor) to cut both taxes and spending, achieve precision in whatever spending did occur, and pay down the nation's long-term debt. In 1802, Republicans repealed all the internal taxes that their opponents had imposed, including a 1798 direct tax that financed expansions of the army and navy (for possible use against France).[21] The regime promptly compensated for this lost revenue by effecting "large reductions . . . in the army and navy[.]"[22] In the executive branch, Albert Gallatin—Jefferson's new Treasury secretary—labored to practice "stringent economy" by "scrupulous[ly] accounting for [expended] funds" and by asking congressional Republicans to appropriate specific funds for specific expenditures.[23] Turning from these here-and-now measures to administration efforts to deal with the residue of previous deficits, Jefferson and Gallatin began earmarking millions in federal revenue each year for the payment of interest *and* principal on the nation's $83 million in long-term debt.[24] What the new regime wanted in these areas—"low taxes, rigid economy, [and] retirement of the Hamiltonian public debt"—is precisely what it got.[25]

While the Republican regime's members appeared more or less united with respect to the fiscal principles announced in Jefferson's inaugural address, the same could not be said of the president's public commitment to an aggressive policing of the line between federal and state power. To be clear, Republicans proceeded to divide on a number of issues during the first decade of the nineteenth century: how to treat Vice President Aaron Burr in the wake of his refusal to step aside after the Electoral College produced a tie between him and Thomas Jefferson,[26] how to deal with the federal judges who had been nominated and confirmed after President Adams and his Federalist majority in the Senate became lame ducks in late 1800,[27] whether to replace all Federalist officers in the executive branch in favor of Republicans,[28] and whether to recognize the property claims of individuals who had innocently purchased land following its initial (and corrupt) sale by the Georgia legislature in 1794.[29] The president, unsurprisingly, mentioned *none* of these issues in his March 1801 address. Conversely, he presented "support [for] the state governments in all their rights" as a regime priority despite the *absence* of real intraparty agreement on this principle.

The conservative or Old wing of the Republican regime offered an un-compromising embrace of Jefferson's preference for government by the states. Norman Risjord has described Old Republicans as classical liberals with respect to the substance of politics and (the heirs of) Anti-Federalists with respect to method; the end was individual freedom, but the primary means of achieving that end was the preservation of local power.[30] This commitment to a strong version of federalism seemed to demand, if nothing else, that the new regime work toward the wholesale destruction of constitutionally suspect federal ventures such as the Bank of the United States.[31] Many of these coalition members were "unreconstructed agrarians" from the South or men who saw "moral and social dangers [as] inherent in the [federally sponsored] expansion of commerce and manufacturing[.]"[32] In this respect, it is worth noting that the subtitle of Risjord's book on the group was "*Southern* Conservatism in the Age of Jefferson."[33] However, Ellis has stressed that this wing of the Republican regime also included "a number of urban radicals" from the North "who, while not agrarians, were political purists."[34]

By contrast, members of the regime's moderate or nationalist wing operated from very different assumptions about government activity generally and the scope of federal power more specifically. Against the classical liberalism of the Old Republicans, regime moderates claimed no a priori animus toward government intervention in community affairs. Moreover, much to the chagrin of agrarians in the regime's conservative wing, moderates displayed little hesitancy in using state governments to support commerce and manufacturing; Republican-led legislatures not only chartered a host of state banks but also "outdid their Federalist predecessors in granting direct state loans to infant manufacturing enterprises."[35] This posture was hardly restricted to the state governments. While Old Republicans interpreted the election of 1800 as a popular call for the immediate elimination of Federalist policies and institutions (including the Bank), moderates construed their opponents' removal from power as "sufficient, by itself, to safeguard liberty while [they] worked toward *gradual* replacement of the Hamiltonian system with one better suited to republican ways."[36] In fact, nationalist Republicans were not inalterably opposed to retaining (or even *expanding*) the federal government's commitments as they stood in 1801. While moderates in the Eleventh Congress offered only limited support for extending the national bank's charter (a fact, as I discuss below, that owed much to their interests in state institutions), members of this wing did press increasingly for "federal initiatives to bolster manufacturing" and fund a series of internal improvements.[37]

The divide between Old and moderate Republicans is surprisingly *un-helpful* for making sense of which party members adopted which positions on the Bank's constitutionality in 1811. Old Republicans' animus toward the institution (and federal power more broadly) certainly found expression in the recharter debate, though members of this cohort were divided on which test of constitutional necessity to impose. Moreover, their nationalist peers failed to divide (as might have been expected) between those who viewed the Bank as constitutional and those who thought it invalid on the basis of the single-prong test (i.e., the functional standard). Instead, the debate reveals a kind of constitutional *polarization* among moderates; members of this wing either had no truck with the Bank whatsoever or joined some of their conservative peers in suggesting that the Necessary and Proper Clause required the institution to clear an especially high bar. The source of this bifurcation, as already noted, was significant political (and probably financial) investment among moderates in state-chartered banks. While my ensuing treatment of the 1811 recharter debate is organized by adopted position on the Bank's necessity, I repeatedly draw attention to the bimodal distribution of moderate Republicans on that question.

TIGHTENING THE FUNCTIONAL STANDARD

The first set of recharter opponents—a small crowd composed largely of Old Republicans—argued that the appropriate test for constitutional necessity was a demanding version of the functional standard. That is to say, means selected by Congress had to be closely related (or even integral) to the exercise of an express power. With one exception, the lawmakers who adopted this constitutional posture openly characterized both the prevailing 1791 interpretation of the Sweeping Clause and the resulting creation of the Bank of the United States as constitutionally mistaken. Ironically, the exception here—the member whose acknowledgment and disapproval of the 1791 results was real but largely implicit—was the man who had arguably the strongest reason to condemn those proceedings: Senator William Branch Giles of Virginia.

Giles, as chapter 1 noted, sat in the First Congress as a member of the House and argued—ultimately to no avail—that constitutional necessity meant something a bit more than being "useful for" or "conducive to" the exercise of an enumerated power. Two decades later, this Old Republican[38] clung to the same argument without explicitly criticizing his former peers; he merely suggested that a bill to incorporate a national bank (or in this particular case, a bill to extend its charter) lacked the requisite "connexion, affiliation, and subserviency, to some enumerated power[.]" Giles conceded Treasury Secretary Albert Gallatin's claim that the institution was "a convenient instrument" for managing the nation's fiscal concerns but made it clear that convenience alone failed to establish constitutional necessity; only means "indispensable" for the achievement of enumerated ends were permitted.[39]

What Senator Giles would not say with respect to the 1791 events, three of his House colleagues would. Richard Mentor Johnson—an Old Republican sympathizer[40] from Kentucky and later Martin Van Buren's vice president—complained that the First Congress, relying on the "odious doctrine of implied powers[,]" had chartered a national bank "in express violation of the constitution."[41] Similarly, John Rhea of Tennessee—yet another Old Republican[42]—argued that because a national bank was merely "convenient" for exercising various Article I powers, "[t]he law creating the Bank of the United States" in 1791 was "not bottomed on the constitution."[43] Finally, William T. Barry of Kentucky, who did not appear strongly affiliated with either wing of the Republican coalition, identified the Bank of the United States as the "illegitimate offspring" of the First Congress.[44]

Not only did these four lawmakers—Giles, Johnson, Rhea, and Barry— implicitly or explicitly reject the 1791 results, but several of them also spent time rebutting a claim that the Bank—even *if* a constitutional bastard in 1791—had been subsequently legitimized. The claim from numerous recharter advocates was simply that the institution's initial critics had hardly treated it as a "nullity"[45] when they seized power following the "Revolution of 1800."[46] Put another way, recharter advocates argued that to whatever extent the constitutional door remained ajar in the early 1800s, it was effectively shut by legislative and executive action that tacitly acknowledged the national bank's constitutionality. In this vein, Representative Jonathan Fisk of New York—a Republican advocate of recharter—stressed that members of his party, including President Jefferson, had "not evince[d] any scruples about the constitutionality of the charter" in 1802, when they sold over two thousand of the federal government's Bank shares. If the national bank "was deemed unconstitutional and dangerous to the liberties and best interests of the people," Fisk continued, "it was not for those who entertained this opinion to give it countenance and support."[47] Similarly, Representative Samuel McKee of Kentucky—another pro-recharter Republican—considered the Bank's constitutionality "confirmed by Mr. Jefferson, and the votes of a republican Congress." More specifically, McKee noted, Congress had passed—and Jefferson had signed—both an 1804 bill authorizing the national bank to establish branches in the territories[48] and an 1807 bill that "subjected the citizens of the United States to capital punishment for counterfeiting the notes of the United States' Bank."[49]

In response to the claims of Fisk, McKee, and other like-minded Bank supporters, this first set of recharter critics insisted that seeming acquiescence to the institution could not paper over the mistaken conclusions of February 1791. Senator Giles, for example, was "disposed to admit the acquiescence in the bank law" but did not see it as "preclud[ing] the present Congress from exercising its sound discretion on the constitutional question." If, he observed, the Eleventh Congress "should be convinced that a former Congress had exceeded its limits, [was] it not bound by every conscientious consideration to *correct the error*[?]"[50] After acknowledging the "doctrine of acquiescence," Representative Barry rejected the suggestion that an initially illegitimate institution could somehow *become* legitimate: "It seems clear to me, that an act of Congress, not originally constitutional, cannot be made so by any lapse of time. If, in 1791, it was unconstitutional, it must be so now. The constitution does not change with the times."[51]

Cognizant of the conclusions reached by the First Congress, convinced that they were erroneous, and unwilling to let post-1791 practice effectively excuse those errors, this cadre of recharter opponents pressed for (1) a definition of constitutional necessity tied to a restrictive understanding of the functional standard and (2) a finding that the recharter bill could not meet that standard. Along these lines, William T. Barry was adamant that "the true exposition of a necessary mean was, that mean without which the end could not be produced."[52] Barry's language here was virtually identical to that used by (then Representative) William Branch Giles in 1791.[53] In the same spirit, John Rhea suggested that whatever aid the institution offered with respect to tax collection, "[i]t will not be said that the Bank of the United States" was "essential" for achieving that end—the correct test for constitutionality under the Sweeping Clause.[54]

I characterize these four Republican lawmakers as committed to a tightened single-prong interpretation of the Necessary and Proper Clause because none of them made *state banks* part of the constitutional equation. In other words, the Bank's constitutionality could be determined without regard for the presence or absence of alternative service providers—that is, without reference to the federal standard. State-chartered institutions, to be clear, were mentioned in the floor speeches of Giles, Johnson, Rhea, and Barry, but for them the only relevant constitutional question was whether a national bank's contribution to the achievement of express federal prerogatives was substantial enough to render its creation a "direct" exercise of the relevant Article I power, or otherwise "indispensable" to the same.

TOWARD ABSOLUTE NECESSITY:
ADDING THE FEDERAL STANDARD

A larger and more diverse set of recharter opponents—roughly ten members of the Eleventh Congress, including both Old and moderate Republicans—pressed for a much more restrictive interpretation of the Necessary and Proper Clause. They argued that means had to satisfy both a demanding version of the functional standard (the requirement suggested by Senator Giles and several of his House colleagues) *and* the federal standard (i.e., Congress could not achieve the same ends via resort to existing means). This was, in essence, a revival of the interpretation that James Madison and Thomas Jefferson had offered back in 1791. Moreover, this two-prong interpretation treated functional necessity as a mere threshold inquiry; establishing that means were sufficiently related to authorized congressional functions would not be enough to establish their constitutionality. Because a second condition would also need to be satisfied, this test threatened to significantly restrain—with respect to the Bank, and more broadly—the exercise of federal power.

Not only did this group of Bank critics seek to impose a two-prong test for constitutional necessity, but each individual member—with the possible exception of Representative William Burwell of Virginia, to be discussed below—contended that the Bank of the United States failed *both* prongs of that test in 1811. Of course, in adopting this interpretation, these members—again, possibly save Burwell—were also suggesting that the Bank had been unconstitutional in 1791. In that sense, they shared something important with the advocates of a demanding single-prong interpretation. However, it is important to emphasize that open criticism of the 1791 outcome was not an especially conspicuous component of this group's constitutional argument.

In fact, only two members of this group—Representatives Adam Seybert and William Crawford, both of Pennsylvania—appear to have made claims to this effect. Seybert suggested that the 1791 "act of incorporation [had been] opposed on constitutional ground" and then proceeded to characterize the arguments of those charter critics as "unanswerable."[55] For his part, Crawford—not to be confused with the Georgia senator (and prominent recharter supporter) of the same name—admonished fellow members of the Eleventh Congress not to palm "this counterfeit *again* upon the nation for twenty years longer."[56]

This group also appeared to agree with, yet ultimately downplay, a second contention from those defending a restrictive single-prong interpretation of the Sweeping Clause: the basic inability of time (coupled with the seeming approbation of other federal actors) to solve the national bank's constitutional problem. In fact, of those defending the two-prong interpretation, only Representative Peter B. Porter of New York—whose floor speech, as I discuss below, was frequently cited as an especially apt statement of the group's position—appears to have gone to the trouble of addressing the "acquiescence" argument on behalf of the Bank of the United States. Porter pointedly rejected Jonathan Fisk's claim that "the constitutional question must be considered as settled, adjudicated, and at rest" and emphasized that it was not an argument deduced "from the provisions of the constitution itself." By contrast, Porter suggested, the Bank's constitutional status in 1811 was "a question *de novo*. It is a question of conscience in the interpretation of the . . . constitution, unembarrassed by any collateral considerations."[57]

These constitutional critics of recharter spent less time dwelling on the past—both the 1791 proceedings and the behavior of Republican officials following the election of 1800—because the real force of their case lay in the present. Put another way, their floor speeches were focused on explaining—frequently in great detail—why the Bank of the United States could not possibly pass constitutional muster *in 1811*. The skeletal logic of their argument, to be fleshed out below, was roughly as follows: First, a national bank could not satisfy the first requirement for constitutional necessity—that is, the tightened functional standard pressed by Senator Giles and others. Second, even if the question of functional necessity were somehow decided in favor of the national bank—a prospect that *only* Representative Burwell appeared willing to entertain—the institution would still unquestionably fail the second requirement of constitutional necessity. That is to say, because Congress could employ alternative means for achieving its varied fiscal ends, the Bank of the United States was not "necessary" in the federal sense of the term. More to the point, Congress could—among other things—store money in, borrow money from, and transfer money between a subset of the hundred-plus state banks that now dotted the American landscape.

The aforementioned Peter B. Porter—a moderate Republican who supported federally financed internal improvements[58] and had both land and transportation interests in the Buffalo region[59]—offered perhaps the most comprehensive exposition of the two-prong interpretation. It was certainly the most popular; no less than four fellow Republican opponents of recharter in the House—moderates William Crawford of Pennsylvania and Isaac McKim of Maryland[60] along with conservatives Joseph Desha of Kentucky and J. W. Eppes of Virginia[61]—explicitly cited the constitutional elements of Porter's January 18 floor speech approvingly. Eppes, for example—Jefferson's son-in-law—contended "[t]hat the power to incorporate a bank is neither delegated, or essentially necessary for carrying into effect any delegated power. For the demonstration, I would insert the speech of a gentleman from New York, (Mr. PORTER) who has combined in a masterly manner on this subject, the purest principles, and most luminous elucidation."[62] Similarly, Crawford suggested that "after the very eloquent and conclusive argument of the gentleman from New York (Mr. PORTER) on the constitutionality of the bill . . . any farther [sic] attempt to elucidate that part of the subject may appear equally unnecessary and impertinent."[63]

What, then, was the structure of Porter's constitutional thinking with respect to the Necessary and Proper Clause? He began by assaulting the lax version of functional necessity that had prevailed in 1791. "[F]ive or six different provisions of the constitution[,]" Porter observed, "are referred to as giving this right" to charter a national bank. The problem, however, was that a list of this sort furnished proof that such an institution bore "no very direct relation to *any* of them[.]"[64] Of course, the Bank might "facilitate, in some greater or less degree," the exercise of these powers, but facilitation and constitutional necessity were not the same thing. For Porter, a closer functional relationship between the mean selected and the end(s) pursued was required. His claim on this point was remarkably clear: "You must show that the plain, direct, ostensible, primary object and tendency of your law is to execute the power, and not that it will tend to facilitate the execution of it."[65] Simply put, Porter was pressing here for the more demanding version of the functional standard.

For Porter, the weak functional relationship between chartering a national bank and exercising the powers of Article I, Section 8 was only the *first* reason that the institution was something less than "necessary." He proceeded to insist that there was "[a]nother ground upon which the constitutionality of this institution has been attempted to be supported[:] that it is necessary to the regular and successful administration of the finances."[66] At first glance, Porter's statement is rather perplexing; it appears to do little more than offer a tautological version of the basic consti-

tutional claim on behalf of the Bank. However, he quickly made it clear
that the specific claim to be rebutted involved the national bank's federal
necessity:

> [I]f these facilities were not to be attained in any other way, I should say
> it would afford an argument in favor of a bank . . . But, sir, is there not,
> in every State in which there is a branch of the United States Bank,
> also one or more State banks, of equal respectability, and of equal secu-
> rity[?] . . . These State banks may be used as depositories for the public
> money, and they will be equally safe and convenient. And, if you will
> give to these State banks the advantages of these deposites [sic], as you
> have hitherto given them to the United States Bank, they will furnish
> means for the transmission of moneys from place to place, equally
> safe, convenient, cheap, and expeditious.[67]

In simpler terms, Porter also rejected the claim of constitutional necessity
because Congress had viable alternatives for the exercise of its fiscal powers: state-chartered banks. This was, in effect, an argument that the Bank
of the United States was *doubly* unconstitutional.

In addition to the four members of the Eleventh Congress who explicitly rallied under Porter's constitutional banner (Crawford, Desha, Eppes,
and McKim), four others—two in the House and two in the Senate—made
floor speeches that reproduced his two-prong vision of constitutional necessity. In the House, for example, Adam Seybert—a moderate Republican
from Philadelphia who had previously spoken in favor of federal support
for manufacturing[68]—confessed that he "never did doubt for a moment,
the *convenience* of a bank, to the moneyed transactions of the Government."[69] This, however, did not meet the bar for functional necessity; Seybert had implied as much—as noted above—in characterizing the claims
of the 1791 constitutional critics as "unanswerable." He then invoked a
January 1811 Treasury Department report—cited briefly in chapter 3[70]—to
establish that a national bank could not meet the federal standard either:

> In the 11th page of that report, we are told, it is one of the duties which
> are assigned to a clerk in the Treasurer's office, to keep a "bank cash
> book, wherein an account is opened with every bank in which the
> United States have money deposited. In 1798, the number of these were
> *five*; they are now augmented to *twenty*." The establishment, consti-
> tuting the United States Bank, and its branches, consists, in all, of nine
> banks; consequently, by the statement just made, it is proved the Trea-

sury Department has been doing business with *eleven* banks, other than those sanctioned by Congress . . . Why, then, pretend, that it is impossible to transact this business through the agency of the State banks, when we have the best authority for asserting, that this has been done already in a majority of cases, with the greatest success, facility, and certainty? . . . After this, will any one pretend to urge the absolute necessity of the United States Bank?[71]

While the mere existence of numerous state-chartered banks was sufficient for Porter to declare the Bank of the United States something less than "necessary," Seybert sought to embellish that argument through recognition that eleven state banks were *already* performing fiscal services for the federal government.

Though Representative Robert Wright and Senator Samuel Smith—both moderate Republicans from Maryland with ties to state banks in Baltimore[72]—also offered floor speeches that reproduced the constitutional thinking of Porter and Seybert,[73] I want to draw particular attention to the February 15 address of Kentucky senator Henry Clay. The young Republican's rejection of the national bank here—based on a two-prong interpretation of the Necessary and Proper Clause—will be carefully contrasted in chapter 5 with his acceptance (in the Fourteenth Congress) of a rechartered institution anchored to the Coinage Clause.

Senator Clay, who had ties to at least two Kentucky banks (and had sat on one's board of directors[74]), opened by characterizing the long-standing effort to legitimize a national bank as essentially quixotic, arguing that "[t]he vagrant power to erect a bank . . . [has] wandered throughout the whole constitution in quest of some congenial spot whereupon to fasten."[75] He then proceeded to reject, and twice over at that, a claim that the Bank of the United States was "necessary" for exercising any power in Article I, Section 8. With respect to functional necessity, Clay emphasized the weak relationship between chartering a national bank (or extending its charter) and collecting taxes: "It would not be difficult to show as intimate a connexion between a corporation established for any purpose whatever, and some one or other of those great powers, as there is between the revenue and the Bank of the United States."[76] The senator then continued his "examination into its necessity" by invoking the federal standard (and finding the institution well short of it): "I will now proceed to show, by fact, actual experience, not theoretic reasoning, but by the records themselves of the treasury, that the operations of that department may be as well conducted *without*, as with this bank."[77] Clay then pointed, as Seybert had, not simply to the existence of numerous state banks but to the employ-ment of several as Treasury depositories.

The man who arguably stood apart among those advancing the two-prong interpretation was William Burwell. An Old Republican from south central Virginia,[78] Burwell opened the House floor debate on January 16. Like a number of representatives and senators who would follow him, Bur-well invoked both functional and federal necessity in his speech. More-over, he agreed with those members that the Bank of the United States ultimately failed this two-prong test. However, Burwell alone seemed to suggest that the institution did not *completely* fail the test for constitu-tional necessity. More to the point, his argument implied that the na-tional bank satisfied the functional requirement in 1811; its constitutional downfall was limited to the existence of state banks.

Respecting Congress's ability to anchor the Bank to the Necessary and Proper Clause, Burwell began with a simple functional claim: "That it may be a useful instrument, I do not deny; it forms depositories conve-nient to the Government[.]"[79] The implication here is simple, and hardly novel given the foregoing material: The national bank might satisfy a lax version of the functional standard but not the tighter version championed by recharter opponents. There are two problems with attributing this meaning to Burwell, however. First, at no point does he claim that means must be "indispensable" or "direct" (the words usually associated with the stronger form of functional necessity). Second, and more importantly, Burwell's discussion of the federal standard all but openly *conceded* the Bank's functional necessity. He opened this portion of his address with a rather stock version of the federal standard: "[I]t must be shown that the bank is necessary to the operations of the Government; without its aid our fiscal concerns cannot be managed. So far from subscribing to the neces-sity of the bank, I believe the revenue would be equally safe in the State banks."[80] In making the same argument with respect to emergency lend-ing, however, Burwell made it clear that the national bank was "neces-sary" in some sense of the term: "The relief which sudden and temporary embarrassments require, can, at all times, be administered by the State banks, and, therefore, *supersedes* the necessity of aid from this bank."[81] Burwell's word choice here is telling; the suggestion is not that the Bank's necessity is altogether nonexistent, only that whatever necessity it does possess—its functional value, in other words—is rendered *moot* by the ex-istence of state-chartered banks. In short, for Burwell, the Bank seems to satisfy the first prong of constitutional necessity—just not the second.

While Burwell's deviation from the standard two-prong argument against recharter is interesting in its own right, there is a second (and far more important) reason to acknowledge his floor speech. Recharter supporters—to whom I turn next—aggressively rejected the two-prong interpretation of the Necessary and Proper Clause; they argued that means need only satisfy the lax version of the functional standard—the meaning that had prevailed in 1791. Part of their rhetorical strategy for defending this permissive single-prong interpretation, as I detail below, involved open distortion of the arguments made by most two-prong constitutional critics. In short, they spoke as if *every* defender of this interpretation had made Burwell's argument—that is, had all but conceded the Bank's functional necessity. For recharter supporters, this effectively conceded the entire constitutional question. Distortion was not the whole of their strategy on behalf of recharter, but it was a significant component.

REBUTTING ABSOLUTE NECESSITY: THE BANK'S DEFENDERS RESPOND

Given the predominance of the two-prong interpretation among recharter critics—in essence, the claim that means must possess "absolute necessity"[82]—it is not surprising that Bank defenders made an aggressive effort to assault it. Those who supported recharter—Federalists coupled with a subset of moderate Republicans—pressed instead for a permissive single-prong interpretation (and did so in at least two distinct ways). First, they misrepresented nearly every two-prong critic as admitting the Bank's functional necessity; this facilitated claims that its constitutionality was clear under their preferred interpretation. Second, they argued that federal necessity was ontologically flawed; it allowed for the possibility that means could be constitutional at one point in time but unconstitutional at some subsequent point (or vice versa). Adoption of this interpretation, they reasoned, would ultimately mean that the powers of Congress would fluctuate according to prevailing conditions—something uncomfortably close to a "flexible" or "living" Constitution.

No less than eight recharter supporters—most of them moderate Republicans, in fact—distorted the arguments of Peter B. Porter, Adam Seybert, and other advocates of a two-prong interpretation of the Sweeping Clause in the course of defending a far more permissive understanding of constitutional necessity. The January 21 floor speech of William Findley, a longtime Republican member of the House from western Pennsylvania,[83] offers an apt introduction to this rhetorical strategy. Findley's speech targeted one (and only one) advocate of the two-prong definition of necessity:

Representative Peter B. Porter of New York. Porter, to recall, had argued that a national bank was "necessary" in neither the functional sense of the term (it bore "no very direct relation" to any enumerated power) nor the federal sense (state banks could provide the same services to the federal government). In Findley's hands, however, Porter's constitutional argument was twisted from this form. According to Findley, "[t]he honorable gentleman from New York . . . has admitted that banks are necessary and proper for [the] collecting, transmitting, and safe keeping of the revenue[.]" Otherwise put, he (falsely) portrayed Porter as conceding the national bank's functional necessity. By Findley's account, Porter's *only* constitutional objection to the Bank of the United States involved federal necessity; the latter "alleges that the State banks are sufficient for" the performance of those functions.[84]

William Findley's behavior here generates an obvious question: *Why* distort the argument offered by Peter B. Porter? What, if anything, would recharter advocates gain from a portrayal of this sort? The answer is relatively simple: Findley—like all Bank defenders—argued on behalf of a single-prong interpretation of the Sweeping Clause. If Findley could portray Porter as (1) committed to the two-prong interpretation but (2) limiting his complaint against the Bank to the second of those prongs (i.e., federal necessity), then the former would have room to argue that the constitutional question had been conceded. That is to say, according to *William Findley's* preferred interpretation of the Necessary and Proper Clause, Porter "was giving up, in a great measure, the [constitutional] point."[85] To concede the Bank's functional necessity, in other words, was to concede its constitutionality. Findley's distortion, therefore, was essentially a device for trumpeting the single-prong interpretation preferred by recharter advocates.

While Findley misrepresented Porter's position alone, every other recharter supporter who adopted their colleague's argumentative strategy distorted the claims of two-prong thinkers *as a group*. In essence, even though William Burwell alone had (arguably) conceded the Bank's functional necessity but disputed its federal necessity, Findley's allies on the recharter question falsely cast *all* supporters of the two-prong interpretation as conceding the first prong in the institution's favor. As with Findley, the point of this rhetorical exercise was ultimately to defend a more permissive understanding of constitutional necessity. Federalist Daniel Sheffey, a member of the House from Virginia, offered a representative version of this argument when he falsely announced on January 22 that "[t]he necessity of a bank to carry on the operations of the Government, seems to have been admitted by all who have spoken in opposition to the bill on your table." With the Bank's functional necessity conceded, Sheffey continued, those arguing on behalf of the two-prong interpretation were left to "insist[] that a Bank created by the United States is not necessary, because State banks will afford us the same conveniences." Having distorted the opposing position—that is, having identified as uniform a concession that perhaps only Burwell had made—Sheffey was then in a position to claim (on the basis of his preferred single-prong interpretation) that the Bank's constitutional critics had "in my humble conception, completely surrender[ed] the question."[86]

Variations on Sheffey's theme came from a number of Republican recharter supporters. Senator William H. Crawford of Georgia, who would later serve as Treasury secretary under President Madison, offered an especially concise version of the distortion when he claimed that "it is contended, that . . . a bank is necessary and proper for the management of the fiscal concerns of the nation, yet Congress has no power to incorporate one, because there are State banks which may be resorted to." Moreover, the distortion once again served as a vehicle for defending a very different interpretation of the Sweeping Clause: "Every man admits, directly or indirectly, the necessity of resorting to banks of some kind. This admission is at least an apparent abandonment of the constitutional objection[.]"[87] Similarly, Richard Brent—Crawford's fellow Republican and Senate colleague from Virginia—falsely suggested that "[o]ne argument, much confided in by gentlemen who have opposed the present bill, is not that banks are not necessary to the collection of the revenue, but, that State banks will answer." Rejecting "[t]his kind of reasoning" as wholly inadmissible, the senator effectively fell back on the functional necessity that he considered conceded: "[I]t appears to me that the only rule, in an instance of this kind, is, to take care that the means used have a necessary reference to the object of the power."[88]

A more abstract—and arguably less dishonest—rejoinder to the two-prong definition of constitutional necessity was offered by two recharter advocates in the House: Republican John Nicholson and Federalist Thomas Gold, both of New York. Instead of openly misrepresenting the opinion of recharter opponents with respect to functional necessity, Nicholson and Gold argued that the mere *discussion* of state banks as alternative service providers effectively conceded that the functional link between chartering a national bank and achieving various Article I ends was sufficiently strong (thus resolving, in their eyes, the constitutional question). In this vein, Nicholson stated that lawmakers "who oppose this bill, have got into a dilemma, in opposing it on the ground that the State banks can be made to answer the purposes of this Government; as they thereby virtually admit that banks of some kind are 'necessary' in managing its concerns."[89]

For his part, Gold suggested that "the whole question of constitutionality" had been "given up" by those pressing the two-prong interpretation, "for the very necessity of the resort to State banks maintains the agency of a bank as necessary in administrating the Government." For a bit of rhetorical flourish on this point, Gold invoked Homer's *The Odyssey*: "In steering clear of Scylla"—that is, in relying on a claim respecting federal necessity—"the argument is lost in Charybdis" (or functional necessity).[90]

Another, albeit less popular, means of defending a permissive single-prong definition of constitutional necessity was tracing out—and then questioning—the full implications of the two-prong interpretation. More specifically, at least three recharter advocates—Representatives Gold and Sheffey along with Senator Crawford—stressed that many of their opponents were logically committed to the possibility that a preferred mean could be constitutional at one point in time (i.e., if no viable alternatives existed) but *become* unconstitutional by a subsequent point (i.e., due to the advent of alternatives).[91] This commitment struck recharter advocates as ontologically flawed. Under an unchanging Constitution, a law was always and forever either constitutional or unconstitutional; its status could not change over time. The two-prong interpretation was thus inconsistent with the very nature of the Constitution.

Along these lines, Gold suggested that the two-prong interpretation, "resting on such contingencies" as the creation of institutions by states, "would at one period make a thing constitutional, which at another would be unconstitutional."[92] What Gold did not say explicitly, however—which Sheffey and Crawford surely did—was that an interpretation of this sort could not be squared with the broader norms of American constitutionalism. Sheffey initially followed Gold's lead in complaining that constitutional necessity—at least as lawmakers like Peter B. Porter, Adam Seybert, and Henry Clay would have preferred to define it—led "to the very extraordinary conclusion, that what is unconstitutional to day [sic] may be unconstitutional to-morrow." For Sheffey, however, this conclusion was problematic and justified further comment: "Can any thing show in a stronger light the untenable position which gentlemen occupy[? They] advance arguments which will make this constitution . . . a *flexible* instrument, to be contracted or extended, to be feeble or strong, as the caprice of State power may direct[.]"[93] Senator Crawford faulted, in a similar spirit, an interpretation that would effectively expand and contract federal

power on the basis of state policy: "The original powers granted to the
Government by the constitution, can never change with the varying circumstances of the country . . . [t]he constitution, in relation to the means
by which its powers are to be executed, is one eternal now."[94]

THE MERITS (AND CONSTITUTIONALITY) OF STATE BANK REGULATION

While members of the Eleventh Congress spent much of the recharter
debate quarreling over the precise scope of federal power, they also acknowledged—and disagreed over the merits of—the Bank's gradual evolution into a monetary instrument. Roughly a handful of lawmakers on
each side of the question invoked the institution's regulatory role, with national bank supporters citing the need for (and value of) restraints on state
bank lending and recharter opponents expressing concern over the potential misuse of such institutional power. Nearly every member of Congress
who discussed the Bank-qua-regulator did so not in the course of offering
thoughts on the constitutional question, but after transitioning—sometimes quite explicitly—to the policy merits of extending the institution's
charter. The lone exception was recharter opponent Henry Clay, who agonized openly about the constitutional dimension of the Bank's conversion.
In language that would haunt him come 1816 (and for decades beyond), the
young Kentucky senator spoke of state bank regulation as an unenumer-
ated (and thus forbidden) object of federal activity.

Recharter supporters recognized the monetary function the national
bank had come to perform by 1811, characterized it as an important con-
straint on state banks, and fretted at the prospect of its removal. Willis
Alston, a House Republican from North Carolina, captured the essence of
the institution's regulatory role when he suggested that "[t]he Bank of the
United States . . . serves as a controlling power, keeps the State banks in
proper bounds; and prevents them from issuing a vast quantity of paper,
which would inundate the country."[95] Not only did the Bank perform this
function, but according to Federalist Benjamin Pickman—Alston's House
colleague from Massachusetts—it was absolutely crucial that *someone*
did: "[I]t is necessary that the [state] banks . . . should have a common
parent to regulate their affairs, and to secure them from ruin from unexpected, and, of course, unprepared for, drafts [for specie]."[96] In other
words, it was important that state institutions be forced to restrict their
lending to a point where regular demands for the conversion of notes and
checks (into gold and silver coin) could be met.

Given the importance attached by recharter supporters to the Bank's monetary function, there was understandable concern at the prospect of its loss. Republican Jonathan Fisk, for example—previously cited for his claim that the behavior of the Jefferson administration all but settled the constitutional question—observed that the national bank "has served as a barometer to ascertain the credit of other banks; as a regulator to keep them within such bounds as might be safe to the community." However, "[s]top this bank, and what check is there then to limit the discounts of all other banks?"[97] Similarly, Fisk's House colleague—Federalist John Stanly of North Carolina—confessed concern that "if we remove the check, the restraining influence, which the . . . Bank of the United States, and its prudent direction . . . exercise over the State banks," then those institutions would be threats to "dishonestly emit[] paper beyond the sum authorized by their capital, and beyond the necessities of the country."[98]

Perhaps the most interesting comment on behalf of the Bank (vis-à-vis its regulatory function) came from Senator Crawford. In his February 11 floor speech, Georgia's senior senator reminded his colleagues that "[t]he State banks, whose credibility, in this case, is unquestioned, have told you that the influence of the Bank of the United States upon them is a beneficial one; that it prevents excessive discounts and emissions of paper, which, but for this check, would inevitably take place in the State banks."[99] Crawford's comment is interesting because, despite his implication of numerous pro-regulation statements from state banks, only one— the Bank of New York—is actually on record as supporting the national bank's monetary activity; its January 1811 memorial to Congress was cited in chapter 3.[100] Two possibilities present themselves here. The first is that Crawford simply overstated the degree of state bank support for the national institution's regulatory behavior. The second is that surviving records do not, in fact, capture the real extent of institutional support for the Bank's restraining influence.

Unsurprisingly, recharter opponents adopted a less sanguine view of the national bank's monetary activity and spoke longingly of its cessation. Michael Leib, a Republican member of the House from the Philadelphia area, acknowledged that the Bank "was a check upon the other banks," but insisted that this was not exactly cause for celebration; in fact, the institution could be analogized to a "shark" antagonizing "the little fish around him." Its ability to behave in this manner, Leib reminded his colleagues, sprang in part from the routine deposit of federal revenue—including state bank notes and checks—in the institution: "It was in the power of the Bank of the United States, by means of its great capital and the Governmental patronage, to prey upon the other banks whenever it pleased[.]"[101] Isaac McKim stressed essentially the same point, arguing that while "these [public] funds are in its hands, [the national bank] can employ the whole pecuniary resources of the nation to coerce other banks . . . into its measures." By the same token, McKim noted approvingly, "[i]f the charter is not renewed, the expiring bank will lose its power of holding other banks in check, by the withdrawing of public and private deposites [sic][.]"[102]

More alarmist rhetoric about the Bank's regulatory power—or rather, the potential abuse of that power—flowed from Representatives William Burwell and William T. Barry. After articulating his unique constitutional position—that a national bank was functionally "necessary" but ultimately illegitimate due to the existence of numerous state banks— Burwell spoke to the "overweening influence it [had] established over the moneyed institutions . . . of the States[.]" Lest this prevailing state of affairs furnish insufficient support for the case against recharter, Burwell emphasized that the Bank of the United States was capable of sins far more egregious than overbearance; its "strength can, at any moment, overthrow whatever State bank [it] may mark for destruction."[103] Barry spoke to the same dark prospect in warning that the institution could, "at any time, be enabled to overwhelm and destroy the small State establishments."[104] Lacking any evidence of actual institutional behavior along these lines, Burwell and Barry were left to convict the national bank of the only remaining crime: *potential* abuse of power.

Standing out among the critics of state bank regulation was Senator Clay, who spoke of the Bank's functional evolution as constitutionally problematic. More specifically, Clay acknowledged that the national bank had come to occupy a monetary role but complained that nothing in Article I, Section 8 actually empowered Congress to pursue that end. In this vein, while the senator (as noted above) had other constitutional misgivings about the institution—it was insufficiently related to an enumerated power, and state banks could perform the same functions—he was willing to concede that many of the federal government's objectives in continuing the Bank (efficient tax collection, safe revenue storage, the timely payment of government creditors, etc.) were perfectly constitutional. However, Clay suggested that

> [U]nder the name of accomplishing one object which is specified, the power implied ought not to be made to embrace other objects, which are not specified in the constitution . . . [it] is mockery, worse than usurpation, to establish it for a lawful object, and then extend it to

other objects, which are not lawful . . . [a] bank is made for the ostensible purpose of aiding in the collection of the revenue, and whilst
it is engaged in this . . . it is made to diffuse itself throughout society, and to influence all the great operations of credit, circulation, and
commerce.[105]

To put the senator's point another way, the national bank's conversion was
a historical fact—but that did not make it constitutional.

CONCLUSION

Given that a number of moderate Republicans in the Eleventh Congress
judged the Bank of the United States to be wholly constitutional, the fact
that so many of their ideological peers found themselves at something
akin to the opposite extreme (arguing that the institution failed both com-
ponents of a two-part test of necessity) invites at least one follow-up inquiry: Was the constitutional position of antibank moderate Republicans
sincere, or a smoke screen for their collective desire to both rid state banks
of their regulator and funnel the federal government's deposits to those
institutions?

Recharter advocates, Federalist and Republican alike, were hardly shy
about asserting that something *other* than constitutional principle was
motivating the position embraced by anti-recharter Republican moderates.
Recharter supporter John Nicholson, for example, tried to pull back the
constitutional veil on fellow Republicans who opposed the Bank: "We all
understand that the stockholders of State banks would be glad [to get] a
slice of the 'loaves and fishes' . . . this preposterous plan of substituting
State banks, has been suggested, and, in some measure, urged, through the
influence of some of those banks."[106] Federalist Benjamin Pickman offered
the same claim in more straightforward language: "[I]t is the *interest* of
the State banks which excites much of the opposition to the renewal of the
charter of the United States Bank."[107]

For their part, subsequent students of the episode have made similarly bold claims. Bray Hammond appeared to draw a distinction between
the antibank arguments of Old and moderate regime members when he
wrote that it was "entirely credible that some of the speakers were sin-
cerely concerned about constitutionality, but one feels some skepticism
when arguments that had been made by James Madison twenty years before were now offered with great earnestness by General Samuel Smith
and [Peter] B. Porter, enterprising business men of Baltimore and Buffalo

respectively[.]"[108] Susan Hoffmann has recently echoed Hammond's claim, suggesting that moderate Republicans "voiced their objection [to recharter] in terms of unconstitutionality and states' rights, but their arguments have a disingenuous ring."[109]

For my purposes, it is not necessary to resolve this sincerity-of-claims question one way or the other. We need only focus on the fact that the broader Republican regime, which included both conservative and moderate elements, was deeply divided over the meaning of the Necessary and Proper Clause in 1811. This division would endure through the conclusion of the War of 1812, a period that also saw the onset of significant economic stress (namely, the suspension of specie payments by state banks located to the south and west of New England). The refusal of these institutions to pay gold and silver on demand for their notes and checks continued into late 1815, when leading Republicans in the executive and legislative branches broached the idea of remedying this national monetary ailment by reviving the Bank of the United States. While a healthy majority of regime members embraced this proposal, no comparable majority could be mustered for pursuing it under the Sweeping Clause; antipathy to federal power was *still* a conspicuous strand in the broader Republican fabric. Regime leaders ultimately built the coalition necessary for creating a new Bank of the United States by forging a constitutional compromise. In a move that delivered the institution's services *without* alienating Republicans with long-term anxieties about federal power, the Bank was chartered under the Coinage Clause. To the story of this "Compromise of 1816" I now turn.

CHAPTER FIVE

The Compromise of 1816

The Conventional Wisdom

In June 1812—just fifteen months following the demise of the Bank of the United States—Congress declared war on Great Britain. Without the institution that Alexander Hamilton had promised would provide "[g]reater facility to the Government in obtaining pecuniary aids, especially in sudden emergencies,"[1] the United States was forced to rely for wartime funding on loans from state banks. This was quite inconvenient for the federal government (and just one of the many economic hardships introduced by the conflict).

In January 1815, looking to provide more reliable funding for the war effort, the Republican-led Thirteenth Congress passed a bill to reestablish a national bank.[2] Owing to the trying economic circumstances, or a widely shared sense that the question had been settled by twenty years of experience (1791–1811), or some combination of the two, most Republicans lawmakers had raised no constitutional objection to the bill. President James Madison ultimately vetoed the bill on policy grounds, but in doing so, made it clear that he "[w]aiv[ed] the question of the constitutional authority of the Legislature to establish an incorporated bank, as being precluded, in my judgment, by repeated recognitions, under varied circumstances, of the validity of such an institution, in the acts of the legislative, executive, and judicial branches of the Government, accompanied by indications, in different modes, of a concurrence of the general will of the nation[.]"[3]

Within three weeks of Madison's veto, the War of 1812 was over (along with its heavy demands on the federal purse). The Treaty of Ghent (signed in December 1814 by American and British negotiators) reached the United States and was quickly ratified by the Senate.

Just over a year later, in April 1816, the Fourteenth Congress—
again controlled by Republicans—passed a slightly different national
bank bill. This time around, President Madison signed the measure—
which offered a twenty-year charter to a new Bank of the United
States—into law.

Casebooks in American constitutional law, whether designed for un-
dergraduates in political science or law school students, appear
strongly committed to some version of the foregoing constitutional narrative on the national bank's 1816 revival. One popular casebook fails to
attribute any constitutional significance to the episode—only "strenuous
political opposition" to the recharter bill is cited[4]—but a handful of others
offer at least a condensed form of this account.[5]

This rendering of the Bank's resurrection is at best incomplete, and at
worst quite misleading. The policy and constitutional facts that it prioritizes—the federal government's difficulties in funding the war, and congressional Republicans' willingness in early 1815 to acknowledge the national bank's constitutional necessity—offer a false sense of both (1) why,
from a policy standpoint, the institution was revived in 1816 and (2) how,
from a constitutional perspective, that revival was justified. A more complete narrative of the 1812–1816 period, one that carefully distinguishes
between the failed midwar and the successful postwar efforts to re-create
the Bank of the United States, can be constructed from scholarship within
law, history, and political science.[6]

The first part of my expanded account, which covers the period between June 1812 and February 1815, aligns with much of the casebook
history offered in the opening vignette. The Twelfth Congress was determined to finance the conflict with Great Britain through the sale of long-
term securities, but even its first effort to raise funds failed to produce the
desired amount.[7] Shorter-term securities bearing a lower interest rate were
sold to make up the shortfall. This latter mode of borrowing quickly became a regular feature of wartime finance, especially as further efforts to
sell long-term securities met with increasing resistance from investors. In
fact, bonds with more distant maturity dates were only sold once the Treasury agreed to accept less than face value for them. It was in this distressed
fiscal context—Treasury Secretary Alexander J. Dallas wrote that "the fiscal operations of the government labor[ed] with extreme inconvenience"—
that President James Madison exercised his constitutional prerogative to
convene lawmakers "on extraordinary Occasions" by calling the Thirteenth Congress back to work in August 1814.[8]

By the time that members of the House and Senate reconvened, fresh economic weights had been added to the government's burden. Within days of the British assault on Washington, DC, in late August, many state banks outside New England had suspended the payment of specie for their notes and checks. This paper began to trade at a discount from face value, which average Americans experienced in the form of price inflation.[9] Congress, however, was fixated less on the newfound monetary disorder and more on its lingering fiscal problems. Moreover, a new national bank had been floated as a solution to the latter. If shares could be purchased in part with wartime bonds, then the institution could (like its 1791 predecessor) help to restore the public's damaged credit. Just as importantly, it could support the war effort through direct loans to the federal government.

The constitutional question loomed, however. In recommending a revived national bank to Congress, Secretary Dallas suggested that twenty years with a national bank—and more than three painful years without one, complete with calls for its restoration—settled the question.[10] In this especially trying fiscal environment, Republican lawmakers—a few members of the party's Old wing excepted—actually said little about the Constitution. The premise for their bill to revive the Bank, passed in January 1815, seems to have been that the fiscal demands of war now rendered the institution far closer to "necessary" than merely "useful."[11] Madison vetoed that bill on policy grounds, arguing that the proposed bank would provide too little short-term support for the war effort, but waived the constitutional question (along Dallasian lines) as settled.

The second part of my expanded account, which runs from Madison's veto through April 1816, offers a significant departure from the standard scholarly narrative. I draw attention to a pair of crucial, related, and much-neglected facts: Relative to the wartime national bank bill that died by the president's pen, the peacetime bill that earned his signature was (1) *grounded in a different policy imperative* and (2) *anchored to a different constitutional provision*. The story here begins with the fact that peace, rather than a national bank, eased the federal government's fiscal burdens; news arrived within weeks of Madison's veto that a treaty between the United States and Great Britain had been signed in Belgium. Peace did little, however, to alleviate the nation's *monetary* suffering; specie payments remained suspended throughout much of the country.[12] In fact, it became increasingly clear to federal lawmakers that the state banks (which were profiting from the ability to lend without restraint) were not going to resume specie payments voluntarily. As members of the Fourteenth Congress considered their options for compelling the restoration of gold and silver to circulation—that is, regulating the state banks—one possibility stood out: reviving the former regulator of those institutions, the Bank of the United States.

President Madison urged Congress to consider this option in the event that state banks refused to remedy the "absence of the precious metals" from circulation, and Secretary Dallas quickly followed up with a report recommending the Bank's revival as a device for restoring the "national currency."[13] That report also seemed to recognize, however, that the arrival of peace had reproblematized the national bank's constitutional status; was the institution "necessary" for collecting taxes or borrowing money now that the conflict with Britain was over? Rather than subject his party to another fight between its Old and moderate wings, Dallas—himself a moderate[14]—proffered an argument designed to appease regime members with federalism concerns. His argument made no reference whatsoever to the Necessary and Proper Clause. Rather, Dallas straightforwardly suggested that national bank legislation would exercise Congress's Article I power to "coin Money, regulate the Value thereof." In essence, he was laboring to shift attention away from the institution's necessity for supporting the federal government's *fiscal* affairs (a controversial subject) and toward its value for regulating the nation's *monetary* affairs (which was far less controversial). Left unclear in the Treasury secretary's report—and in the floor statements of prominent Republicans who would echo his constitutional thinking—was whether Congress would directly exercise its power under the Coinage Clause in chartering a national bank (that is, no recourse to the Sweeping Clause was required) or act in a manner that was manifestly "necessary" for exercising its power to coin money. Either way, however, Dallas's argument left regime members who were opposed to a broad understanding of federal power in the long term free to support a national bank in the short term.

Scholarly treatment of the national bank's constitutional status has been blind not simply to Dallas's constitutional position—which I have labeled the "Compromise of 1816"—but to the fact that leading moderate Republicans in the Fourteenth Congress openly embraced it. A careful reading of the 1816 debate, in fact, leaves little doubt that the Coinage Clause was the textual anchor for the revived Bank of the United States. The regime's constitutional compromise was not immune to criticism, however. While several prominent Republicans had embraced it on originalist grounds, arguing that the framers had intended (via the Coinage Clause) to grant Congress plenary power over the nation's currency, Federalists protested that this claim offered an example of overly abstract originalist thinking. To their eyes, the specific intent behind the provision had been to authorize the physical creation of coins and the assignment of monetary value to them; chartering a national bank was beyond the constitutional pale. This objection did little, however, to halt Republican plans for reviving the Bank. And eight months after signing the recharter bill into law, President Madison invoked the Compromise of 1816 in his final annual message to Congress.

This chapter replicates the previous one in that it offers an oft-forgotten scene in the Bank's longer constitutional drama the kind of critical analysis usually reserved for moments when Alexander Hamilton, John Marshall, or Andrew Jackson occupy the stage. Much of the chapter documents (and distinguishes between) the economic factors that gave rise to the failed wartime drive to revive the national bank in the Thirteenth Congress and the successful peacetime effort to do the same in its successor. American economic historians are familiar with these facts, but my ensuing treatment of the 1816 recharter debate explains why they are important for constitutional scholars. In short, we cannot understand the textual basis for the Bank's revival without acknowledging both the difference between fiscal and monetary policy *and* (just as importantly) the Republican regime's willingness to leverage that distinction for the sake of internal peace. I close the chapter by briefly speaking to the import of the president's decision to invoke the Coinage Clause in his 1816 annual message for our understanding of him as a constitutional thinker.

FINANCING THE WAR OF 1812

Though scholars have traditionally been preoccupied with either the causes of America's second war with Great Britain[15] or the military campaigns—by land or by sea—that were waged during the same,[16] a small but growing body of work is devoted to chronicling the federal government's struggle to finance the War of 1812.[17] This section does not explore that work at any length, but it does review both the core element of the wartime financing scheme and its growing ineffectiveness over time. In short, both the Twelfth (1811–1813) and the Thirteenth (1813–1815) Congresses largely eschewed new domestic taxes as a funding tool in favor of selling 6 percent bonds, but the Treasury's ability to sell them (at least at face value) only diminished over time.

In November 1807, roughly five months after the USS *Chesapeake* was attacked by the HMS *Leopard* off the coast of Virginia—an incident that ratcheted up existing tensions between the United States and Great

Britain[18]—Treasury Secretary Albert Gallatin submitted a report to the Tenth Congress that included thoughts on the funding of a prospective war.[19] He wrote that if an armed conflict would not "materially affect" the domestic economy, or if the government could not secure loans on decent terms, new taxes would represent the appropriate funding tool; they would spread the war's costs across the "great mass of the citizens." Gallatin, however, argued that a maritime war with Britain *would* adversely affect the economy; it would (for example) reduce domestic profits from foreign commerce. In that situation, new taxes would only aggravate the "losses and privations caused by the war." Moreover, since the public's credit was "unimpaired" in late 1807, the principal alternative with respect to funding—borrowing via bond sales—was doubly attractive.[20] Less than two years after authoring this report, Gallatin was retained as Treasury secretary upon James Madison's ascension to the presidency. As such, it is not surprising that Congress ultimately adopted (in 1812 and beyond) a financing scheme along the lines suggested in late 1807.

Anticipating a formal declaration of war, and working from Gallatin's estimate of more than $10 million in war-related expenses for 1812 alone,[21] the Twelfth Congress authorized a bond issue of $11 million on March 14 of that year (with the securities paying 6 percent interest).[22] Though the Treasury secretary had been optimistic enough to outline a procedure for reducing subscriptions to the loan in the event that *more* than $11 million was committed,[23] only $6.12 million was raised when the books opened in early May—$4.19 million from state banks and $1.93 million from individual investors.[24] These figures, however, actually overstate the real willingness of state banks to invest in the $11 million loan. Of the $4.19 million in institutional subscriptions reported by Secretary Gallatin, just 62 percent—$2.58 million—was offered on the Treasury's terms (i.e., the principal would not be paid back for at least twelve years). The remaining 38 percent—$1.61 million—was lent by state banks "[o]n special contract"; the principal would need to be repaid after just one, two, or five years.[25]

Despite Gallatin's praise for the initial fund-raising effort—he suggested that $6.12 million was "as great as might have been expected within so short a period"[26]—it was clear that auxiliary measures were required to meet the $11 million mark. Consequently, the remainder of 1812 saw both Congress and the Treasury Department labor to make up the $4.88 million shortfall. In June—right around the time war was formally declared—Congress authorized the sale of up to $5 million in Treasury notes, or one-year bonds that paid 5.4 percent interest. In essence, Congress was expressing a formal willingness to borrow for a shorter length of time

(though it would compensate by paying a slightly lower rate of interest).
That fall, approximately $3.54 million was raised through the sale of these
securities—$3.18 million from state banks and $355,000 from individuals.[27]
Moreover, in August, the Treasury Department formally reopened the subscription books from early May; this yielded an additional $3.45 million
in funds—$1.86 million from state banks and $1.59 million from individuals.[28] In short, the federal government ultimately raised $13.1 million be-
tween May 1812 and the end of the calendar year, or more than the $11 mil-
lion needed to finance its estimated expenses for that period.

By the end of 1812, the problem was less the federal government's
backward-looking struggle to raise $11 million and more the forward-
looking need to raise *additional* funds. The Treasury secretary estimated
that more than $20 million in new borrowing would be needed to both
fund regular federal operations and prosecute the ongoing war with Britain. Moreover, even that figure presumed that a proposed expansion of the
navy would be delayed.[29] The Twelfth Congress, cognizant of the fact that
it would be impossible to borrow this sum entirely in long-term 6 percent
securities, responded by approving two borrowing bills in early 1813: a
$16 million loan on February 8 and another $5 million in one-year Treasury
notes on February 25.[30] Though $3.93 million in new Treasury notes were
ultimately sold by the conclusion of 1813,[31] the real story of federal wartime
finance in early 1813—and the beginning of the government's fiscal troubles
for the remainder of the war—was the abject failure of the $16 million loan.

Two days after the subscriptions books opened in mid-March 1813, just
$3.96 million had been committed—a mere quarter of the requested sum.[32]
Opponents of the war reveled in the failure of "Mr. Madison's Loan," re-
printing in local newspapers the *New-York Gazette*'s poetic commentary
of March 17: "To BORROW—not to TAX—the GOVERNMENT was prone:
The people, not Subscribing, left it quite A-LONE."[33] Moreover, just as the
Treasury Department had reopened the $11 million loan in August 1812,
it reopened the $16 million loan in late March 1813. This time around,
however, it communicated a willingness to receive offers for the residual
$12.04 million *below par*.[34] In other words, the federal government was
desperate enough for funding to sell the remaining securities at a discount
from face value.[35] This proved to be a successful gambit; a trio of wealthy
Americans—Stephen Girard, David Parish, and John Jacob Astor—bought
the bulk of the remaining securities at a price of $88 per $100 bond.[36] In essence, the federal government agreed to pay 6 percent interest for the sake
of securing $88—an effective interest rate of 6.8 percent. All told, the cost
of wartime borrowing had begun to climb.

The Treasury's spring 1813 acceptance of below-par offers on the $16 million loan was only, it turned out, a harbinger of things to come. In July of that year, two months after Albert Gallatin resigned his position to join an American delegation negotiating for peace in England,[37] acting Treasury Secretary William Jones requested an *additional* $7.5 million from Congress to both raise new troops and fund the war for the first quarter of 1814.[38] The House and Senate obliged less than two weeks later, but this time, the Treasury immediately assumed that the loan would not be subscribed at par value. Its initial advertisement of the $7.5 million loan solicited proposals (at some discount from par value) from "any person or persons, body or bodies corporate, who may offer . . . to loan [money] to the United States[.]"[39] Ultimately, the Treasury was able to raise $6.62 million in additional funds; it sold the available securities to a set of wealthy individual investors at the price of $88.25 per $100 bond—a slight improvement over the previous sale.[40] As before, however, it effectively paid a heightened rate of interest—just shy of 6.8 percent—for those funds.

The cost of borrowing would only increase throughout 1814, and with good reason. By the time the Thirteenth Congress reconvened in December 1813, the military situation of the United States looked exceedingly grim. As War of 1812 historian Donald Hickey has noted, "Canada was still in British hands, the British fleet had invaded American waters, and the tide of the war appeared to be turning against the United States."[41] Not only was the military scene rather gray—Republican William Murfree, a member of the House from North Carolina, volunteered that "the result of the last campaign had disappointed the expectations of every one"[42]—but the fiscal picture was even darker. Tens of millions had already been borrowed (with little to show for it), but the acting Treasury secretary communicated in January 1814 that an additional $29.4 million—a staggering sum relative to the 1812 and 1813 loan totals—would need to be borrowed for the coming year's expenses.[43] War critics were predictably irate; one editorial reprinted in Goshen, New York's *Orange County Patriot* mockingly complained that "Different acts of congress have authorized the loan of *Thirty Eight Millions Five Hundred Thousand* dollars . . . [b]ut Mr. Madison proposes . . . to borrow still more . . . So far all the money borrowed by government . . . is thrown away . . . [W]hat have government to show for it? Why they have *re*-conquered a part of our own territory. Michigan is ours again. They possess Lake Erie!"[44] More importantly, it was during this season of national distress that the first clear call was heard for a new national bank—an institution that could help remedy the federal government's fiscal woes by both raising bond prices (provided that these securities, as in 1791, would be accepted for the purpose of purchasing bank stock) and lending directly to it. On January 10, a petition authored by Jacob Barker—one of the wealthy individuals who invested in the $7.5 million loan—and signed by 120 fellow New Yorkers was communicated to Congress; it "pray[ed] for an act of incorporation, authorizing them to establish a national bank[.]"[45]

Given the price for 6 percent securities in 1813—somewhere between $88 and $88.25 for a $100 bond—federal lawmakers in early 1814 concluded that $29.4 million could only be raised by authorizing borrowing far in excess of that amount. Consequently, the Thirteenth Congress approved the issuance of $10 million in new Treasury notes on March 4 and a $25 million loan on March 24.[46] On the premise that $25 million in new 6 percent securities could not be sold at once—at least at reasonable prices—in the current climate, the newly confirmed Treasury secretary (George W. Campbell) elected to pursue a partial sale of $10 million in late April and early May. Technically speaking, all of these securities were sold—the bulk ($9.23 million) at a price of $88 and the remainder ($730,000) at prices between $85 and $88. To secure these funds, however, the Treasury had to accept a condition attached to more than half ($5 million) of the $88 bids: If another portion of the $25 million loan was subsequently sold at a rate "more favorable to the lenders" (i.e., below $88), that rate would be retroactively applied to the older bond sales.[47] These sophisticated sale terms aside, the broader inference to be drawn is not especially complex: Increasingly desperate for funding, the Treasury Department had begun (by the spring of 1814) to pay even higher effective rates of interest *and* accept specialized terms favorable to lenders.

The condition attached to the spring sale was ultimately activated in August, when the Treasury attempted to sell a $6 million portion of the $25 million loan. This occurred in the midst of a national humiliation—arguably the worst of the post-1789 era. An advertisement for the sale of the $6 million tranche had been circulated in late July, just as the British navy began to charge up the Chesapeake Bay and toward the nation's capital. On August 19, three days before bids on the bond offering were due, the British began to land troops in Maryland and advance on foot toward Washington, DC.[48] In this troubled atmosphere—the White House, the Capitol building, and the Treasury Department would all be burned within a few days' time[49]—the Treasury was probably lucky to secure any bids at all. It received offers for approximately $2.82 million in these securities, or just under half of the available total. The bulk of these offers came in at $80—some were below $80 and others as high as $88—and Secretary Campbell wound up accepting all bids tendered at $80 or above.[50] While this secured some immediate funding for the war—roughly $2.34 million[51]—it also cost the Treasury (via the retroactive price reduction) $400,000 from the spring sale.[52] In short, the government was now borrowing money—to the extent funds were even offered—at an effective interest rate of 7.5 percent. A newspaper in Windsor, Vermont—the *Washingtonian*—remarked soon after the conclusion of the August sale that "we are in the very jaws of national insolvency—the loan drags—Stock is low, down to 80 or 81—money grows fearce."[53]

From the standpoint of national banking, two important events followed the August 1814 bond sale. First, given the lackluster result of this funding effort coupled with the unceasing fiscal demands of the war, the recently recalled Thirteenth Congress began serious consideration of a proposal to reestablish a national bank. President Madison, perhaps sensing that serious financial and military trouble lay ahead, had called members back to Washington on August 8—two weeks before the troubled bond sale and sixteen days before the British burned portions of the capital.[54] However, the special session of Congress did not convene until September 19, or several weeks *after* the tumultuous August events. One day later, Madison delivered his annual message to Congress—a full six weeks early. The president acknowledged that the winter session of Congress did not normally begin until early December but suggested that he "was induced to call" members so that "any inadequacy in the existing provisions for the wants of the Treasury might be supplied[.]"[55] Notwithstanding some subsequent consideration of new taxes as a funding source,[56] after mid-October members largely turned their attention to the Madison administration's preferred fiscal solution: a revived Bank of the United States.

Second, within ten days of the August 22 bond sale—and arguably in consequence of the August 24 assault on Washington[57]—many state banks south and west of New England halted the payment of gold and silver for their paper. Perhaps the most important consequence of this development was the immediate depreciation of their notes and checks, which consumers experienced in the form of price inflation. As a result, after Alexander J. Dallas replaced George W. Campbell as Treasury secretary in early October—the latter had resigned after less than eight months in office, "[s]hattered in health and spirit" by the war[58]—the former reported to the House Ways and Means Committee that turmoil in public finance was no longer the sum total of American economic woes; "[t]he condition of the circulating medium of the country present[ed] *another* copious source of mischief and embarrassment."[59].In simpler terms, monetary disorder was now supplementing fiscal distress. Nevertheless, the ensuing (but ultimately failed) drive in late 1814 and early 1815 to revive the Bank of the United States was focused less on restoring monetary order and more on funding the ongoing conflict. Once the war concluded—a development that eliminated the short-term financial pressure—members of the Fourteenth Congress would revisit the proposal for a national bank. This time, however, their object was the nationwide resumption of specie payments; they sought to "settle the currency, which *remained* in the utmost disorder."[60]

A QUESTION "FOREVER SETTLED AND AT REST"?

On October 17, precisely four weeks after President Madison advised the recalled Thirteenth Congress to address the wartime "wants of the Treasury[,]" Secretary Dallas formally proposed that it charter a national bank. Such an institution, he wrote, was absolutely crucial for achieving the Madison administration's short- and long-term fiscal goals: "plac[ing] the public credit upon a solid and durable foundation . . . provid[ing] a revenue commensurate with the demands of a war expenditure; and . . . remov[ing] from the treasury an immediate pressure[.]"[61]

Exactly four months later—February 17, 1815—the House of Representatives tabled a national bank bill in light of the newly received Treaty of Ghent.[62] Formally, the administration's effort to improve its fiscal predicament had failed. In real terms, however, the premise for that effort—a costly war with Great Britain—had simply been removed. Political and economic historians have chronicled much of the action between the Treasury secretary's October 1814 proposal and the February 1815 decision by the House to suspend renewed consideration of it. In short, two national bank bills had quickly emerged. First, there was an administration-supported bill that offered Republicans structural advantages in terms of both ownership and management.[63] It also guaranteed the federal government a quick and sizable loan ($30 million), but lending on that scale might have immediately threatened the nascent institution's ability to pay specie for its paper.[64] Second, there was a "radically different bill"[65]—the brainchild of John C. Calhoun, a young South Carolina Republican in the House—designed to appease Federalists with respect to both stock purchase rules and decision-making structures.[66] Moreover, by removing the forced loan and promising (at least on paper) the continuous payment of specie, Calhoun sought to win over Republicans who were wary of producing a stillborn financial institution. Protracted debate in Congress ultimately led to passage of a compromise national bank bill in January 1815.[67] That institution, however, was not slated to go into operation until 1816—a full year away. Secretary Dallas—desperate for more immediate fiscal support—urged the president to veto the bill on policy grounds,[68] and Madison obliged. Several weeks later, as the House began renewed debate on the administration's bank bill, news of the Treaty of Ghent arrived.

The politics of institutional design and performance aside, the administration's effort to reestablish a national bank was constitutionally memorable. Not four years earlier, in early 1811, a collection of Old and moderate Republicans had assaulted the Bank of the United States as beyond the scope of congressional power under the Necessary and Proper Clause. As discussed in chapter 4, a handful of recharter opponents had also rejected the claim that evidence of post-1801 acquiescence among Republicans in power eliminated the Bank's constitutional problem. The subsequent advent of an extended and costly foreign conflict, however—one that the federal government struggled to fund—made a national bank an increasingly attractive policy option for the Republican regime. From a constitutional standpoint, its members had two options: (1) subordinate fiscal need for the sake of constitutional consistency or (2) find one or more ways to swallow their long-standing objections. On the whole, they chose the latter.

The need to overcome the legacy of Republican constitutional opposition to a national bank was manifest in Alexander Dallas's October 1814 proposal to revive the institution. Writing to House Ways and Means chairman John W. Eppes—one of the Bank's constitutional foes in 1811— the Treasury secretary openly acknowledged that doubts about the institution's status still existed; "[i]t would be presumptuous to conjecture that the sentiments which actuated the opposition have passed away[.]" He stressed, however, that even those who harbored such sentiments needed to recognize that the "contest" was now over; "there must be a period when discussion shall cease and decision shall become absolute."[69] To justify his claim that the constitutional question was settled, Dallas began with the evidence of acquiescence that fellow Republicans had recently acknowledged but ultimately rejected. "We have marked," he said, "the existence of a national bank for a period of twenty years, with all the sanctions of the legislative, executive, and judicial authorities[.]"

Dallas did not, however, rest his case solely on the behavior of federal officials between 1791 and 1811 (and especially the post-1801 period). Those considering the question in 1814, in short, also had access to infor-

mation about current public opinion. "[W]hen we have seen the dissolution of one institution," the Treasury secretary wrote, "and heard a loud
and continued call for the establishment of another . . . can it be deemed a
violation of the right of private opinion, to consider the constitutionality
of a national bank, as a question forever settled and at rest?"[70] It is worth
noting here—and I return to this point below in discussing James Madison's thought—that Dallas's acknowledgment of these forces and their relevance for resolving the institution's status hardly meant that he *personally* had embraced a broad understanding of the Sweeping Clause.

The ensuing debate in Congress—which commenced on November 14
following the introduction of a bill[71] that conformed to Dallas's report of
October 17—was not completely devoid of constitutional content, but that
element was far less conspicuous than it had been in either the 1791 or the
1811 proceedings. Federalists, of course, had no constitutional truck with
a national bank; their opposition to the administration's bill (as noted
above) was rooted in two provisions that would have facilitated Republican ownership and management of the institution. Republican advocates
of a national bank, especially those with prior constitutional misgivings,
were altogether *silent* on the question. This silence has been construed not
as an embrace of Dallas's claim that the question was "settled" but rather
as an implicit argument that present demands on the Treasury rendered
the Bank "necessary" in a way it had not been before. In this vein, Keith
Whittington has written that the war "persuaded many Jeffersonians of
the necessity of a bank, at least within that immediate context . . . circumstances [had] changed, rendering a Bank 'necessary and proper' where
it might once have been merely expedient[.]"[72]

Given their silence on the constitutional question, there is really no
way to know for sure whether the recent Republican converts to the national bank cause understood the institution's legitimacy in Dallasian
terms or along the lines suggested by Whittington. Old Republican John
Clopton,[73] a persistent constitutional critic of the national bank, appeared
curious on this point himself. Speaking on the House floor, Clopton confessed that he "would have been glad if some gentleman who patronize[d
the administration bill], would have presented to us his views of the authority which he conceives the constitution has given us to pass such a
bill as this[.]"[74] The indirect evidence here points, I think, to the conclusion that Dallas and recent converts on the Bank had *different* understandings of its constitutionality. Had Dallas's argument been widely accepted,
we would not have seen an extended discussion of the constitutional question a year and a half later; there would have been agreement that it was

still "settled." The very genesis of the Compromise of 1816 suggests (along Whittington's lines) that many Republicans viewed the institution as "necessary" during the war but something less than that after the arrival of peace.

This is getting ahead of the story, however. While probank Republicans were silent on the constitutional question, their intraparty opponents were not.[75] Joseph Hawkins of Kentucky, for example, suggested that he "entertained constitutional objections to the establishment of any bank[.]"[76] In accordance with the two-prong interpretation of the Necessary and Proper Clause, members of this cohort argued that the federal government's ability to finance the war through the sale of short-term Treasury notes rendered a national bank something less than "necessary."[77] This opposition notwithstanding, a compromise bill passed Congress in January 1815.

President Madison vetoed that bill on policy grounds, stressing that it did "not appear to be calculated to answer the purposes of reviving the public credit [and] . . . affording to the public more durable loans."[78] Perhaps to make it clear that a different national bank bill would have earned his signature, the president began his veto message by "[w]aiving the question of the constitutional authority of the Legislature to establish an incorporated bank[.]" Moreover, he did so in a manner that was consistent with the constitutional thinking of Secretary Dallas. Madison claimed that the question was "precluded, in my judgment, by repeated recognitions, under varied circumstances, of the validity of such an institution, in acts of the legislative, executive, and judicial branches of the Government, accompanied by indications, in different modes, of a concurrence of the general will of the nation[.]"[79] Like Dallas, the president invoked both past acquiescence by federal officials and current public opinion. However, as several students of Madison's thought have recently suggested, there is no evidence that the president's *own* position on the meaning of the Sweeping Clause had changed.[80] Rather, he was willing to permit certain forces to trump fidelity to the text as he understood it.

If the House and Senate majorities mustered in January 1815 to pass the ill-fated Bank bill included two types of moderate Republicans— those who had long been at ease with more expansive conceptions of federal power and those who viewed the Bank's necessity as a wartime phenomenon—then those majorities presumably fell apart with the arrival of peace. The latter crowd retreated to the claim that a peacetime national bank was not (and never had been) valid under the Sweeping Clause. Otherwise put, peace with Great Britain had the perverse effect of restoring war among Republicans over the scope of federal power. This intraparty civil

war would soon produce a separate peace on the Bank question, however—
one facilitated by the Fourteenth Congress's desire to solve a very different
kind of economic problem.

TOWARD THE RESUMPTION OF SPECIE PAYMENTS

In early December 1815, nearly ten months after the arrival of peace and
more than fourteen months since his anguished (and early) annual message to the Thirteenth Congress, President Madison could offer its successor more cheerful news on the state of the Union. The war's conclusion, along with a subsequent commercial agreement that facilitated the
resumption of transatlantic trade with Great Britain, had produced an
impressive "revival of the public credit."[81] Not only were the federal government's expenditures lower, but its income—which came in large part
from import taxes—was higher. Erastus Root, a Republican member of
the House from New York, later captured the essence of Madison's sentiment; he recalled that during the war, "the credit of the Government was
weak . . . now it is strong."[82]

The president acknowledged, however, that the state of the Union was
not uniformly strong. More specifically, the payment of specie remained
suspended for many state banks outside New England. Economic historian Edwin Perkins has argued that most Americans were willing to endure monetary disorder during the war but expected a quick restoration of
specie to circulation with the arrival of peace.[83] In this spirit, a May 1815
editorial in the New Haven–based *Connecticut Journal* expressed "belie[f]
and trust, that the banks will soon resume their accustomed payments
in specie."[84] The resumption of payments did not follow on the heels of
peace, however. In early August, almost six months after the Treaty of
Ghent had been publicized, an editorial in Trenton's *True American* reported that "[c]omplaints prevail very generally thro' the country" about
the continued refusal of state banks "to pay specie for [their] notes. There
is no doubt that this refusal produces very serious inconvenience; and
that it is very desirable the payment of specie should be resumed by the
banks[.]"[85] The endurance of these conditions into early December was
recognized by Madison, who suggested that the "benefits of an uniform
national currency should be restored to the community."[86]

Suspension generated economic winners and losers—a fact that no
doubt explains the cresting political desire to address it. American consumers got the short end of the suspension stick; they encountered the
depreciation of state bank paper in the form of price inflation. Burent Gar-

diner spoke to this state of affairs in an August 1815 essay for the *Rhode-Island American*. Despite the public's monetary expectations during a time of peace, he wrote, "the cessation of war produced no specie payments. The banks went on in their old way." Moreover, that "old way" was adversely affecting countless lives: "All men who have regular stated prices for their labor, all salarymen, all who live on income, are obliged to live at an expense of fifteen per cent. greater than they would do, if the banks paid specie for their notes."[87] A version of the same claim—though likely quite exaggerated—appeared in the *Baltimore Patriot* on December 16; an anonymous editorial complained that due to the "absence of the precious metals, we now pay *double* prices for almost all the comforts and necessaries of life. To those who have . . . [set] salaries, this state of things is peculiarly oppressive and distressing."[88] A satirical piece in the October 20 issue of the Georgetown-based *Federal Republican* was less focused on the extent of price inflation and more on the attitude it cultivated toward the notes and checks of state banks. Its main character—a French visitor to the United States—"never paid or received [his paper] without a vast deal of shrugging up of his shoulders and other tokens of dissatisfaction, and whenever he handled a bank note, eyed it with a look of most sovereign contempt."[89]

Faring far better in the midst of monetary turmoil—at least according to many observers—were the state banks. Far from crippling their operations, suspension enabled these institutions to expand their lending (and thus their profits). Whereas regular calls to convert state bank paper into gold and silver coin had forced institutions to limit their demand liabilities to some multiple of their held specie, the suspension of payments effectively empowered these state banks to lend *without* regard for their hard assets. Otherwise put, the prevailing monetary conditions permitted state banks to enjoy what Mathew Carey called a "great harvest of large dividends[.]"[90] Burent Gardiner's essay emphasized the relationship between the state banks' gain and consumers' pain, arguing that "the community is paying at a horrific rate for the profits *they* make."[91] Moreover, there was a sense—one that later found expression on the floor of the House—that suspension endured not because the state banks could not pay specie but "because [they] ha[d] no interest to reduce their excessive issues."[92] That is to say, if simply left to their own devices, state banks might *never* resume the payment of gold and silver coin.

The question, of course, was how—if at all—these institutions could be forced to "reduce their business" and then restore the convertibility of their paper.[93] The Madison administration's answer was built on what one

Republican senator—James Barbour of Virginia—would later call the "lessons of experience."[94] The political logic of those lessons was reasonably clear: If the old Bank of the United States had contributed to the nationwide maintenance of specie payments (by restraining the lending of local institutions), but that state of affairs had been compromised in its absence, then a new national bank would revive its predecessor's regulatory activity and thereby facilitate both the restoration of the precious metals to circulation and the preservation of that important monetary achievement.

The impulse to treat a national bank as a cure for present ills was even strong enough to inspire counterfactual thinking about the failed 1811 recharter effort. Thomas Willing, president of the Bank of the United States between 1791 and 1807, wrote John Sergeant—a Federalist member of the House from Pennsylvania—after a peacetime national bank had been proposed to suggest that "[h]ad the old Institution been cherished, modified and its Capital enlarged, the present state of things as it respects our money circulation . . . might have been avoided."[95] A few days earlier, an editorial in the Albany Daily Advertiser had speculated in the same manner; its author wrote that had the Bank "been in existence during the late war . . . it would have prevented all the vexations, and mortifications, and losses, which individuals constantly sustain, from a confused, and depreciated paper currency."[96] Condy Raguet, who later became president of the nation's first savings bank—the Philadelphia Saving Fund Society[97]—alluded to the prevalence of this thinking in writing that "[i]t has been frequently asserted . . . that had the charter of the late bank of the United States been renewed, we would have experienced none of those difficulties to which we are now exposed[.]"[98]

The president's annual message, communicated to the Fourteenth Congress on December 5, did not explicitly call for the chartering of a national bank. By contrast, he merely suggested that if "the operation of the State banks c[ould] not produce" the resumption of specie payments—that is, if they would not voluntarily resume the payment of gold and silver coin—then a national bank bill would "merit consideration[.]"[99] The next day, however, Treasury Secretary Dallas made it abundantly clear that the administration was going to proceed on the assumption that voluntary resumption was *not* forthcoming. In a lengthy report to Congress on the state of the nation's finances, Dallas—citing "the state of the national currency"—concluded that it was his "duty respectfully to propose [t]hat a national bank be established at the city of Philadelphia, having power to erect branches elsewhere[.]"[100] Perhaps unsurprisingly, within days Congress was flooded with supportive petitions from citizens of that city. Each cited the "fluctuating and interrupted state of the circulating medium of the country"—the petitions only differed with respect to their signatories—as a troublesome condition that justified the establishment of "a National Bank with branches[.]"[101]

Before turning to Republicans' postwar constitutional argument on behalf of a national bank, several points about this second (and ultimately successful) post-1811 effort to revive the institution are worth noting. First, there was a crucial shift in policy rationale between the midwar and the postwar proceedings in Congress. As Roy Douglas Womack has noted, during the war, "Secretary Dallas and the administration had wanted a bank primarily to provide financial assistance to the government." After the war, by contrast, it was sought for monetary purposes—to "restore order to the currency and banking system."[102] Second, this latter fact also rendered the postwar effort meaningfully different from the initial 1791 push to charter a national bank. In the midst of floor debate in late February 1816, Representative Sergeant admitted that "[h]e saw a wide distinction between the bank now proposed to be established, and the old Bank of the United States; the object of the latter was to increase the active capital of the country, and to facilitate the operations of the Government in the collection of the taxes, whilst the motive of this bank was directly the *reverse*; it was not to increase, but to diminish the paper medium of the country."[103] Finally—and as a means of broadening out Sergeant's point—the eventual passage and signing of a national bank bill aimed at solving monetary problems reinforces a more general claim about institutional development: The "processes responsible for the genesis of an institution" are sometimes "different from the processes responsible for the reproduction"—even, as here, the *belated* reproduction—of that institution.[104]

THE COINAGE CLAUSE: ONE OF THE "HIGHEST POWERS OF THE GOVERNMENT"

In early April 1816, just over four months after Secretary Dallas formally proposed a peacetime national bank (and just over five years after the dissolution of the Bank of the United States), President Madison signed legislation that reestablished that institution.[105] As with the failed effort between October 1814 and February 1815 to charter a national bank, political and economic historians—not to mention political scientists[106]—have offered detailed accounts of the politics between December 1815 and April 1816 that ultimately produced the Bank's revival.

Questions of institutional ownership and management loomed just as large in the postwar setting as they had during the wartime proceedings. The administration's preferred scheme, outlined in a memorandum from Secretary Dallas to the House of Representatives, called for a $35 million national bank.[107] It also included provisions designed to appease some— but clearly not all—Federalist lawmakers: (1) stock purchase rules that did not discriminate in favor of the investors (mainly Republicans) who had funded the War of 1812[108] and (2) a managerial plan that included government-controlled seats on the board of directors but diluted their influence relative to the wartime bank proposal.[109] The bill reported by the House Select Committee on a Uniform National Currency was "substantially what Dallas had recommended[,]"[110] and that bill—despite significant Federalist opposition on account of the management provision[111]— was substantially what the Fourteenth Congress passed (and President Madison signed) that spring.

These distributive aspects of the Bank's revival notwithstanding, the constitutional dimension of the postwar proceedings warrants special attention. As noted earlier, it appears that a number of moderate Republicans with genuine anxiety about the scope of federal power agreed to support the wartime bank bill on the premise that fiscal pressures on the Treasury rendered it "necessary." That constitutional argument became a veritable nonstarter, however, once the Treaty of Ghent was signed; going forward, only bona fide nationalists in the Republican coalition could be expected to support a peacetime national bank anchored to the Sweeping Clause. Accordingly, when Secretary Dallas brought his proposal forward in December 1815, he did so with a novel constitutional argument attached. Functionally, the argument was rooted in knowledge of the national bank's past performance as a monetary authority and expectations of its future return to that same role. Politically, it was rooted in the desire of Dallas and other nationalist Republicans to win crucial support for their proposal *without* forcing party members with lingering anxieties over federal power to implicitly sanction a host of future lawmaking. With nary a mention of Congress's powers to lay and collect taxes, borrow money, or make laws "which shall be necessary and proper for carrying [those powers] into Execution[,]" the Treasury secretary's report instead presented a national bank as an exercise of the branch's Article I, Section 8 authority to "coin Money, regulate the Value thereof."

The Coinage Clause, to be clear, had *never* been proposed as an anchor for the national bank. It had been mentioned in both the 1791 and the 1811 Bank debates, but not as a potential source of congressional authority on the subject.[112] How, then, could its employment possibly be justified in late 1815?

The Treasury secretary began his subsection on a "national circulating medium" with a simple observation: Under Section 10 of Article I, the states were prohibited from "emit[ting] Bills of Credit[,]" or fiat currency.[113] The states had chartered many banks since the adoption of this provision, and those institutions had circulated notes and checks that were convertible upon demand into specie. Dallas did not consider paper of this sort to violate the prohibition in question. However, he noted, "[d]uring the last year the principal banks, established south and west of New England, resolved that they would no longer issue coin in payment of their notes, or of the drafts of their customers[.]" For Secretary Dallas, this behavior had constitutional consequences. "By this act," he wrote, "corporations, erected by the several States, have been enabled to circulate a paper medium, subject to many of the [same] practical inconveniences [as] the prohibited bills of credit."[114] In essence, state banks that had suspended the payment of specie but were continuing to circulate their paper were *now* violating the Constitution.

Correcting this violation, Dallas stressed, was within the Article I, Section 8 powers of Congress. That body had previously exercised its Coinage Clause authority in making metallic coins the "money of the United States." However, the suspension of payments by numerous state banks meant that specie—or paper redeemable on demand in specie—had effectively "ceased to be the circulating medium of exchange[.]" In essence, the inconvertible paper of state banks had "supersede[d] the only legal currency of the nation." As such, if Congress believed—on the basis of past experience with the institution—that a new Bank of the United States would produce both the "restoration of [that] national currency" and its protection going forward, then a charter for the same could be granted pursuant to the Coinage Clause.[115] As the Treasury secretary would privately communicate to Representative Calhoun a few weeks later, a national bank would now be directly implicated in the "exercise of some of the highest powers of the Government."[116]

The constitutional argument offered by Dallas was not explicitly originalist; it included no claim about the intent of those who framed and ratified the Coinage Clause. At least three Republicans in Congress, however, both anchored a national bank to this provision *and* did so on originalist grounds.

John C. Calhoun, whose past differences with Dallas over the proper form of a national bank had been "wiped out" by the arrival of peace,[117] both chaired the House Select Committee that reported a bill in line with Dallas's recommendations and opened floor debate on that bill in late February 1816. During his first years in Congress, Calhoun was an "eager nationalist intent on strengthening the powers of the federal government[.]"[118] As such, there was every reason to expect a claim from him that the Bank was "necessary" for exercising the federal government's fiscal powers. Calhoun eschewed this approach, however, opting instead for a claim that would appeal to Republicans with greater anxiety about federal power.

He began by suggesting that "the state of things at the time of the adoption of the constitution" furnished an argument on behalf of anchoring the national bank bill to the Coinage Clause. The framers, Calhoun noted, labored in a monetary environment marked by a "depreciated paper currency[.]" The textual provision in question, in short, was their collective response; through it, "the money of the United States was intended to be placed entirely under the control of Congress." Federal lawmakers had subsequently chosen the precious metals as the country's money, and state "bank notes represent[ing] gold and silver" were not inconsistent with that choice. However, Calhoun continued, of late there had "been an extraordinary revolution in the currency of the country . . . [this] turns you back to the condition of the Revolutionary war, in which every State issued bills of credit[.]" A national bank that worked to restore and maintain the circulation of gold and silver, it followed, would redeem the "object the framers of the constitution" had in view—congressional control over money—when writing the Coinage Clause.[119]

William Bibb, a Republican representing Georgia in the Senate, similarly explained the Bank's constitutionality. He argued that "the leading objects which produced the adoption of the constitution" in the 1780s included restoring "confidence among the citizens of the country in regard to pecuniary transactions" and preventing "any thing but gold and silver from being a legal tender[.]" Empowering the federal government to regulate the "general currency of the country" was crucial for the achievement of these ends; without that authority, the "attainment of these great objects [would have been] impracticable." Congress had used its power to secure these monetary objects for a time, but a "combination of circumstances" had resulted in their being "at this moment lost to the nation." Otherwise put, the banks outside New England—by virtue of their conduct since late August 1814, but especially since the war's conclusion—had effectively "taken from the [federal] Government" its power to regulate the "currrency [sic] of the country[.]"[120] Just as importantly, Bibb made it clear that he agreed with "a large majority of the Senate": A national bank offered the "best possible means of restoring the country to the old state of things."[121] That is to say, a revived Bank would help to reestablish congressional control over the currency (and thereby secure anew the framers' monetary objects).

The most famous originalist claim on behalf of Congress's authority to charter a national bank under the Coinage Clause came from Henry Clay, Speaker of the House. Five years earlier, as a United States senator from Kentucky, he had both assaulted claims that the Bank could be anchored to the Necessary and Proper Clause and criticized its evolution into a regulatory power as constitutionally suspect.[122] This time around, Clay did more than simply reverse his basic position on the constitutional question; he also made the institution's regulation of state banks the very *foundation* of its constitutionality. In a March 9 floor speech[123] that would dog Clay for the rest of his political career—it was the first great flip-flop in American politics, and none of his opponents ever let the public forget it[124]—the Speaker openly eschewed what he called the "pride of consistency" and announced his belief in the constitutionality of a national bank (not to mention his support for its revival).

The Speaker, nationalist Republican that he was, could have simply recanted his former position on the meaning of the Sweeping Clause.[125] That would have reflected his understanding of the Constitution in 1816, but it would have done little to win support for the Bank bill among more conservative Republicans. As such, Clay—like his fellow nationalist Calhoun—took an altogether different (and constitutionally narrower) approach. The Speaker suggested that he and other members of the Eleventh Congress had failed to examine the Constitution closely enough to appreciate the full scope of congressional power; "provisions of the [text], but little noticed, if noticed at all, on the discussions in Congress in 1811" spoke to the national bank question. His constitutional myopia, however, had been corrected by "events of the utmost magnitude." Once state banks had suspended specie payments, it became clear to Clay that these institutions were effectively exercising "one of the highest attributes of sovereignty—the regulation of the current medium of the country."[126] More importantly, he could now infer from the Coinage Clause (coupled with the ban on state bills of credit) that "the subject of the general currency was intended to be submitted exclusively to the General Government." As such, chartering a national bank for the purpose of restoring and maintaining specie payments was little more than Congress seeking to "recover the control which it had lost, over the general currency[.]"[127]

At least one Federalist in the Fourteenth Congress, Senator William Wells of Delaware, took issue with Republican efforts to anchor a national bank to the Coinage Clause. Wells argued that while the provision invested Congress with the power to "make a metallic money[,]" it did not authorize the regulation of institutions whose behavior was impairing the circulation of that money. "So far . . . as honorable gentlemen say this measure is intended . . . to operate upon what is called the national currency," he remarked, "it is warranted by no part of the constitution."[128]

The character of Wells's constitutional critique invites a number of observations. First, the disagreement between Wells and congressional Republicans who defended the Compromise of 1816 highlights the distinction (for students of constitutional interpretation) between "original principles originalism" and "original expected applications originalism."[129] Senator Wells was suggesting, in short, that the Coinage Clause had a "specific intended application[]": the minting of gold and silver coins and their valuation in dollars. As a result, when Republicans spoke as if the provision offered a "statement[] of broad principle" from the founding generation—complete congressional control over monetary affairs—they committed an error of abstraction.[130]

Second, his criticism of the Coinage Clause argument should not be construed as a claim that the national bank bill was unconstitutional. Federalists like Wells had never objected to the Bank on constitutional grounds, viewing it as "necessary" for the execution of Congress's fiscal powers. What he objected to, in essence, were Republican efforts to have their constitutional cake (secure a national bank's services) and eat it too (avoid a broad interpretation of the Necessary and Proper Clause). If the regime wanted the institution, its members should have simply admitted that a national bank represented "nothing more than the employment of a 'necessary and proper' mean 'for carrying into execution'" the power to lay and collect taxes.[131]

Finally, the fundamental lack of interparty disagreement in 1816 on the national bank's constitutional status—Republicans and Federalists simply differed with respect to explaining that status—underscores the fact that opposition among the latter to the postwar bill was principally *political*. As already noted, Federalists hardly relished the prospect of a Bank board that included Republican appointees.[132]

JAMES MADISON AND THE COMPROMISE OF 1816

President Madison signed the bill reviving the Bank of the United States on April 10 but said nary a word in doing so about the constitutional question. Though he was certainly under no obligation to do so, the president subsequently broke his silence. In early December 1816, with his time in office running short (James Monroe would take the oath three months later), Madison delivered his eighth and final annual message to Congress. Before concluding that message by reflecting on his pending exit "from the public theater[,]" the president took a moment to praise the work of the Fourteenth Congress with respect to a national bank. In doing so, Madison invoked the Compromise of 1816: "[I]t is essential that the nation should possess a currency of equal value, credit, and use wherever it may circulate. The Constitution has intrusted Congress exclusively with the power of creating and regulating a currency of that description, and the measures which were taken during the last session *in execution of the power* give every promise of success."[133] The resulting question, simply put, is whether the president's commentary represents a personal embrace of the Coinage Clause argument or little more than recognition that fellow Republicans (in both his cabinet and Congress) had adopted it. The answer is less obvious than one might think.

If the president's message communicated personal support for the Compromise of 1816—and that seems to be the natural import of his words—then he, like Secretary Dallas, offered one view of the Bank's constitutionality during the War of 1812 (it was "settled") but a very different one following the end of hostilities (it was sanctioned by the Coinage Clause). That finding would break significant new ground with respect to our understanding of his decision to sign the national bank bill. If, by contrast, the president was doing little more than acknowledging the constitutional work of a coordinate branch, then our traditional understanding of his decision—that it followed from his January 1815 waiver—survives.

And there is a case to be made that it should. It is a backward-looking case built on three statements made by Madison—one in 1817 and two in 1831. Because the 1831 statements directly address his decision to sign the Bank bill, I begin with them. In February 1831, the ex-president explained in a letter to C. E. Haynes that his assent to the work of the Fourteenth Congress "was given in pursuance of my early and unchanged opinion that, in the case of a Constitution as of a law, a course of authoritative expositions sufficiently deliberate, uniform, and settled, was an evidence of the public will necessarily overruling individual opinions."[134] Toward the end of that year, he offered the same explanation for his April 1816 behavior in a letter to N. P. Trist.[135] Madison's words in retirement, of course, do a better job of tracking his January 1815 veto message than his December 1816 annual message.

If two letters penned by a man in his late seventies, both recalling the basis for behavior that took place fifteen years earlier, were the only evidence in support of the idea that Madison signed the Bank bill due to cross-branch practice and public opinion, we might be tempted to dismiss it as flowing from an imperfect memory. That evidence is supplemented, however, by a statement made much closer to the events of April 1816. In March 1817, on the final day of both his presidency and the Fourteenth Congress, Madison vetoed legislation that would have offered federal support for internal improvements.[136] More importantly, he attached a message explaining that decision on constitutional grounds.[137]

The president wrote that "a power [to support internal improvements] is not expressly given by the Constitution, and . . . cannot be deduced from any part of it without an inadmissible latitude of construction and a reliance on insufficient precedents[.]"[138] Madison thus appears to suggest that his personal conviction respecting Congress's authority to pass the Bonus Bill—namely, that it possessed none—could have been overcome by a long history of cross-branch support for internal improvements. However, no such history existed. The president's ultimate decision to veto the bill is less important (at least for my purposes here) than his reasoning. If Madison had waived the question of the Bank's constitutionality in January 1815 partially on the basis of institutional practice, and rejected the Bonus Bill in March 1817 due to the absence of such practice, then there is reason to believe that his behavior *between* those dates—which would include April 1816—reflected the same constitutional thinking.

What we have, then, is a conflict between the natural import of Madison's December 1816 commentary on the Bank's revival and both (1) his general mode of thinking about questionable exercises of federal power in the 1810s and (2) his specific memory of signing the recharter bill. Otherwise put, insofar as Madison's peers observed[139] (and generations of scholars have discussed[140]) an apparent inconsistency between his 1791 opposition to a national bank and his 1816 willingness to sign legislation creating one, we now have two competing explanations for it. All told, the question of *why* Madison signed the 1816 Bank bill is now an open one.[141]

CONCLUSION

Congress's decision to revive the Bank of the United States following the War of 1812, far from being (as scholarly tradition would have it) a constitutional nonevent, actually yielded a novel textual anchor for the institution: the power to "coin Money, regulate the Value thereof." This chapter has documented the role played by the Coinage Clause in the national bank's revival and explained how a confluence of institutional, ideological, and economic factors led federal lawmakers to assign it that role. After state-chartered banks outside New England proved reluctant to voluntarily resume specie payments in the postwar period (and thus curb the menace of price inflation), members of Congress sought means for compelling resumption. This led them back to the idea of a national bank, as the institution that existed between 1791 and 1811 had evolved into a regulator of state banks. While Republicans dominated the Fourteenth Congress, many in their coalition were unwilling to concede that a peacetime national bank was "necessary" for managing the federal government's fiscal affairs; doing so would all but openly encourage future lawmakers to exercise federal power aggressively. Leading regime figures responded by suggesting that Congress, in reviving the Bank of the United States for the purpose of restoring gold and silver coin to circulation, would be exercising its power to coin money. Either because Congress's power would be directly exercised or because a national bank was manifestly "necessary" for achieving the resumption of specie payments, the Sweeping Clause formed *no part* of their discussion—and thus generated no coalition-dividing debate.

Because Republicans developed a line of constitutional thought that secured a national bank's services *without* embracing either a broad or a strict understanding of federal power under the Necessary and Proper Clause, I have characterized their work as the Compromise of 1816. Drawing belated attention to it is about more, however, than reinforcing the idea—first advanced in the previous chapter—that the period between Alexander Hamilton's February 1791 memorandum to President Washington and John Marshall's March 1819 decision in *McCulloch v. Maryland* included constitutional drama worthy of our attention. To recognize that Republican lawmakers crafted a novel understanding of the Bank's constitutionality in the mid-1810s is also to invite a fundamental reconsideration of the Supreme Court's work in *McCulloch*. If, for example, both Republicans and Federalists agreed that the Bank was constitutional, then why was the question of congressional power even on the Court's agenda? And in answering that question, why did the justices eschew the Compromise of 1816 in favor of general reasoning about federal power and a lengthy discussion of the Sweeping Clause? Rereading *McCulloch* in the shadow of postwar Republican constitutionalism is the subject of the next chapter.

CHAPTER SIX

McCulloch (1819) in the Shadow of the Compromise

The Conventional Wisdom

Not long after the rebirth of the national bank, the American economy experienced a severe downturn. Some observers considered the Bank directly responsible for the turmoil because it had recently contracted its lending. Others located the source of the strife elsewhere—the institution's contraction was merely an effect of that cause—but considered the Bank of the United States guilty of unnecessarily exacerbating the economic pain. Eager to hold someone *accountable, Americans (and their elected representatives) targeted the national bank. Many states proceeded to levy heavy taxes on the institution. Maryland's lawmakers, for example, voted to institute a $15,000 yearly tax on the Bank's Baltimore branch.*

After the cashier of that branch—James M'Culloh[1]—issued Bank notes without paying the tax, Maryland imposed the statutory fine for behavior of that sort: $100. The state's courts upheld the tax (and M'Culloh's fine for failing to pay it), but the US Supreme Court quickly agreed to hear the case on appeal. Just three days after oral arguments in McCulloch v. Maryland *concluded, the Court unanimously ruled— through an opinion authored by Chief Justice John Marshall—that (1) Congress had acted constitutionally in chartering the Bank of the United States, and (2) Maryland had acted unconstitutionally in taxing it. The first part of Marshall's opinion—by "almost any reckoning the greatest . . . [he] ever handed down"[2]—offered general reasoning in support of a capacious understanding of federal power* and *embraced a broad interpretation of the Necessary and Proper Clause. In the eyes of the Court, the final provision in Article I, Section 8 authorized Congress to pass laws that were "convenient, or useful[,] or essential" for*

exercising the powers enumerated in that section's foregoing clauses.[3]
Many Republicans, incensed at the Court's understanding of fed-
eral power, applauded pseudonymous assaults on Marshall's opinion
in print—assaults that led the chief justice to respond in the same
fashion.[4]

The first part of this chapter-opening vignette offers a fairly standard
account of the economic and political action that led to *McCulloch
v. Maryland* (1819). It posits, in essence, a cause-and-effect relationship between the national bank's lending behavior and the imposition of Maryland's tax (not to mention many others).[5] In recent years, however, new
scholarship on the origins of *McCulloch* has revealed the fundamental in-
accuracy of this account. The taxes of several states, Maryland included,
were enacted months *before* the Bank of the United States contracted its
lending and public opinion began to turn against the institution.[6] The
Supreme Court heard arguments in *McCulloch* at a time (February 1819)
when hostility toward the Bank was cresting, but that hostility can no
longer be taken as an explanation for Maryland's tax.

If the first part of the vignette is flawed on the basis of what it contains, then the second part—which focuses on the constitutional action in
early 1819—is flawed on the basis of what it omits. The standard account
of *McCulloch*, in short, fails to recognize that postwar Republicans eschewed discussion of a national bank's necessity for exercising Congress's
fiscal powers in favor of an argument that the institution enabled federal
lawmakers to redeem their constitutional prerogative to "coin Money,
regulate the Value thereof."[7] This chapter corrects that omission and assesses *McCulloch* anew in light of the Compromise of 1816. Acknowledging the constitutional shadow cast by the Republican regime has the effect
of both raising new questions about the case (only some of which can be
answered) and explaining the fallout from it.

The questions raised about *McCulloch* by the constitutional drama
of 1816 form the focus of my discussion here. Republicans' resort to the
Coinage Clause in reviving the national bank forces us, for example, to
ask why the institution's lawyers avoided that provision in defending their
client's constitutionality before the Court. It also demands that we appreciate (and interrogate) the pronounced gap between political and judicial
understandings of the Bank's constitutionality in the 1810s. What made
it possible for the Marshall Court to substitute its own answer to the congressional power question for that of elected officials? Why did the justices
do so? And how is that portion of *McCulloch* to be characterized relative

to the preferences of the Republican regime? That is to say, did the Court act in a majoritarian, a countermajoritarian, or a nonmajoritarian fashion? The available evidence cannot furnish answers to all these questions, but each warrants attention in the ongoing study of this landmark in American constitutional law.

With respect to explaining the fallout from *McCulloch*, the Coinage Clause argument helps us to make sense of the fact that many Republicans accepted the Bank's constitutionality in 1819 but nonetheless greeted the Court's reasoning on that subject with great hostility. Former president James Madison arguably represents the poster boy for this crowd; he had no objection to the Marshall Court's conclusion about the Bank of the United States but nonetheless protested that "the occasion did not call for [a] general & abstract doctrine" respecting federal power to be announced.[8] The whole point of postwar Republicans employing the power to coin money, to borrow language from one of John Marshall's pseudonymous post-*McCulloch* essays, had been to "furnish an argument which shall . . . prove the Bank to be constitutional" *without* resort to controversial claims about the meaning of the Necessary and Proper Clause.[9] The Court, by sharp contrast, had resolved this part of the case in a manner that jettisoned the Republican regime's carefully wrought constitutional compromise and thereby reaggravated intracoalition tensions over federal power.

THE ORIGINS OF *MCCULLOCH* (AND ITS AGENDA)

In late 1817, members of Maryland's General Assembly began consideration of a bill to tax any bank (or branch of a bank) operating within the state that it had not chartered. "The only bank that fit this description," as scholars have long noted, was the Baltimore branch of the Bank of the United States.[10] Several months later, in February 1818—or four months *before* the July reduction in lending[11] that would (rightly or wrongly) turn the public against the national bank—the bill was passed by the state legislature and signed by Federalist governor Charles Ridgely.[12]

The legislature's rationale here, according to historian Richard E. Ellis, was purely fiscal; the state had incurred debts in fielding its militia during the War of 1812—debts that it hoped the federal government would eventually pay—and taxed a variety of institutions after the war to help service them in the short term.[13] More importantly, at least with respect to the Supreme Court's treatment of *McCulloch*, Ellis has noted that no advocate of the tax in the Maryland Senate or House of Delegates openly challenged the underlying constitutionality of the Bank.[14]

Maryland's statute went into effect in May 1818, and soon thereafter, James M'Culloh—cashier of the Baltimore branch—issued notes without having paid the tax. As a result, the state quickly initiated legal proceedings against the Bank (in M'Culloh's name) in Baltimore County Court. That tribunal's judgment in favor of the state was upheld by the Maryland Court of Appeals (the state's supreme court) in June.[15] Governor Ridgely later noted that Maryland's supreme court had considered the statute's consistency with the US Constitution and had concluded that it was not in violation of the same.[16] Following that decision, M'Culloh asked the US Supreme Court to review the case under Section 25 of the 1789 Judiciary Act. Section 25, whose own constitutionality had been defended by the Court barely two years earlier in *Martin v. Hunter's Lessee* (1816), authorized the institution to hear appeals from state supreme courts when the meaning of the Constitution, a treaty, or a federal law was at issue.[17] In September 1818, the Court agreed to hear *McCulloch* on appeal and set oral argument for February 1819.[18]

What happened over the ensuing five months has never been established with any degree of precision. We know that "[t]he central issue in the dispute between Maryland" and the Bank of the United States— indeed, the reason the US Supreme Court was able to hear *McCulloch* at all—was "the constitutionality of the state's tax on the bank" (or, technically speaking, the fact that the state's supreme court had made a claim respecting its constitutionality).[19] We also know that when oral arguments in *McCulloch* commenced in February 1819, the very first lawyer to speak—former New Hampshire congressman Daniel Webster, representing the Bank—immediately began to address a very different (and logically prior) constitutional question: Did Congress have the power to charter a national bank? Simply put, how is the seemingly sudden appearance of this question to be explained?

It is possible, of course, that one or more of Maryland's attorneys— Joseph Hopkinson, Walter Jones, and state attorney general Luther Martin—informed both the Court and opposing counsel in advance that they would question the constitutionality of Congress's behavior in 1816. This would represent odd behavior coming from three Federalists; their party had long defended congressional authority in this area.[20] The bigger problem with this account, however, would be its inconsistency with Maryland's established fiscal interests. As already noted, the legislature had imposed the tax to pay the interest on debts incurred during the War of 1812. Were the Court to hold that the Bank of the United States was unconstitutional, Maryland would *lose* this source of revenue. Working to undermine the institution, in other words, would be a patently irrational strategy for servicing the state's wartime debt.

By the same token, it is also possible that one or more of the Bank's attorneys—Daniel Webster, William Pinkney, and William Wirt—were responsible for raising the congressional power question. On the one hand, *McCulloch*'s written record does not absolutely foreclose this possibility. Oral arguments began on February 22, and Webster opened these proceedings by claiming that "the question whether congress constitutionally possesses the power to incorporate [the institution], might be raised upon this record[.]"[21] On the other hand, there are good reasons to conclude that the Bank's legal team was merely responding to someone else's initiative. First and foremost, it is not clear how the institution's interest in operating without state interference could be advanced by having its lawyers instigate debate over the legitimacy of its existence. Second, correspondence between two of those lawyers in late December 1818 implies an external source for the question. After learning that he and Webster were to be "on the same Side" in *McCulloch*, Pinkney intended to ask his co-counsel for "an interchange of Ideas" on Maryland's power to tax the institution. However, he now supposed that exchange unnecessary, "since *it is said* that little else than the threadbare topics connected with the constitutionality of the establishment of the Bank will be introduced into the argument[.]"[22] Pinkney's language here suggests that *McCulloch*'s agenda had been set (and was being discussed out of doors) before the Bank's team had even been assembled.

This leaves us with the veritable third party in the dispute between the Bank of the United States and Maryland: the Supreme Court itself. It is possible that the institution's leader, Chief Justice John Marshall—acting on his own or on behalf of his colleagues—instructed both sides to address the congressional power question. To be clear, there is no documentary evidence (e.g., a pre-February 1819 memorandum to the parties from the Court) available to substantiate this account. Ellis has expressed real doubt, however, that "anyone else but Chief Justice John Marshall had the stature, the influence, or the power to operate behind the scenes" and adjust the case agenda.[23] This claim, of course, does not resolve the question of *why* the Supreme Court requested argument on the Bank's constitutionality.

ARGUMENTATIVE ODDITIES

Counsel on both sides took the Court's instruction seriously. Much of the oral argument, which lasted for a total of nine days between February 22 and March 3, addressed the Bank's constitutionality. However, given my account of both pre-*McCulloch* constitutional politics and Maryland's rationale for taxing the institution, at least two aspects of that discussion now seem odd: (1) the decision by national bank counsel to rely exclusively on an argument rooted in the institution's necessity for exercising the federal government's fiscal powers and (2) the decision by state counsel to contest the congressional power question at all.

The first oddity flows from constitutional positions already outlined. By 1816, Federalists and a majority of Republicans agreed that Congress was authorized to charter a national bank and disagreed only on *why* that was the case. Federalists saw the institution as "necessary" for laying taxes and/or borrowing money, while Republicans spoke of the same as an exercise of Congress's power to coin money. Conversely, Federalists in the Fourteenth Congress had openly criticized the Coinage Clause argument, and Republicans eager to avoid internecine strife had eschewed any reference to the Sweeping Clause (out of a sense either that the power to coin money could be directly exercised or that a national bank was so manifestly "necessary" for exercising the power as to obviate the need for discussion).

Given these dueling perspectives on the source of the Bank's constitutionality, we might have expected the institution's lawyers to advance both a primary and a secondary argument to the Supreme Court. The primary claim, and the one with a lineage dating to 1791, would involve fiscal powers and the Necessary and Proper Clause. The secondary claim, of far more recent vintage, would posit that the Court could (and should) uphold the Bank of the United States under the Coinage Clause in the event that it declined to offer the Sweeping Clause a broad interpretation. This argumentative approach would simultaneously recognize the historical reality of competing justifications for the Bank and serve the institution's interests by offering the Court *multiple* options for validating its existence.

This was not, however, the approach adopted by the institution's attorneys; their defense of the Bank only addressed the more traditional constitutional argument on its behalf. Daniel Webster, for example, claimed that the final provision in Article I, Section 8 authorized Congress to choose means "suitable and fitted" for achieving enumerated ends. Just as importantly, a national bank was a "proper and suitable instrument" for exercising a number of congressional powers.[24] For his part, Attorney General William Wirt volunteered that Congress was permitted to adopt means that were "needful [for] and adapted" to the exercise of enumerated powers. This understanding of constitutional necessity was confirmed,

he added, "by the best authorities among lexicographers[.]"[25] And William
Pinkney, himself a former attorney general, openly admonished the Court
to "construe the constitutional powers of the national government liber-
ally[.]" He would, in effect, have left it to Congress to determine the "degree of political necessity which will justify a resort to a particular means,
to carry into execution the [various] powers of the government."[26]

The second oddity flows from historical context already reviewed.
Maryland's rationale for taxing the Bank of the United States was not to
destroy the institution; it was to raise revenue. That revenue, of course,
would *disappear* if the Bank were held to be unconstitutional. As such, if
the first obligation of Maryland's lawyers was to defend their client's interests (including its fiscal interests), then we might have expected them to
concede the Bank's constitutionality and make the state's power to tax the
whole of their argument.

Far from conceding the constitutional question, Maryland's lawyers
argued that Congress was *not* empowered to charter a national bank. Joseph Hopkinson, for example, rejected the Bank's constitutional necessity
for exercising fiscal powers on the strength of the two-prong test applied
by many Republicans during the 1811 recharter debate: Means selected
by Congress had to satisfy both the functional and the federal standards.
Moreover, he argued (as Representative William Burwell had eight years
earlier) that while the Bank might have passed this test at a previous point
in time, it no longer could: "The argument might have been perfectly
good, to show the necessity of a bank . . . in 1791, and entirely fail now [in
1819], when so many facilities for money transactions abound, which were
wanting then."[27]

Hopkinson's co-counsel agreed that a national bank was not "necessary" for conducting the federal government's fiscal affairs, but arrived at
this shared end point via different routes. Walter Jones thought of constitutional necessity in terms of the functional standard alone, albeit a demanding version of that standard. He told the Court that the Bank required
a "natural connection" to one or more of Congress's enumerated powers.
Jones argued, however, that, at best, the institution was something less:
"convenient" for exercising those powers.[28] Luther Martin's understanding of the Bank vis-à-vis the Necessary and Proper Clause, by contrast,
was decidedly novel; it flowed from a self-made and seemingly binary distinction between less and more important powers. He argued that many
provisions in Article I, Section 8 (e.g., the power to borrow money) were
actually means for Congress to exercise more important powers (e.g., the
power to declare war). In addition, Martin contended that Congress was

categorically precluded from exercising any of these more important powers—he called them "more sovereign" powers—unless they had been specifically enumerated. Otherwise put, a more sovereign power could never
be treated as incident to (or "necessary" for) the exercise of a less sovereign
power. Martin believed that "the authority of establishing corporations"
was clearly "one of [those] great sovereign powers of government[.]" Since
all agreed that such authority was *not* specifically enumerated, Congress
was simply not at liberty to charter a national bank.[29]

While there is certainly room to speculate on (1) the reasons for the
Bank's failure to offer a fallback justification for its existence and (2) Maryland's decision to challenge the legitimacy of an institution that it was
seeking to extract tax revenue from, there is little hard evidence with
which to resolve these questions. For example, although it might have
been the case that Daniel Webster eschewed a Coinage Clause claim because he considered the provision utterly unrelated to the congressional
power question, there is simply nothing in his published correspondence
that speaks to his strategy for arguing *McCulloch*.[30] Similarly, while
Maryland's attorneys may have contested the national bank's status for
the benefit of sister states that *were* taxing with the intent to destroy,[31]
here, too, we lack empirical insight into their thinking. Absent evidence
on these scores, we can only consider the Court's response to the proffered
arguments.

MCCULLOCH IN THE SHADOW OF THE BANK'S REBIRTH

On March 6, or just three days after the conclusion of oral arguments, the
Supreme Court rendered its decision in *McCulloch*. It famously held—in
a unanimous opinion authored by Chief Justice John Marshall—that Congress was empowered to charter the Bank, but neither Maryland nor any
other state was empowered to tax it. While the circumstances surrounding the national bank's rebirth in April 1816 fail to shed greater light on
the basis for Marshall's conclusion that it was constitutional, they do
work to (1) highlight the role of legal factors in the development of the
Bank controversy, (2) identify *McCulloch* as an unappreciated instance of
departmentalism in constitutional interpretation, (3) problematize a traditional mode of classifying Supreme Court decisions, and (4) invite fresh
thinking about the Court's motive for resolving the congressional power
question as it did.

John Marshall's answer to the question of where, precisely, the Constitution empowers Congress to charter a national bank has been in dispute

for close to half a century. This part of his opinion for the Court tends to be treated, even today, "as if it rested on certain explicit constitutional clauses."[32] More to the point, observes Akhil Reed Amar, if you ask "a lawyer or a knowledgeable layperson to name the basis for Marshall's decision . . . he will probably point you unhesitatingly to the necessary-and-proper clause."[33] The tendency here no doubt arises from both the chief justice's extended discussion of the clause's meaning—it is no fewer than nine pages in length[34]—and his Hamiltonian contention that "if reference be had to [the meaning of "necessary"] in the common affairs of the world or in approved authors, we find that it frequently imports no more than that one thing is convenient, or useful, or essential to another."[35] Marshall did not go on to specify which of the foregoing seventeen powers the Bank was "necessary" for exercising, but an earlier passage in his opinion had alluded to the federal government's "great powers," including those "to lay and collect taxes; to borrow money; to regulate commerce; to declare and conduct a war; and to raise and support armies and navies."[36]

The tendency to read the first part of Marshall's opinion as resting on a claim about the meaning of the Sweeping Clause was challenged by Charles L. Black Jr. in *Structure and Relationship in Constitutional Law* (1969). He argued that the chief justice all but resolved the congressional power question *"before* he reache[d]"* that specific provision.[37] Black pointed to Marshall's "general reasoning" about federal power earlier in *McCulloch*, and more specifically the claim that a government "intrusted with such ample powers" as those listed in Article I, Section 8 "must also be intrusted with ample means for their execution."[38] Amar, a student of Black's and an open partisan of his teacher's understanding of the case, has written that while the chief justice has traditionally been "depicted as a narrow textualist" in *McCulloch*, "building his constitutional church on the solid rock of an explicit clause[,]" his textual analysis was actually preceded by an effort to construe the document as a "whole rather than as a jumble of discrete clauses." Otherwise put, before Marshall offered one word about the meaning of the Necessary and Proper Clause, he issued a preemptive declaration that the "Constitution *as a whole* seemed to empower Congress to create a national bank[.]"[39]

Nothing about the fact that the Fourteenth Congress chartered the Bank pursuant to its power to coin money helps us to adjudicate this dispute over what Marshall said. It does, however, help us to understand something just as important: what he *failed* to say. Just as counsel on both sides ignored the Compromise of 1816 in arguing *McCulloch*, the Court resolved the national bank's constitutional status without mentioning the Coinage Clause. As Bray Hammond noted in his *Banks and Politics in America* (1957), far from "establish[ing] the Bank's constitutionality on [this] narrow, specific ground[,]" John Marshall and his colleagues "took no account [whatsoever] of the Bank as a monetary agency[.]"[40] In fact, their only reference to the circumstances surrounding the institution's revival was at best silent on, and at worst distorted, Congress's understanding of the textual basis for its work: "The original [charter] was permitted to expire, but a short experience of the embarrassments to which the refusal to revive it exposed the Government convinced those who were most prejudiced against the measure of its necessity, and induced the passage of the present law."[41] This statement offers either no claim respecting the textual foundation for the 1816 law *or* falsely implies that the law was considered "necessary" for executing Congress's fiscal powers.

To recognize that the Marshall Court embraced an understanding of the national bank's constitutionality that departed from that of the Fourteenth Congress is to invite, in the first instance, an inquiry into why it was able to do so. Given that the Coinage Clause had been recognized as the basis for the Bank bill by a wide range of legislative and executive actors—the secretary of the Treasury, the chairman of the House Select Committee on a Uniform National Currency, the Speaker of the House, sundry members of the House and Senate, and even the president of the United States—why was the Court in a position to decide the first part of *McCulloch* with at least partial reference to controversial claims about the meaning of the Sweeping Clause? The answer to this question flows less from ordinary politics than from law—namely, two features of the Constitution. First, Article VI states that all members of Congress, "and all executive and judicial officers, both of the United States and of the several states, shall be bound by Oath or Affirmation, to support this Constitution." Second, that same Constitution famously fails to .explicitly identify a supreme interpreter. As such, not only is a member of the Supreme Court committed to supporting the Constitution, but the justice is ostensibly committed to supporting it *according to his or her best understanding of it*. If the justices in *McCulloch* were, for example, convinced that the political branches had misidentified the textual basis for the 1816 national bank bill, then the Constitution certainly permitted (and perhaps even compelled) them to correct that error.

By presenting its own understanding of the Bank's constitutionality, the Court rendered *McCulloch* an example of departmentalism in constitutional interpretation. We tend to think of departmentalism—which limits a particular institution's interpretive supremacy to some parts of the Constitution, and in extreme form, denies it to any institution over any matter[42]—as a theory designed to underwrite legislative and executive conclusions about the Constitution that are at odds with those of the judiciary. Andrew Jackson's 1832 contention, contra *McCulloch*, that a national bank was unconstitutional—a contention that I review in the next chapter—furnishes an especially prominent example of this. The Compromise of 1816 helps us to recognize that the Supreme Court is *equally capable of reaching conclusions at odds with those of Congress or the president*. In essence, we might imagine Chief Justice John Marshall in 1819 penning the very argument that President Jackson would not deploy for another thirteen years: "The Congress, the Executive, *and the Court* must each for itself be guided by its own opinion of the Constitution. Each public officer who takes an oath to support the Constitution swears that he will support it as he understands it, and not as it is understood by others."[43]

The gap between political and judicial understandings of the Bank's constitutionality in the mid- to late 1810s does more than bring a hidden moment of departmentalism to light. It also poses a challenge to scholars who routinely classify Supreme Court decisions as majoritarian, countermajoritarian, or even nonmajoritarian.[44] Decisions have traditionally been classified on the basis of *outcomes*.[45] If Congress passes a bill, the president signs it into law, and the Supreme Court subsequently strikes the act down, then an unelected judiciary is thought to have "thwarted the will" of the elected branches.[46] Conversely, if the Court declares that those same branches have acted constitutionally, then its decision is considered majoritarian. Finally, when members of the judiciary weigh in on an issue that has "internally divide[d] the existing lawmaking majority"—think here of southern Democrats' resistance to federal civil rights legislation in the years following World War II, and the executive branch's resulting call for the Court to take action—we classify its work as nonmajoritarian.[47]

When measured against this outcomes-based standard, *McCulloch* appears to be a majoritarian decision. Republicans in the Fourteenth Congress passed legislation to charter a new Bank of the United States, President Madison signed it into law, and the Court declared their work to be constitutional. Otherwise put, insofar as John Marshall and his colleagues sanctioned the Bank's existence, they did not thwart the will of the "dominant national alliance."[48] While this may strike readers as an obvious conclusion, it is worth noting that *McCulloch* has long been construed as *counter*majoritarian. As Mark Graber notes, the "inherited wisdom" has been that *McCulloch* was a Federalist decision that imposed an expansive conception of federal power on a Republican regime that was committed to a far more limited understanding.[49] The easiest way to account for this divergence is to recognize that the traditional construction of *McCulloch* is rooted not in its outcome (the act chartering the national bank was upheld) but rather in its *reasoning* (the Necessary and Proper Clause gives Congress considerable latitude in exercising its powers under Article I, Section 8).

Graber's reassessment of *McCulloch*, however, did not result in a conclusion that the Marshall Court had acted in a majoritarian manner. Rather, he characterized its work in the case as *non*majoritarian. Graber suggested that the Republican regime of the 1810s, far from being united in its opposition to an active federal government, included a "moderate" wing that was composed of "Jeffersonians who became reconciled to [national] commercial policies by 1815, former Adams Federalists who increasingly saw the Democratic-Republican party as the better vehicle for their nationalistic and political ambitions, and westerners who were eager to gain national support for an extensive program of internal improvements."[50] As such, *McCulloch*'s understanding of federal power under the Sweeping Clause did not so much "run counter to the 'mandate of the supposedly sovereign people'" as attempt to resolve one of "the conflicts that divided members of the dominant [Republican] coalition[.]"[51] This construction of the Court's work, like the "inherited wisdom" that Graber set out to criticize, prioritizes judicial *reasoning* over outcomes. If we draw attention back to the traditional basis for classifying decisions and consider *only* the fact that the justices upheld the national bank legislation recently enacted by the Republican regime, then we must conclude that their decision was majoritarian.

There is something deeply unsatisfying, however, about classifying *McCulloch* on the basis of its outcome and calling it a day. Yes, the Marshall Court concluded (as a majority of Republican lawmakers had three years earlier) that Congress was empowered to charter a new Bank of the United States. However, in doing so, it at best ignored—and at worst silently rejected—the reasoning offered by those legislators. And in this particular case, the reasoning very much mattered. The whole point of anchoring a national bank to the Coinage Clause had been to forestall infighting among Republicans over the question of what Congress could and could not do under the Necessary and Proper Clause. To answer that question would have been, in effect, for the regime to settle some of the issues that most divided it: Congress's ability to support internal improvements and its ability (by way of a future northern majority) to "threaten slavery in the states where it existed or . . . abolish it by statute in the new territories."[52] The Court's decision, far from honoring this textual "avoidance strategy" for the maintenance of intraregime peace, actually shone a bright light on the eschewed and contested provision. *McCulloch*, in short, fanned the very flames that Republicans had sought to douse in 1816.

McCulloch requires us to acknowledge that there will be times when the Court acts in a traditionally majoritarian manner (i.e., by upholding the dominant coalition's work) *but does so for reasons that can only be characterized as countermajoritarian or nonmajoritarian.* Choosing between the two is surprisingly difficult here. On the one hand, members of the Fourteenth Congress clearly viewed the national bank bill as an exercise of their power to "coin Money, regulate the Value thereof." Because the Court upheld the Bank on alternate grounds, we could characterize its reasoning as countermajoritarian. On the other hand, Republicans only sought recourse to the Coinage Clause because they were hopelessly divided on the meaning of the word *necessary*. Insofar as the Marshall Court actually sought to resolve this question, we could characterize its reasoning as nonmajoritarian.

It bears emphasis that *McCulloch* is not the only landmark case in which the Court has upheld the work of federal lawmakers but done so for reasons that failed to match its own. Consider the far more recent example of *NFIB v. Sebelius* (2012). In 2010, the 111th Congress passed—and President Obama promptly signed—the Patient Protection and Affordable Care Act (PPACA). When the constitutionality of the PPACA's "individual mandate" to purchase health insurance was subsequently challenged before the Supreme Court, lawyers for the federal government pointed first and foremost to Congress's power to "regulate Commerce . . . among the several States[.]" Their opponents argued that if the Court interpreted that provision as permitting Congress to regulate an individual's decision not to purchase health insurance, it would "not be able to stop" a future Congress from compelling people to engage in other forms of commerce.[53] The Court's opinion in *Sebelius*, authored by Chief Justice John Roberts, rejected the Commerce Clause as an anchor for the PPACA. Following the line of constitutional thought drawn by the law's opponents, Roberts wrote that accepting the government's argument would have opened a "new and potentially vast domain to congressional authority."[54] He nevertheless upheld the PPACA on the basis of a fallback argument that the federal government's lawyers had offered but "seemed to have little confidence" in: Congress was empowered to impose the individual mandate under the Taxing and Spending Clause.[55]

To bring my broader point full circle: We could classify *Sebelius* solely on the basis of its outcome. Since the PPACA was upheld, the decision was majoritarian in the traditional sense of the term. Doing so, however, would be just as unsatisfying as classifying *McCulloch* solely on the basis of its outcome. Part of what Chief Justice Roberts did in *Sebelius*—and the conservatives who claimed victory in the case would call it a large part[56]—was reject the reasoning of the liberal majority that enacted the PPACA. And just as in *McCulloch*, the majority's reasoning very much mattered; for Roberts, it threatened to "justify a mandatory purchase to solve almost any problem" identified by a future Congress.[57] It reflected, in short, a problematic vision of constitutional governance. We can only capture this crucial dimension of *Sebelius* by distinguishing between the majoritarian character of the outcome and the countermajoritarian character of the Court's reasoning.

The Compromise of 1816 does something more fundamental, however, than ask us to understand the roots of the Supreme Court's capacity to reason about the Bank's constitutionality differently than the political branches, or appreciate the departmentalist character of its decision to do so, or carefully distinguish between the majoritarian and nonmajoritarian[58] dimensions of its work in *McCulloch*. The fact that a national bank was revived pursuant to Congress's power to "coin Money, regulate the Value thereof" invites us to place a new spin on a very old question: *Why*, exactly, did John Marshall and his colleagues resolve the congressional power component of the case in the manner that they did? This question has traditionally been asked with reference to the meaning of the Sweeping Clause: What led the justices to embrace a broad rather than a strict interpretation of the provision? Was this Republican-heavy Supreme Court, for example, merely expressing the preference of the dominant Republican coalition? By contrast, were the justices expressing not partisan but *personal* preferences with respect to federal power? And setting aside instrumental perspectives on judicial decision-making, is there evidence that their conclusion about the meaning of the Necessary and Proper Clause flowed from objective analysis of the "plain meaning of . . . the Constitution, the intent of the Framers, and/or precedent"?[59] My account of the Bank's rebirth forces us to supplement this traditional inquiry with a second (and logically prior) question: What led the justices to resolve *McCulloch*'s congressional power question at least in part with controversial claims about the meaning of the Sweeping Clause rather than with a Coinage Clause argument that was uncontroversial among members of the dominant regime? *Why*, in short, did the Marshall Court reject the constitutional thinking of the political branches?

The available evidence does a better job of foreclosing certain answers to this question than of firmly establishing a specific motive for the Court's rejection of the Compromise of 1816. Just as students of judicial behavior can evaluate partisan, attitudinal, and legal explanations (among others) for the Marshall Court's decision to interpret the word *necessary* as it did, they can also consider a parallel set of explanations for the justices' antecedent decision to answer the congressional power question by discussing the Necessary and Proper Clause rather than the Coinage Clause. I describe and briefly consider these competing explanations below. I find that while a partisan explanation can be dismissed, the same cannot be said for either an attitudinal or a legal account. Of course, one's inability to dismiss an account of judicial behavior cannot be construed as evidence of its explanatory power. Neither the attitudinal nor the legal model, for reasons I lay out below, are susceptible to formal evaluation here. However, we can and should begin the process of identifying circumstantial evidence that works to strengthen or weaken the case for each account. This discussion, all told, serves as a kind of first stab at the question of why the Marshall Court rejected the constitutional thinking of the Fourteenth Congress.

Evaluating a partisan explanation for the Court's decision to eschew a holding rooted in the Coinage Clause in favor of one focused on the Sweeping Clause involves comparing the composition of the Court (as measured by which party's presidents had filled the seats) with the preferences of the dominant political regime. As Thomas M. Keck has written, "[w]hen a Republican judicial coalition invalidates a Democratic statute, the Court's decision is consistent with a partisan account."[60] To begin, the Court that decided *McCulloch* had largely been constructed by the Republican regime. While Bushrod Washington and John Marshall had been nominated by Federalist John Adams (in 1798 and 1801, respectively), the remaining five members of the Court had been appointed by two Republican presidents. Thomas Jefferson was responsible for naming three of these justices to the bench (William Johnson in 1804, Brockholst Livingston in 1806, and Thomas Todd in 1807). The other two took their seats following nominations from James Madison (Gabriel Duvall and Joseph Story, both in 1811). As such, the Court that sat in 1819 was a regime-affiliated one.

The Republican regime, of course, had a clear preference for how the Bank's constitutionality should be understood. Its preference for the Coinage Clause steered clear of the coalition's Scylla (a broad reading of the Sweeping Clause) *and* its Charybdis (a range of more restrictive readings of the same). If the regime had anything approaching a preference with respect to the meaning of the Necessary and Proper Clause, it would have

been leaving the same as something akin to a "political question."[61] Since
a Republican judicial coalition rejected Republicans' preferred anchor for
the Bank of the United States *and* treated the meaning of the Sweeping
Clause as a question ripe for judicial resolution, *McCulloch* does not appear consistent with a partisan account.

Graber's theory of nonmajoritarian decision-making raises the prospect of salvaging a partisan account of the Court's behavior. Such decision-
making requires, at minimum, that a regime both find itself incapable of
resolving a constitutional question and actively seek its resolution in the
courts. If, therefore, the Republican regime intended the Coinage Clause
less as a permanent solution to the problem of the Bank's status and more
as a placeholder argument designed to support the institution in the short
term while inviting the Court to decide its long-term fate with reference
to the Necessary and Proper Clause, then *McCulloch* could be read (consistent with a partisan account) as a regime-affiliated court resolving a
regime-dividing constitutional question.

One major problem with this reading of *McCulloch* is the absence of evidence suggesting that members of the Republican regime in any way "invited" an affiliated Court to resolve the meaning of the Sweeping Clause.
Graber implies that invitations of this sort tend to come in the form of
litigation initiated by party "extremists" or "insurgents."[62] As applied to
the Republican coalition in the late 1810s, this would mean that members
of the party's Old wing challenged the Bank's constitutionality as a means
of asking the Court to weigh in on the meaning of the word *necessary*.
As already noted, however, the backstory to *McCulloch* involved neither
Republicans nor a challenge to the Bank's constitutionality; it involved
Maryland's decision to tax the Baltimore branch of the institution and the
ensuing claim (from Bank officials) that such a tax was unconstitutional.
The question of Congress's authority to charter a national bank in the first
place came along only later, and probably at the behest of the Court itself.[63]

While a partisan account of the Marshall Court's decision to resolve
the congressional power question with partial reference to the institution's
constitutional necessity cannot be squared with the available evidence, an
attitudinal (or policy) explanation for the same cannot be dismissed. To
paraphrase Jeffrey Segal and Harold Spaeth, an argument of this sort posits
that the justices eschewed the Coinage Clause as a textual anchor for the
national bank because they favored more federal regulation of the economy and wished to validate the institution in a manner that would provide
judicial sanction for such regulation.[64] Any attempt to determine whether
their decision is explicable on such grounds is complicated by the absence

of a measuring stick: data on the policy preferences of Marshall Court members. For modern justices, that stick is usually provided by a Segal-Cover score, which measures individual ideology on the basis of "judgments in newspaper editorials that characterize [Court] nominees prior to confirmation as liberal or conservative[.]"[65] As of late 2016, however, only post-1937 nominees to the Supreme Court had Segal-Cover scores.[66]

Even if we cannot (at present) formally evaluate a claim that the Court's liberal account of congressional authority to charter a national bank flowed from the economic liberalism of its members, we can and should take note of two related observations that militate against this reading. First, it is difficult to believe that the Court that heard *McCulloch* was actually composed of seven "aggressive nationalis[ts.]"[67] That would mean, for example, that all three of Thomas Jefferson's appointees were personally supportive of an active federal government with respect to the economy. Second, even more realistic assumptions about the Court's composition and behavior here—namely, that it contained only a *majority* of nationalists and that justices who wished to concur or dissent opted instead to line up behind their colleagues[68]—fail to square with the manifest importance of the case. In short, it is also difficult to believe (given that Marshall's opinion embraced an expansive conception of federal power *beyond* the Bank controversy) that (1) more economically moderate justices would have eschewed a concurring opinion focused on the Coinage Clause, and (2) conservative justices would have refrained from dissenting with respect to the meaning of the Sweeping Clause.[69]

When scholars ask whether judicial behavior is consistent with the legal model of decision-making, they are usually trying to determine (as already noted) whether a justice's interpretation of a constitutional provision is consistent with the plain meaning of the text, the intent of the framers, and/or existing precedent. In many cases, neither the plain meaning of the clause in question nor the intent of those who wrote and ratified it can "be established a priori[.]" As a result, claims that justices adhere to these two sources cannot be falsified.[70] Students of the legal model have thus focused on the influence of precedent, which is measurable; they have asked how frequently justices who dissent from the Court's creation of a precedent vote to affirm that precedent in a subsequent case.[71]

The question raised here, strictly speaking, is *not* whether the Court's pronouncement about the meaning of the Sweeping Clause is consistent with the legal model. It is, instead, whether the justices' decision to eschew the Compromise of 1816 (and resolve the Bank's status with partial reference to the question of whether it was "necessary" for executing various federal powers) is consistent with that model. In simpler terms, did the Court reject the Coinage Clause argument because it considered the provision wholly unrelated to the subject of Congress's authority to charter a national bank? To borrow the logic of falsification cited above, a legal explanation for the Court's behavior here cannot be evaluated because we cannot establish, a priori, which clauses could (and could not) support the Bank's creation. If, by contrast, we somehow knew (say, by reference to the framers' intent) that the Coinage Clause simply did not speak to the national bank question, we could argue that the Marshall Court's preference for one provision over another was consistent with a legal explanation.

As with the attitudinal explanation, even if we lack the benchmarks required to formally evaluate a claim that legal concerns led the Court to reject the Compromise of 1816, we should take note of circumstantial evidence that might bear on its veracity. In this instance, however, the most noteworthy piece of it cuts in no obvious direction. The evidence itself is simple: On the surface, the Coinage Clause appeared to play no role in the resolution of *McCulloch*. It is not that Marshall mentioned the provision and then rejected it as a source of congressional authority; *he did not mention it at all*. While this fact could serve as an indication of just how little the justices thought of the idea that Congress could "coin Money" by chartering a national bank, it could just as easily be cited for the proposition that we have no direct evidence of the Court rejecting the Coinage Clause for legal reasons.[72]

The overall effect of this discussion—which has dismissed a partisan account of the Court's behavior and found that the available evidence does not permit formal evaluation of either an attitudinal or a legal account—is to leave us (1) uncertain as to whether the justices' decision to discuss the Sweeping Clause in the course of deciding the first part of *McCulloch* was more a product of politics than of law and (2) in need of evidence that will help us resolve that question. Students of judicial behavior will surely recognize this predicament. Rather than simply lament its existence, we should clearly identify the types of evidence that (if developed or discovered) could help to rectify it. Given the standard approach to attitudinal analysis among judicial behavioralists, evaluating that type of account will require the development of an "exogenous measure of the justices' attitudes" toward federal power in 1819.[73] Something akin to Segal-Cover scores for members of the early Court would fit the bill. Effective evaluation of a legal account will be intrinsically more difficult. Since *McCulloch* was the *first* opportunity for the Court to weigh in on the source of Congress's power to charter a national bank, we cannot ask whether the majority's reasoning in a prior case swayed the justices. The best we can hope for is the discovery of primary source material (e.g., correspondence) that speaks to how members of the Marshall Court viewed the Compromise of 1816.

CONCLUSION

This chapter has demonstrated that two hundred years after the fact, we still have much to learn about the Court's landmark decision in *McCulloch v. Maryland* (1819). Students of the case have historically paid little attention to the constitutional dimension of the national bank's rebirth—in particular, the Republican regime's decision to justify the institution with reference to the Coinage Clause. This has blinded us to several crucial aspects of the Marshall Court's work, including the historical reality that the justices offered a very different justification for the Bank and the fact that several features of the Constitution made their deviation possible. These aspects of *McCulloch*, in turn, invite us to acknowledge two others. First, because the Court's answer to the congressional power question differed from that of the political branches, it represents an exercise in departmentalism. Second, while the Court's first major conclusion in the case—that Congress was empowered to charter the Bank of the United States—squared with the preferences of the dominant political coalition, the reasoning behind that conclusion surely did not. Students of judicial behavior tend to classify decisions solely in terms of their outcome, but doing so here—that is, simply characterizing *McCulloch* as majoritarian—would fail to capture why the case was anathema to so many Republicans.

It may be too much, however, to claim that the Compromise of 1816 ultimately helps us make better sense of what occurred in *McCulloch*. In truth, the events surrounding the Bank's revival raise as many questions about the case as they answer. Even if the institution's attorneys, for whatever reason, preferred to defend their client as "necessary" for exercising one or more of Congress's fiscal powers, why did they fail to cite the Coinage Clause as a fallback claim on the national bank's behalf? More importantly, why did the Court prefer to resolve the congressional power question on its own constitutional terms rather than those supplied by the Fourteenth Congress? For both questions, the available evidence does a better job of inviting speculation (and future research) than of furnishing an answer. All told, it is safer to conclude that the Compromise of 1816, rather than helping us make better sense of *McCulloch*, invites us to appreciate new aspects of it.

CHAPTER SEVEN

A Tale of Two Clauses

The Conventional Wisdom

In July 1832, over thirteen years after the McCulloch *decision, the Twenty-Second Congress passed a bill to extend the national bank's charter—which was not set to expire until March 1836—for an additional fifteen years.[1] President Andrew Jackson rejected that bill a week later, in part on constitutional grounds. His veto message asserted that decisions of the Supreme Court "ought not to control" the behavior of elected officials in the federal government who were bound by oath to support the Constitution; Jackson would thus be "guided by [his] own opinion" of the Bank's constitutionality. The president went on to argue that his veto was justified because the institution was neither "necessary" nor "proper."[2]*

Like several of the vignettes that have opened chapters in this book, the foregoing account—which describes a critical juncture in American constitutional history—contains no falsehoods. President Jackson, for example, surely embraced departmentalist thinking in the course of rejecting a charter extension for the Bank of the United States. Like those same vignettes, however, it is also flawed on account of several important omissions.

Those omissions all spring from a common source: the Compromise of 1816. While the Bank's constitutional affairs between 1829 and 1832— beginning with President Jackson's first annual message (December 1829) and ending with his Bank veto (July 1832)—are routinely presented as little more than another round of squabbling over the meaning of the Necessary and Proper Clause,[3] in reality they were also informed by claims respecting Congress's power to "coin Money, regulate the Value thereof." There is, moreover, good reason for this: While members of the Fourteenth Congress had hoped that a revived Bank of the United States would restore and maintain the nationwide circulation of specie (i.e., vindicate the monetary choices made by Congress soon after ratification), the institution's performance in the mid- to late 1820s had *realized this hope*; the "objective of sound money" led it to routinely curb "the loans and discounts of the state banks[.]"[4] After Jackson expressed constitutional doubts about the institution early in his presidency, the Coinage Clause argument was discussed in print and in the halls of both the Twenty-First and the Twenty-Second Congresses. Just as importantly, those discussions led the president to address the provision in his veto message. In short, the standard narrative for the 1829–1832 period omits the fact that General Jackson had to fight the early battles of his "Bank War"[5] on not one but *two* constitutional fronts.

It is well known, for example, that Jackson's first annual message included a suggestion that Congress's authority to create and maintain a national bank was "well questioned by a large portion of our fellow-citizens[.]"[6] What seems to be less well known is the fact that many of the president's fellow Democrats in the Twenty-First Congress—where the new party, a partial outgrowth of the defunct Republican regime's Old wing,[7] enjoyed both House and Senate majorities—labored to rebut his claim by pointing not only to *McCulloch* but also to the Coinage Clause. An April 1830 report of the House Ways and Means Committee suggested that the monetary turmoil that began in August 1814 had "furnished a most pregnant commentary" on the meaning of that provision.[8] More to the point, the revived institution was helping to secure the clause's core prerogative: congressional control over the nation's money.[9] This particular line of constitutional thinking endured into the Twenty-Second Congress, where supporters of legislation to extend the Bank's charter defended their efforts by invoking the Article I, Section 8 power to "coin Money, regulate the Value thereof[.]" All told, the first-term president faced more than straightforward claims that Marshall's opinion in *McCulloch* had settled the Bank's constitutional status; many members of his own coalition were offering a second defense of the institution.

Even if scholars have proven inattentive to claims respecting the Coinage Clause in the early 1830s, the fact remains that Jackson *himself* took notice of them. The president's July 1832 veto message not only rejected the argument that *McCulloch* settled the national bank's status but separately recognized (and quickly dismissed) the power to coin money as an alternative justification for the institution. The president's approach here was not to argue (as Senator Wells had sixteen years earlier) that an originalist reading of the clause would not support the chartering of a national bank, but rather to suggest that any congressional power over the nation's currency beyond the creation of metallic coins could not be delegated to a corporation.[10]

Scholars seem at best uninterested in this element of the broader Bank drama; the editors of several prominent constitutional law casebooks that include the president's veto message have *excised* the passage in which he discusses the Coinage Clause.[11] As such, their coverage begins with Jackson's contention that neither the executive nor the legislative branches of the federal government were bound by the Supreme Court's understanding of the Constitution and ends with his assertion that the Bank of the United States was both "unnecessary and improper[.]"[12] Given the importance of the Coinage Clause argument in 1816 and its resurgence in the constitutional politics of national banking a decade and a half later, one function of this chapter is to defend a claim that Jackson's discussion of the provision deserves inclusion in future casebooks.

More broadly, just as the appearance of a regime-supplied solution to the national bank problem calls for a reassessment of the justices' behavior in *McCulloch v. Maryland* (1819), its reappearance in the constitutional politics of the early 1830s calls for a reassessment of both the run-up to Jackson's veto message and its constitutional content. This chapter provides that reassessment. It also begins the process of explaining how the Compromise of 1816, despite the Marshall Court's refusal to embrace (let alone acknowledge) it, has shaped the post-*McCulloch* constitutional politics of national banking. In that sense, the chapter helps further underwrite a claim that the genesis of the Coinage Clause argument deserves belated recognition as an important juncture in American constitutional development.

FISCAL SUPPORT AND STATE BANK
REGULATION IN THE 1820S

Chapters 2 and 3 of this book chronicle slow-moving changes in American banking between 1791 and 1811. The former helps explain why the recharter debate of 1811 offered something more than a constitutional rerun of 1791, while the latter furnishes a partial explanation for the constitutional novelties on display in 1816. Pushing the same analytic task forward in time, it seems fair to ask (before delving into the debates of the 1829–1832 period) whether there were any changes in American banking between 1816 and 1829 with the potential to further alter the trajectory of the Bank's constitutional politics.

The answer to this question appears to be no. To be clear, I am not suggesting that the period between 1816 and 1829 is completely devoid of change in American banking; the mid-1820s, for example, saw the birth of the "Suffolk System," which enabled larger banks located in regional centers to accept and circulate the paper of their smaller and more remote peers at par value.[13] By contrast, I am merely positing that no change in the national bank during this period (or to the institution's place in the broader banking industry) stood to reframe the debate over its constitutional status.

Because the proliferation of state banks between 1791 and 1811 informed subsequent debate in Congress over the meaning of the Necessary and Proper Clause (1811), and the national bank's functional evolution during that same period led to suggestions that the Coinage Clause could anchor the institution (1816), a defense of this claim ought to include assessments of (1) how the size of the banking industry changed between 1816 and 1829, and (2) how the functions of the Bank in 1829 compared with those envisioned by members of the Fourteenth Congress.

The story with respect to state-chartered institutions is not devoid of change, but the force of that change appears to have been (preemptively) blunted by the Marshall Court. On the one hand, the number of state banks continued to grow between 1816 and 1829. While older and newer datasets differ with respect to the number of institutions operating in 1816 (Joseph Van Fenstermaker counted 212 in 1965, while Warren E. Weber reported 205 just over forty years later), and also offer different figures for 1829 (355 for Fenstermaker, compared with 318 for Weber), they both suggest significant industry growth during the period.[14] In that sense, we might expect a post-1829 debate over the Bank's constitutionality to include a revival of the 1811 claim that the sprinkling of state banks throughout the nation rendered the institution less than "necessary" for meeting the federal government's fiscal needs. On the other hand, not only was a discussion of state banks conspicuously absent from the postwar deliberations over a national bank bill, but John Marshall's opinion for the Court in *McCulloch* all but declared their existence (and number) to be constitutionally irrelevant. The chief justice, after presenting the bulk of his argument in favor of congressional power to charter the Bank, closed by suggesting that "it can scarcely be necessary to say that the existence of State banks can have *no possible influence on the question.* No trace is to be found in the Constitution of an intention to create a dependence of the Government of the Union on those of the States, for the execution of the great powers assigned to it."[15] Insofar, then, as we would expect *McCulloch* to be invoked in a new round of debate over the Bank's constitutionality, we should construe its presence as (at least in part) analogous to the 1811 claim that state bank proliferation was irrelevant to the constitutional question. All told, there is little reason to expect expansion in the banking industry after 1816 to fundamentally alter (come 1829) the terms of debate over the national bank's status.

As for the institution's functions at the commencement of President Jackson's assault, they matched both those carried out by the first Bank at the time of its demise (1811) and those envisioned for the second by members of the Fourteenth Congress (1816). In short, there is no evidence of functional change in the national bank between 1816 and 1829. Part of the reason federal lawmakers sought to revive the institution following the War of 1812 was its sound record of fiscal service to the nation between 1791 and 1811: providing occasional loans to the Treasury, safeguarding the revenue collected by that department, and serving as the federal government's fiscal agent. Although the second Bank certainly performed these functions,[16] they did not represent its principal raison d'être. As detailed in chapter 5, postwar lawmakers recalled the first Bank's gradual development of regulatory power over state-chartered peers and saw a revived institution as first and foremost a tool for restoring and maintaining their payment of specie. In short, a new national bank was sought more for monetary purposes than for fiscal ones.

Two facts about the Bank's monetary performance between its formal reopening and 1829 are reasonably clear. First, it proved unable to single-handedly secure the resumption of specie payments by state banks in early 1817; that outcome was only achieved after both the national bank and Madison's Treasury Department offered "substantial concessions" to those institutions at a February 1 conference with leading bankers from Philadelphia, New York, Baltimore, and Richmond.[17] Second, the Bank's inability to unilaterally *restore* specie payments notwithstanding, it did help *maintain* the payment of gold and silver by state banks throughout the 1820s. As a veritable army of economic historians have noted, the Bank of the United States during the early years of Nicholas Biddle's institutional presidency (1823–1829) routinely "kept state banks in line by returning their notes to them for redemption in specie."[18]

When it comes to the national bank's monetary performance during the 1820s, we need not rely exclusively on secondary sources. Biddle[19] authored over three thousand official letters during his time as the Bank's president (1823–1836), and they were copied into numerous "Letterbooks" principally by his longtime secretary, George W. Fairman. Only a small subset of these have been published to date,[20] but I read and cataloged the entire collection as part of a separate project on Biddle's management of the institution.[21] Among other things, the collection confirms that insofar as members of the Fourteenth Congress sought to create an institution that would help maintain nationwide convertibility of state bank paper into specie, they succeeded.

Biddle was hardly shy, for example, about identifying the national bank's regulatory function or characterizing it in positive terms. To John Cumming, president of the institution's Savannah branch, he wrote in early 1825 of the broader Bank's influence "in sustaining the currency and *protecting* the property of the country."[22] A few years later, Biddle suggested to Joseph Hemphill—then a member of the House from Pennsylvania—that there could "be little danger to the community while the issues of the [state] banks are restrained from running to excess by the *salutary control*" of the national bank.[23] There is even evidence (albeit outside the collection of letters under discussion) that the Bank's president thought of this function as the institution's most important. In response to a formal inquiry from the Senate Finance Committee of the Twenty-First Congress in early 1830, Biddle wrote that the "great object" of the national bank was "to keep the state banks within proper limits; to make them shape their business according to their means."[24]

The Letterbooks of Nicholas Biddle also reveal (1) how decisions to regulate state bank behavior were made and (2) how they were executed. As to the former, his letters suggest that decisions to exercise monetary power in specific locales—namely, those where the Bank had a branch—were made from the institution's headquarters in Philadelphia. What is not clear from Biddle's letters to members of the Bank's main board of directors—which constitute roughly 10 percent of the collection[25]—is whether the president made these decisions more or less unilaterally (with an expectation that the board would then validate them) or permitted open discussion of institutional policy and submitted it to the judgment of the group. Far clearer, by contrast, is the fact that decisions made in Philadelphia were then communicated by Biddle to peripheral officers (branch presidents, cashiers, and directors). For example, in a July 1823 letter to Charles Nicholas—cashier of the Bank's branch in Richmond—Biddle opened by suggesting that the parent office was ordering the adoption of "certain measures to change the relations in which you stand to the [state] Banks of Virginia which are injurious in themselves and require to be corrected."[26]

As for how monetary policies adopted in Philadelphia were to be implemented, Biddle often instructed branch officials to (1) remain or become the creditor of state banks in their vicinity and then (2) force those institutions to reduce their lending by demanding specie in payment of their debts to the branch. One easy way for the New York City branch to "turn the scale in [its] favor with the other Banks" in Manhattan, Biddle explained to Isaac Lawrence (its president) in April 1825, was to engage in a simple "diminution of [its] discounts"; this would lead to more state bank paper in the branch's possession and less branch paper in the possession of those institutions.[27] Biddle's July 1823 letter to Nicholas also clarified how branches were expected to press their advantage once it was established; the branch cashier was instructed to "[w]rite to the . . . branches [of the Bank of Virginia] that you have a certain amount of their notes on hand which you desire them to pay [in specie.]"[28]

These excerpts from Biddle's Letterbooks, in conjunction with secondary sources, should be sufficient to establish that far from undergoing further functional change between 1816 and 1829, the Bank of the United States realized both the fiscal and the monetary ambitions of its postwar founders. Given that federal lawmakers' desire for effective state bank regulation helped inspire the Coinage Clause arguments of 1815 and 1816, and that institutional performance during the mid- to late 1820s met that objective, we might expect a post-1829 debate over the Bank's constitutionality to again include claims respecting that provision (especially from people sympathetic to the institution but wary of embracing *McCulloch* and its capacious understanding of federal power). In short, as with state bank proliferation, nothing about the national bank's functions between 1816 and 1829 stood to alter the terms of debate over its status.

FROM RECALCITRANCE TO RECHARTER

The long road to President Andrew Jackson's July 1832 veto of a Bank recharter bill began nearly four years earlier, in the first days following the 1828 presidential election. The supporters of "Old Hickory" were convinced that the Bank of the United States had labored to secure the reelection of incumbent John Quincy Adams.[29] Samuel Ingham, Jackson's first Treasury secretary, later registered this complaint with Nicholas Biddle rather obliquely; he suggested that the national bank had been "made an instrument for the accomplishment of [objects other] than those for which it may be legitimately exercised."[30] Just as importantly, one of Jackson's supporters in the federal government—Postmaster General John

McLean—offered Biddle a bold suggestion in January 1829 for how to avoid similar problems in the future: select members of both parties—National Republicans[31] *and* Democrats—as directors of Bank branches.[32] McLean's letter was, in Bray Hammond's words, a rather transparent effort "to fetch [the institution] within the party pale as spoils of victory."[33]

Biddle's response to this passive-aggressive overture was polite but dismissive. He thanked McLean for his thoughts concerning the composition of branch boards but confirmed that "the first considerations" with respect to director selection were "integrity, independence & knowledge of business. No man should be excluded, no man should be sought, merely on account of his political sentiments." Only in cases where the institution had a choice between "persons equally competent" would the value of political diversity be considered.[34] The Bank's initial recalcitrance about making partisanship a factor in institutional decision-making was only reinforced several months after the new president's inauguration. Secretary Ingham, in the aforementioned July 1829 letter that accused the national bank of participation in the recent election, also shared with Biddle accusations of partisan discrimination in lending at branches in New Hampshire, Kentucky, and Louisiana.[35] The national bank's president, reading Ingham's language (rightly or wrongly) as including a revival of McLean's proposal for partisan balancing in director selection, curtly replied a week later that "the [institution] owes allegiance to no party, and *will submit to none.*"[36]

The epistolary back-and-forth between Secretary Ingham and President Biddle continued through early October 1829, with the former invoking (at minimum) the administration's right to "suggest its views" on the Bank's management and the latter repeatedly asserting the institution's complete independence from the executive branch.[37] In the coming years, Biddle would frequently attribute President Jackson's initial public expression of constitutional and policy hostility toward the national bank to the "intractable spirit" he had adopted with Ingham.[38] That expression came in early December 1829 with the new president's first annual message. Despite the fact that the charter granted to the Bank of the United States in April 1816 had more than six years left to run—it would not expire until March 1836—Jackson reminded members of Congress that its stockholders would "probably apply for a renewal of their privileges." Given the "important principles" and "deep pecuniary interests" involved, the president did not think it too early for Congress to begin considering the recharter question. Jackson then famously set the agenda for those discussions: "Both the constitutionality and the expediency of the law creating this bank are well questioned by a large portion of our fellow citizens[.]"[39]

The president's revival of the congressional power question—which had lain dormant for more than ten years since *McCulloch* (1819)—was greeted with raised eyebrows by many members of the Twenty-First Congress, including some Jackson supporters. The House Ways and Means Committee, chaired by Democrat George McDuffie of South Carolina, issued a report in April 1830 that tried to offer the question a quick re-retirement. McDuffie and his fellow committee members—a group consisting of five Democrats and two National Republicans—addressed two potential textual anchors for the Bank: the Sweeping Clause and the Coinage Clause.

The committee's treatment of the former appears to reproduce the intraregime quarrel among Republicans that led to the Compromise of 1816. On the one hand, McDuffie's committee was willing to recognize the long-standing argument that the Bank was constitutional under the Necessary and Proper Clause: "In the discussion of 1791, and also in that before the Supreme Court [in *McCulloch*], the powers of raising, collecting, and disbursing the public revenue, of borrowing money on the credit of the United States, and paying the public debt, were those which were supposed most clearly to carry with them the incidental right of incorporating a bank, to facilitate these operations."[40] On the other hand, it was unwilling to *endorse* that argument. This fact probably owes much to the presence of five Democrats on the seven-man committee—lawmakers who (like their forerunners, more conservative Republicans) had little interest in facilitating future exercises of federal power. With a majority of its membership unwilling to openly equate utility with constitutional necessity, the committee simply stated that this perspective on the meaning of the Sweeping Clause had been fully explained in "former discussions, familiar to the House[.]"[41]

McDuffie and his colleagues appeared far more willing to openly embrace the Coinage Clause as a basis for extending the institution's charter. Their argument here tracked, in all important respects, that offered back in late 1815 and early 1816: Congress had previously chosen gold and silver to be the "money of the country" (a choice surely contemplated by the provision), but the state banks' refusal to resume specie payments following the arrival of peace with Great Britain in February 1815 had effectively "taken from Congress" this "great and essential power[.]" This state of monetary affairs meant that the Fourteenth Congress "not only had the power, but . . . [was] under the most solemn *constitutional obligation*[] to restore the disordered currency"; a revived Bank of the United States—on the basis of its past regulation of state-chartered institutions—was selected as the means of restoration.[42] As had been the case fifteen years earlier, it was not clear from the committee's report whether (1) power under the Coinage Clause was directly exercised by Congress or (2) a national bank was manifestly "necessary" for exercising its power to coin money. If the committee's treatment of the Necessary and Proper Clause vis-à-vis Article I's fiscal provisions offers proof that the members of Jefferson's party were still fighting over the scope of federal power in the early 1830s (albeit under new labels), then its discussion of the Coinage Clause suggests that constitutional compromise among probank lawmakers was still possible.

Others who chose to comment on the constitutional question mimicked McDuffie's committee, at least in that their discussions were not restricted to *McCulloch* or the Bank's necessity for exercising Congress's fiscal powers. In late June 1830, Nicholas Biddle learned that Albert Gallatin—now almost twenty years removed from his wartime service as Madison's Treasury secretary—was planning his own written response to the president's commentary on the Bank. Biddle proceeded to encourage Gallatin's effort, in part by volunteering to serve as his research assistant; offering "my humble assistance in collecting materials for you[,]" the Bank's president wrote the aging statesman thirty-five letters over the remaining six months of 1830.[43] That December, the fruit of Gallatin's labors was published in the *American Quarterly Review*; an expanded version was published two months later in pamphlet form.[44] In that pamphlet, he noted that Alexander Hamilton's original proposal for a national bank had been defended on the ground that it was "necessary" for exercising the federal government's fiscal powers.[45] While clearly sympathetic to this position, Gallatin also stressed that it was *"far from being on that ground alone,* that the question of constitutionality is now placed." The current Bank of the United States had been proposed not as "incident" to the fiscal powers, but "for the express purpose of regulating the currency"—that is, as an exercise of Congress's monetary power under the Coinage Clause.[46]

A comparable vote of constitutional confidence came from William B. Lawrence, a former diplomat practicing law in New York City. In April 1831, the *North American Review* published Lawrence's thoughts on the national bank. To be clear, his article—titled simply "Bank of the United States"—was not organized around the constitutional question. Lawrence devoted most of his space to reviewing—and ultimately praising—the institution's monetary performance; at one point he characterized it as the "ultimate regulator of the currency."[47] Nevertheless, he offered two discrete claims respecting its constitutionality. First, Lawrence argued that this could "no longer . . . be considered a doubtful question"; the Supreme

Court's decision in *McCulloch* had merely reinforced a conclusion previously established by the words and acts of elected officials.[48] In a postscript, he offered a second claim on behalf of the Bank; Lawrence wrote that "[i]f we suppose, with Mr. McDuffie, that the power 'to coin money, and regulate the value thereof,' implies an authority to regulate the currency . . . it is the duty of Congress not to omit to legislate on the subject."[49] His language here, like that employed by McDuffie's committee a year earlier, treated the Coinage Clause less as a power granted to Congress and more as an obligation imposed on it.

These initial responses to President Jackson's first annual message notwithstanding, the prediction that gave rise to his constitutional claim—that the Bank's stockholders would apply for an extension of their charter—was not borne out until January 1832. At that point, Nicholas Biddle (on behalf of the "President, Directors, and Company of the Bank of the United States") submitted a memorial to Congress on the subject.[50] What followed (in the late spring and early summer) was debate in the Twenty-Second Congress on an uncomplicated bill to extend the Bank's charter by fifteen years. That debate, in a functional rebuttal of the president's claim respecting public opinion, actually included very little discussion of the constitutional question at all (and certainly less than its 1791, 1811, or 1816 iterations). Moreover, it ended with little fanfare in early July with congressional passage of the recharter bill.[51]

What recharter advocates in the Twenty-Second Congress said about the Bank's constitutionality is consistent with the published responses to Jackson's first annual message. There was at least one effort, for example, to defend the Bank as "necessary" for exercising Congress's fiscal powers. Oddly enough, it came from a Democrat. More oddly still, it came from a Democrat who had previously stated that a national bank was *not* "necessary" for achieving those prerogatives. Senator Samuel Smith of Maryland, who had opposed the 1811 recharter bill by invoking the two-prong test of constitutional necessity,[52] completed his Clay-like flip-flop on the question by suggesting that absent a national bank, the "Government [could not], in my opinion, carry on its fiscal operations in safety[.]"[53]

Legislation designed to extend the national bank's life beyond 1836 was more frequently defended, however, as an exercise of Congress's power under the Coinage Clause. George Dallas, a Democratic senator from Pennsylvania and son of the Treasury secretary who had both drafted the postwar Bank bill and grounded it in that provision, was given the honor of opening floor debate in his chamber. If the father's bill had been designed to *restore* the payment of specie by state banks, and thereby redeem the currency choices made by Congress in the first few years under the Constitution, then the son's support for a charter extension envisioned the *"maintenance* of a uniform, sound currency[.]"[54] Dallas found an unlikely constitutional ally in the man who followed him on the Senate floor: Daniel Webster of Massachusetts. Thirteen years earlier, as counsel for the Bank of the United States in *McCulloch*, Webster had argued that the Sweeping Clause granted Congress ample means for managing the nation's fiscal affairs. Now, however, the National Republican opted for a much narrower argument; he claimed that the monetary objective identified by Dallas was "sufficiently prominent on the face of the constitution itself."[55]

For my purposes here, the respective rationales for Smith's flip-flop and Webster's shift are ultimately less important than the constitutional corner into which their positions backed the president. If Andrew Jackson was going to argue that Congress lacked the power to extend the national bank's charter, he would need to openly grapple with not one but *two* provisions from Article I, Section 8.

JACKSON'S VETO MESSAGE: BEYOND DEPARTMENTALISM

President Jackson's July 10 veto of the recharter bill, issued in part on constitutional grounds, "burst like a thunderclap over the nation."[56] Arguably the "most important veto ever issued by a president,"[57] it tends to be treated today as a classic statement of departmentalism with respect to interpretive authority.[58] As Gerard Magliocca has recently noted, however, the portion of the message that questioned the Supreme Court's ability to "control the coordinate authorities of [the] Government" with respect to textual meaning received "relatively little notice from Jackson's peers[.]" That is to say, this Court-centric perspective on the veto is a distinctly modern phenomenon.[59] The president's message deserves still further reassessment, however. For one thing, despite Jackson's denial of *McCulloch's* authority, he never actually rejected Chief Justice Marshall's claims respecting the Necessary and Proper Clause. If anything, he leveraged them to his own advantage. Moreover, despite the reductionist tendencies of casebook editors with respect to the veto[60]—a manifestation, no doubt, of Magliocca's point—Jackson's written claims were hardly restricted to the Bank's necessity for exercising the government's fiscal powers. Later in the message, the president addressed the argument that the institution could be anchored to the Coinage Clause. Unlike many of his fellow Democrats, Jackson proved unwilling to accept a national bank even on narrow constitutional grounds.

The bulk of Jackson's departmentalist language is contained in a single paragraph of the veto message; he acknowledged the Court's opinion in *McCulloch* but argued that it did not preclude his own judgment about the constitutionality of the recharter bill. It is important to clarify, however, that the president did not simply dismiss the Court's work out of hand and then proceed to evaluate the constitutional question from scratch. By contrast, he closed the paragraph by suggesting that the Court's opinion must "have only such influence as the force of [its] reasoning may deserve."[61] What followed, in short, was less a de novo assessment of the Bank's status and more an effort to hoist John Marshall on his own constitutional petard.

The president began this portion of the veto message by glossing the *McCulloch* opinion: "I understand [the Court] to have decided that inasmuch as a bank is an appropriate means for carrying into effect the enumerating powers of the General Government . . . the law incorporating it is in accordance with" the Necessary and Proper Clause. More specifically, Jackson added, members of the Court had "satisfied themselves that the word 'necessary' . . . means 'needful,' 'requisite,' 'essential,' [and] 'conducive to,' and that 'a bank' is a convenient, a useful, and essential instrument in the prosecution of the Government's 'fiscal operations[.]'"[62] At this point, Jackson might have—in the best tradition of antibank constitutional thinking—taken issue with the Court's permissive interpretation of the Sweeping Clause. The president did no such thing, however. Instead, he actually delved *deeper* into John Marshall's opinion, quoting it directly: "[W]here the law is not prohibited and is really calculated to effect any of the objects intrusted to the Government, to undertake here to inquire into the degree of its necessity would be to pass the line which circumscribes the judicial department and to tread on legislative ground."[63]

Jackson's rationale for reproducing, rather than repudiating, the Court's reasoning was quickly made clear. "The principle here *affirmed*," he wrote, is that the "degree" of a national bank's necessity "is a question exclusively for legislative consideration . . . [u]nder the decision of the Supreme Court, therefore, it is the exclusive province of Congress and the President to decide whether the particular features of this act are necessary and proper" for the institution to perform its assigned duties.[64] In essence, the president argued that the Court *itself* had sanctioned his constitutional review of the recharter bill. Otherwise put, instead of articulating and applying a more restrictive interpretation of constitutional necessity (and thus maintaining a schism over textual meaning that dated to the year 1791), Jackson eschewed that battleground altogether and instead treated *McCulloch* as a more or less explicit act of interbranch deference; the Court had (in his eyes) confirmed that the meaning of the Sweeping Clause was a political question.[65] Working from this premise, the president spent much of his remaining space explaining why the Bank was neither "necessary" nor "proper."[66]

The constitutional commentary offered by members of three separate Congresses—the Fourteenth, the Twenty-First, and the Twenty-Second— virtually required Jackson to address the argument that a national bank could be anchored to the Coinage Clause. This the president did following his analysis of the Bank's constitutional necessity; he acknowledged that it was "maintained by some that the [institution] is a means of executing the constitutional power 'to coin money and regulate the value thereof.'"[67] Jackson's first move here was to gesture in the direction of a claim (first offered by Federalist senator William Wells back in 1816) that the provision only empowered Congress to take specific weights of the precious metals and assign them monetary values. After noting that Congress had established a mint and passed laws on the value of its output, the president remarked that "[t]he money so coined, with its value so regulated . . . [is] the only currency known to the Constitution." Jackson, however, refused to categorically deny that the Coinage Clause might also sanction *other* forms of federal activity. This led to the president's second move; he claimed that if Congress possessed "other power to regulate the currency, it was conferred to be exercised by themselves, and not to be transferred to a corporation." If—to invoke the most salient example—Congress was also authorized to take measures designed to maintain the nationwide payment of specie, it had to act directly on state banks; lawmakers could not delegate or "part[] with their power for a term of years[.]"[68]

Readers who are familiar with modern constitutional history, especially early twentieth-century separation-of-powers controversies, may recognize here that bringing Jackson's Coinage Clause commentary back into the Bank veto has important implications beyond documenting the legacy of the Compromise of 1816. Doing so alerts us to the fact that the Taft Court's decision in *J. W. Hampton, Jr. & Co v. United States* (1928), which suggested that Congress was free to delegate its power so long as its delegatee was provided with an "intelligible principle" for action,[69] did not mark the beginning of debate over delegation and nondelegation among federal officials.[70] Nearly a century earlier, the president of the United States had suggested that (1) the Constitution prohibited the delegation of powers, and (2) Congress had violated that prohibition. Moreover, he almost certainly implied that (3) the Marshall Court had not viewed Congress's delegation of its own power as a constitutional problem. Just as the debate over George Washington's Neutrality Declaration (1793) demonstrates that federal officials were thinking about implied presidential power long before Harry S. Truman's seizure of the nation's steel mills during the Korean War (1952),[71] Andrew Jackson's Bank veto demonstrates that some were troubled by the prospect of the "administrative state" long before the Sixty-Seventh Congress spurred the *Hampton* controversy by delegating its power to tax imports to the US Tariff Commission and the president.[72]

The delegation component of President Jackson's commentary on the Coinage Clause also works to expose the cost of our collective tendency to ignore this portion of his Bank veto. In *Creating the Administrative Constitution* (2012), Jerry Mashaw sought to make the case that "[f]rom the earliest days of the [American] Republic, Congress [has] delegated broad authority to administrators[.]"[73] At least with respect to the law establishing the second Bank of the United States, Andrew Jackson would not have disagreed. Mashaw opened his chapter on the "Bank War" by asserting that its "constitutional dimensions . . . highlight important and continuously contested issues of administrative law[.]"[74] Jackson's discussion of delegation certainly leaves me inclined to agree. However, Mashaw's treatment of the Bank veto (pp. 159–61) did not focus on this aspect of the president's message. In fact, it failed to mention Jackson's discussion of the Coinage Clause at all. The lessons that Mashaw drew with respect to the "administrative constitution" all came from the president's discussion of the Necessary and Proper Clause. The point warrants special emphasis: In discussing the Bank veto's relevance for administrative law, the one passage that spoke directly to delegation *was never mentioned*. My assumption here is not that Mashaw read the full text of Jackson's veto message but somehow missed the critical passage. Rather, it is that he worked with an edited version of the president's message. Reductionism with respect to Jackson's Bank veto, in short, appears to have impoverished the study of delegation as a site of constitutional controversy.

One final observation about the president's Coinage Clause commentary warrants mention. As already noted, Jackson's contemporaries took far less notice of the departmentalism on display in his veto message than have modern students of American constitutionalism. That element of the message, in other words, actually fails to capture what made it so radical at the time it was issued. As for the true source of its radicalism, Keith Whittington has argued that "[t]he rejection of judicial supremacy was a necessary step in Jackson's argument, but the main target of his ire was the [B]ank and its Whig supporters."[75] It was, then, the president's basic willingness to judge the Bank of the United States unconstitutional that gave the veto message its radical edge. That, in turn, underscores the importance of Jackson's Coinage Clause commentary. It was one thing for the president to conclude that the institution was both "unnecessary" and "improper." There were certainly members of the Democratic coalition who would have gone further, to the point of openly repudiating Marshall's opinion from *McCulloch*. It was quite another thing, however, for Jackson to simultaneously reject the Coinage Clause as a narrower justification for the institution. A number of Democrats in the early 1830s, like their Republican forebears in the 1810s, were willing (and perhaps even eager) to have a national bank if having it did not require an abandonment of their broader commitment to limited federal power. President Jackson's veto message was thus radical because independent of his thoughts on the Necessary and Proper Clause, Jackson *also* rejected the Coinage Clause as a textual anchor for the institution.

CONCLUSION

This chapter has demonstrated that the argument for chartering a national bank under the Coinage Clause, born in 1816 to Republicans seeking a narrow justification for the institution, did not die when the Marshall Court failed to embrace it in *McCulloch v. Maryland* (1819). It was revived in the early 1830s following President Andrew Jackson's suggestion that "a large portion" of Americans questioned the Bank's constitutionality. A report from the House Ways and Means Committee of the Twenty-First Congress cited the provision approvingly, as did several articles published in periodicals. Just as importantly, members of the Twenty-Second Congress invoked the power to "coin Money, regulate the Value thereof" when discussing (and ultimately passing) a bill to extend the national bank's charter until 1851. All of this meant that if Jackson intended to veto the bill on constitutional grounds, he would need to reject not simply the idea that the Bank of the United States was "necessary" for exercising one or more Article I fiscal powers, but an independent claim that the institution was essential for the effective exercise of Congress's monetary powers.

This is precisely what the president proceeded to do. Despite the fact that casebook editors tend to reduce Jackson's Bank veto to (1) his rejection of *McCulloch* as a binding resolution of the institution's status and (2) his assertion that it was neither "necessary" nor "proper" for exercising the federal government's fiscal powers, the full message also included (3) his

rejection of the Coinage Clause as an independent basis for the institution. Though we have never recognized it as such, the Bank-related constitutional drama of Andrew Jackson's first term is actually a tale of two
clauses rather than one.

I suggested at the start of this chapter that it would *begin* the process
of explaining how the Coinage Clause argument continued to inform the
constitutional politics of national banking long after the Marshall Court
failed to embrace it. The conclusion will bring that process to a close,
demonstrating that modern efforts to defend the constitutionality of the
Federal Reserve—efforts that invariably reference Congress's power to
"coin Money, regulate the Value thereof"—are traceable to post–Civil War
jurisprudence that itself appears indebted to the work of Republicans in
the Fourteenth Congress. In essence, not only did the Coinage Clause play
a heretofore unappreciated role in the Early American Republic's conflict
over a national bank, but that same role *continues* to inform our constitutional politics.

A Revisionist Bank Narrative— Lessons Timely and Timeless

There is scant evidence that the December 1913 passage of the Federal Reserve Act by the Sixty-Third Congress, and President Woodrow Wilson's signing of the same, occasioned any sort of constitutional drama. A recent history of the struggle to create the Federal Reserve—which has been called the "third Bank of the United States"[1]—makes no mention of constitutional concerns on the part of federal lawmakers,[2] and the president said nary a word about the Constitution in signing the bill into law.[3] Even the period preceding the institution's birth fails to yield evidence on this score. While the National Monetary Commission—which was formed in the aftermath of the Panic of 1907 to study potential reforms to American banking laws—solicited the first scholarly histories of the first and second Banks of the United States,[4] there is nothing to suggest that these monographs were commissioned to allay anxieties over federal power.

The constitutionality of the Fed has, however, periodically been questioned *since* 1913. Just as importantly, institution-affirming answers to that question—whether coming from scholars, lawmakers, or institutional officers—have always cited the Coinage Clause. An exchange of this very nature, in fact, took place in a congressional hearing during the worst days of the 2008 financial crisis (a point I return to below). This prompts a rather obvious question: Is the modern constitutional defense of the Federal Reserve fairly traceable to the events of the Early American Republic, or is the symmetry between nineteenth- and twentieth/twenty-first-century constitutional thinking coincidental?

The symmetry, I will argue, is not coincidental. Evidence suggests a real (but heretofore unrecognized) connection between the Compromise of 1816 and modern invocations of the Coinage Clause, with the Supreme Court's Reconstruction-era jurisprudence serving as the crucial link in this constitutional chain. The justices ruled in *Knox v. Lee* (1871) that Congress was empowered to require creditors to accept Treasury notes (which were not redeemable on demand in specie) in the payment of debts. The majority opinion in *Knox* did not rest upon the Coinage Clause, but it did stress that the provision could only be fairly construed as supporting the case for blanket congressional power over money.[5] Most importantly for my purposes, the argument on this point appears to invoke at least two distinct claims from the 1816 national bank debate.

.   To establish *Knox*'s connection to the debates of the 1810s, however, is to complete but half of the constitutional chain. The other half comes from establishing the role of that case (and its Coinage Clause commentary) in defending the Federal Reserve. On this point, federal judges and lawmakers have frequently suggested that *Knox* offers *doctrinal* support for congressional authority to establish the Fed (and more broadly, to make choices about money). It is also the case that a broader set of actors have pointed to the Coinage Clause as *textual* support for the Federal Reserve. Because these invocations of the power to "coin Money" represent attempts to reduce *Knox* to a clause-based argument (for they have no other obvious source), they are faulty: The justices (as noted above) *declined* to rest upon that provision. Nevertheless, whether by way of direct citation or an erroneously derivative textual claim, the Court's decision in *Knox* has been repeatedly deployed to justify our contemporary monetary system.

While this skeletal account of the connection between the Compromise of 1816 and constitutional claims on behalf of the Federal Reserve (and the more comprehensive version offered below) rests in part upon inferences from limited evidence, there are two important reasons to offer it here. First, published material on post-1789 development[6] in the meaning of the Coinage Clause is in rather short supply, and that which exists either (1) takes no notice of arguments from the mid-1810s[7] or (2) briefly acknowledges them but assumes that they had no bearing on subsequent episodes (e.g., *Knox*).[8] As such, any evidence suggesting that the first instance of significant executive and legislative commentary on the meaning of the power to "coin Money" influenced the first instance of significant judicial commentary on the same (and ultimately constitutional claims about contemporary arrangements) would represent a nontrivial contribution to this literature.

The second reason is arguably a broader version of the first. Practitioners of American Political Development (APD) have largely eschewed studies of the Early American Republic in favor of work on the post-1865 period.[9] Those who pursue projects focused on the antebellum era informally face the challenge (rightly or wrongly) of explaining how their work helps us better understand *modern* political behavior and institutional arrangements. The challenge implies that notwithstanding the field's announced ahistorical commitment to explaining both "individual cases of political development" and "patterns of development in the polity as a whole,"[10] there seems to be an expectation that APD scholars will always (irrespective of their project's formal cutoff date) seek to render the present day their real end point. My effort to establish that arguments on behalf of the Federal Reserve have roots running to the constitutional politics of the 1810s both recognizes this challenge and labors to meet it.

This book does not simply conclude, however, with an effort to buttress the constitutional résumé of the Compromise of 1816 by suggesting that we are banking on it even today. Taken as a whole (i.e., as a single, complex case of American constitutional development), the national bank controversy reinforces and refines the idea that such development routinely owes as much to the messy interplay of forces typically associated with "politics"—long-simmering ideological tensions within a governing majority, short but acute episodes of economic stress, and gradual but significant change both within institutions and to institutional landscapes— as to those that fall under the heading of "law" (e.g., the text of the Constitution, or evidence respecting the intent of the founding generation, or precedents established by the Supreme Court). In simpler terms, the story of the Bank between 1791 and 1832 *also* speaks to APD's aforementioned ahistorical search for general developmental propositions. Accordingly, after addressing what might be called the "historical" import of this antebellum account of constitutional development—its relevance for understanding modern American politics—I make a final analytic turn toward its ahistorical lessons (and the specific line of research that they invite students of APD-themed public law to pursue).

THE SUPREME COURT AND LEGAL TENDER, 1870–1871

With respect to Congress's authority (or lack thereof) to charter a national bank, the first post-1832 juncture with long-term significance was actually not President John Tyler's decision to veto two bank bills in 1841 on constitutional grounds; the messages accompanying those vetoes did little more (in terms of shaping future debate over the institution's status) than quickly retire the argument that Congress could charter a national bank in Washington, DC, pursuant to its Article I, Section 8 power to govern the capital "in all Cases whatsoever[.]"[11] That juncture came, by contrast, during (and more importantly, in the early years after) the Civil War.

The question of interest here involved not Congress's authority to charter a national bank but rather its authority to compel the receipt of Treasury notes as a legal tender. If Madison's Treasury Department had trouble funding the War of 1812, it was nothing compared to the difficulties that Lincoln's would experience during the early days of the Civil War. In late 1861, Treasury Secretary Salmon Chase offered the Thirty-Seventh Congress a grim take on the nation's finances; he reported that estimated federal expenditures outpaced estimated federal revenues by a *ten-to-one* margin ($532 million versus $55 million).[12] Unable to close this gap through borrowing from state banks and private parties at favorable interest rates,[13] Congress passed a stopgap measure that authorized Secretary Chase to issue $50 million in Treasury notes—paper money that was not redeemable upon demand in gold and silver coin—and made such notes a legal tender in the payment of all public and private debts.[14] Abraham Lincoln signed the Legal Tender Act in February 1862.

The Supreme Court heard a challenge to the constitutionality of the Legal Tender Act in 1869. In June 1860, nearly two years before the law was enacted, Susan Hepburn had agreed in writing to pay Henry Griswold 11,250 "dollars" by a specified date in 1862. That date came and went without payment from Hepburn. In 1864, Griswold brought suit in Louisville's Chancery Court to enforce the terms of their written agreement. That court judged Hepburn's debt to Griswold satisfied after she paid the principal owed (plus interest accrued) with Treasury notes. Griswold, whose contract with Hepburn had been made at a time when the word *dollars* unquestionably meant gold and silver coin (or paper money redeemable in the same), refused to accept this resolution of his suit. Appealing the judgment to Kentucky's Court of Errors (then the state's supreme court), Griswold argued that the Legal Tender Act was unconstitutional as applied to contracts made *before* its enactment. In essence, he claimed that the Chancery Court had erred in accepting anything other than specie (or its equivalent) for the purpose of satisfying Hepburn's debt. After the state supreme court accepted this argument and reversed the Chancery Court's judgment, Hepburn appealed its decision to the US Supreme Court.[15]

The early fiscal demands of the Civil War had rendered Secretary Chase—a longtime defender of bank paper redeemable in specie—a reluctant advocate of both issuing Treasury notes and giving them status as legal tender.[16] By the time the Court decided *Hepburn v. Griswold* (1870), however, the war was over and Salmon Chase occupied a very different role in the federal government: chief justice of the United States. He authored the Court's opinion in *Hepburn*, which declared (consistent with the Kentucky Court of Errors conclusion) that the Legal Tender Act was unconstitutional as applied to "debts previously contracted[.]"[17] In simpler terms, as a peacetime chief justice, Chase worked to roll back the programs he had endorsed as a wartime Treasury secretary.

Writing for himself and at least three other justices,[18] Chase offered four basic claims in *Hepburn*. First, making Treasury notes legal tender was not incident to Congress's power to "coin Money, regulate the Value thereof[.]" For Chase, that provision only empowered Congress "to determine the weight, purity, form, impression, and denomination of the several coins" to be used in exchange nationwide.[19] Second, it was not especially clear what other enumerated power the legal tender provision might be "necessary" for exercising. In this vein, the chief justice argued at length that it would not facilitate the exercise of Congress's power to "declare War." Giving Treasury notes status as legal tender might offer the federal government more money in nominal terms to purchase war-related goods and services, but that benefit would be offset by a rise in nominal prices (because the notes would increase the overall money supply).[20]

Third, even if the legal tender provision *was* incident to one or more enumerated powers, that fact was not sufficient to establish its constitutionality as applied to existing debts. On this point, Chase began by invoking Chief Justice John Marshall's famous claim from *McCulloch v. Maryland* (1819): "Let the end be legitimate, let it be within the scope of the constitution, and all means which are appropriate, which are plainly adapted to that end, which are not prohibited, but consist with the letter and spirit of the constitution, are constitutional."[21] On the strength of this argument, Chase asserted that the legal tender provision was inconsistent with the *spirit* of the Constitution. Even though states alone were expressly prohibited from "impairing the Obligation of Contracts"[22]— an outcome that Griswold's forced receipt of Treasury notes would produce—the chief justice thought it "clear that those who framed and those who adopted the Constitution intended that the spirit of this prohibition should pervade the *entire body of legislation*[.]"[23] No supporting evidence was offered by Chase on this point. Perhaps recognizing the weakness of this argument, the chief justice offered his fourth and final claim: The legal tender provision was also inconsistent with the *letter* of the Constitution; the Fifth Amendment forbade the federal government from depriving persons of "life, liberty, or property, without due process of law[.]"[24] For Chase, the Due Process Clause could not "have its full and intended effect unless construed as a direct prohibition of the legislation which we have been considering."[25]

Hepburn had a remarkably short shelf life, a fact attributable to change in the size and composition of the Court in the late 1860s and early 1870s. In 1866, the Republican-controlled Thirty-Ninth Congress passed (and Democratic president Andrew Johnson signed) legislation that would gradually reduce the Court's membership; the next three vacancies on the ten-member bench would *not* be filled.[26] The Judiciary Act of 1866 immediately reduced the Court's membership to nine, as the seat opened by Justice John Catron's death the previous May was simply eliminated. That number slipped to eight in 1867 with the death of Justice James Wayne.[27] Two years later, in April 1869, the Republican-controlled Forty-First Congress engaged in a broad reorganization of the federal judiciary. Among other things, the Judiciary Act of that year—signed in mid-April by the new Republican president, Ulysses S. Grant—pushed the Court's membership back up to nine, effective in December.[28] The new seat had not been filled as of late January 1870,[29] when Justice Robert Grier retired from the bench. This left the president with not one but two Court vacancies. On February 7, he nominated Republicans William Strong and Joseph Bradley for these seats. On the very same day, Chief Justice Chase announced the Court's 5–3 decision in *Hepburn*; the now-departed Justice Grier had been part of the majority.[30] Because both Strong and Bradley were understood to view the legal tender provision as constitutional (even as applied to "debts previously contracted"), the *Hepburn* decision was essentially ripe for reconsideration from the moment of its announcement.[31]

The Court's reconsideration of *Hepburn* came just one year later, in *Knox v. Lee* (1871). In March 1863, Confederate officials had confiscated livestock in Texas owned by Phoebe Lee, a loyal citizen of the Union then residing in Pennsylvania. Her animals had subsequently been sold to William B. Knox.[32] At the war's conclusion, Lee brought suit against Knox in federal court for damages. As Jerre Williams has noted, there was no real question at the trial that the Confederacy's confiscation had been "improper, and that the defendant [Knox] was liable. The only issue was whether the defendant could discharge" his impending obligation by paying Lee in Treasury notes.[33] The trial judge, convinced that Knox could do this, admonished the jury to "recollect that whatever amount they may give by their verdict can be discharged by the payment of such amount in legal tender notes of the United States."[34] In essence, they were all but openly invited to award Lee a higher nominal amount on the premise that specie traded at a premium to Treasury notes. Knox responded to the jury's ensuing award of damages by filing a writ of error with the Supreme Court, arguing that the trial judge erred in implying that Treasury notes were not equal to specie (i.e., the nominal award should have been lower).[35] The nine justices heard argument in *Knox* in February 1871 and issued their decision on the first of May.

That decision offered a ringing vindication of the Legal Tender Act's constitutionality. Court newcomer William Strong authored the majority opinion, writing for himself, the three dissenters in *Hepburn*, and Joseph Bradley (the other recent Grant appointee). Strong and his colleagues, technically speaking, need not have overruled *Hepburn* in deciding *Knox*; because Knox's debt to Lee was incurred *after* passage of the Legal Tender Act, the Court might have simply distinguished the two cases.[36] Strong, however, wrote that *Hepburn*'s holding was ripe for reassessment in *Knox* because the case had been decided without the benefit of a full Court. Consequently, his majority opinion declared the act "constitutional as applied to contracts made either before or after [its] passage."[37]

For my purposes here, the crucial part of *Knox* is Justice Strong's lengthy discussion of the Coinage Clause. In *Hepburn*, Chief Justice Chase had categorically rejected a claim that the provision empowered Congress to assign Treasury notes the quality of legal tender. In *Knox*, by contrast, Strong merely declined to "rest [his] assertion" about legislative authority on the power to "coin Money, regulate the Value thereof[.]"[38] This decision did not, however, amount to an outright rejection of the clause as a basis for congressional action. This fact is crucial, as I explain below, for understanding twentieth- and twenty-first-century claims about the constitutionality of the Federal Reserve.

Strong's opinion offered a direct response to Chase's claim from *Hepburn* respecting the absolute irrelevance of the Coinage Clause to the legal tender controversy. The chief justice and others, he recalled, had argued that "the clause which conferred upon Congress power 'to coin money, regulate the value thereof, and of foreign coin,' contains an implication that nothing but that which is the subject of coinage, nothing but the precious metals can ever be declared by law to be money, or to have the uses of money."[39] Strong made it clear that he was not comfortable with the idea that the Coinage Clause precluded any monetary activity beyond giving value to certain weights of specie. In defense of a broader understanding of congressional power, he wrote that "[s]o far from . . . containing a lurking prohibition, many have thought that [the clause] was intended to confer upon Congress that general power over the currency which has always been an acknowledged attribute of sovereignty in every other civilized nation than our own."[40]

I want to carefully draw out what might be called the *past, present,* and *future* dimensions of Strong's commentary. With respect to the *past,* at no point does he identify the source for this claim respecting the intent behind the Coinage Clause. In this vein, there is no footnote attached to his "many have thought" language; it appears to represent a naked assertion. The omission of supporting evidence, however, does not necessarily mean that Strong was incorrect. In fact, there is evidence that an older generation of constitutional thinkers conceived of the clause in *precisely* these terms—evidence furnished by the national bank debate of 1816.

In short, Justice Strong's language in *Knox* appears to splice the constitutional arguments offered by John C. Calhoun and Henry Clay during floor debate over the postwar national bank bill. Representative Calhoun, who chaired the House Select Committee that reported the bill and then proceeded to open floor debate on it, explained the prevailing state of monetary affairs to his colleagues in the Fourteenth Congress. Due to the refusal of state banks outside of New England to resume specie payments for their notes and checks, Americans had "in lieu of gold and silver, a paper medium, unequally but generally depreciated[.]" The state banks, in other words, were effectively "regulat[ing] the currency of the United States"—a reality that Calhoun considered "opposed to the principles of the federal constitution." There was no doubt, he added by way of explanation, that the "money of the United States was intended to be placed entirely under the control of Congress" via the Coinage Clause.[41] Just over a week after Calhoun's debate-opening speech, Speaker Henry Clay offered his (in)famous about-face on the national bank question. For his part, Clay agreed with the notion that the effective power of state banks notwithstanding, "the subject of the general currency was intended to be submitted exclusively to the General Government."[42] There is no definitive proof that Justice Strong had either John C. Calhoun or Henry Clay in mind fifty-five years later when he wrote that "many have thought that [the Coinage Clause] was intended to confer upon Congress [a] general power over the currency[.]" However, the remarks of Calhoun and Clay certainly represent a possible source for Strong's claim.

The case for connecting Strong's commentary to the 1816 national bank debate is only strengthened when the second half of his statement is considered—the idea that "general power over the currency has always been an acknowledged attribute of sovereignty in every other civilized nation than our own." Henry Clay's speech had spoken to this point as well; the House Speaker had observed that the state banks were currently, "in fact, exercising, what had been considered at all times, and in all countries, one of the highest attributes of sovereignty—the regulation of the current medium of the country."[43]

Not only did Justice Strong employ language consistent with that used in February and March 1816, but the range of alternative sources for his claim appears to be quite narrow. In fact, there is no evidence of significant debate—in Congress or federal courts—over the meaning of the Coinage Clause in advance of the Civil War *outside* the national bank controversy.[44] In all likelihood, then, the "many" to whom Strong referred were early federal lawmakers looking to leverage the national bank's functional evolution into a narrow case for its constitutionality. On the whole, Richard Timberlake probably erred when he wrote that claims respecting the Coinage Clause in the mid-1810s "*anticipated* like remarks from some Supreme Court justices fifty years later" in *Knox*.[45] Rather than anticipating Justice Strong's language, there is a good argument to be made that the words of Calhoun, Clay, and others *inspired* it.

As for the *present* dimension of Strong's Coinage Clause commentary, the justice made it clear that despite the existence of expansive thinking about the provision's meaning, the Court's conclusion in *Knox* was *not* built upon the power to "coin Money, regulate the Value thereof[.]" Having laid out what "many have thought" respecting the Coinage Clause, he volunteered that "[w]e do not, however, rest our assertion of the power of Congress to enact legal tender laws upon this grant. We assert only that the grant can, in no just sense, be regarded as containing an implied prohibition against their enactment, and that, if it raises any implications, they are of complete power over the currency, rather than restraining."[46]

Where, then, did Justice Strong rest the Court's assertion respecting congressional power? In other words, which enumerated power was being exercised when Congress assigned Treasury notes the quality of legal tender? In principle, the justice did not have a single answer to this question. He appeared to rest, as the Court would later note in *Norman v. Baltimore & Ohio Railroad Co.* (1935), on the "*aggregate* of the powers granted to the Congress[.]"[47] Strong understood those powers, which included, but were not limited to, "the power to levy and collect taxes, to coin money and regulate its value, to raise and support armies, [and] to provide for and maintain a navy," as means or "instruments" for accomplishing the Constitution's "paramount object": the establishment of "a government, sovereign within its sphere, with [the] capability of self-preservation, thereby forming a union more perfect than that which existed under the old Confederacy."[48] Given that premise, a legal tender provision adopted in the midst of a civil war was a "necessary and proper means" for achieving the Constitution's "ultimate end[.]"[49]

KNOX TODAY: THE FEDERAL RESERVE
AND THE COINAGE CLAUSE

This leaves the *future* dimension of Justice Strong's commentary in *Knox*. The Court's decisions in *Knox* and *Juilliard v. Greenman*[50]—the 1884 case that upheld the issuance of legal tender Treasury notes in peacetime—have been construed as doctrinal support for Congress's creation of the Federal Reserve.[51] Strong, as already noted, refused to ground *Knox* in the Coinage Clause alone. Justice Horace Gray displayed a similar reluctance in *Juilliard*, resting his opinion for the Court jointly upon Congress's powers to "borrow Money on the credit of the United States" and "coin Money, regulate the Value thereof[.]"[52] *Despite* this clear unwillingness to employ the Coinage Clause alone, the Court's legal tender precedents have repeatedly been reduced to a textual claim that the power to coin money authorizes the Federal Reserve.

This account of the Fed's constitutionality has prevailed, both in and out of the federal government, since at least the early 1970s. In 1973, for example, University of California, Berkeley professor Sherman Maisel—who had recently completed a seven-year stint as a Federal Reserve governor—wrote that Congress had "delegated its constitutional power to coin money and control its value to the Federal Reserve through the Federal Reserve Act of 1913[.]"[53] That same year, an official at the Federal Reserve Bank of New York similarly suggested that the Federal Reserve System as a whole derived its power "from the Congress, which has been given the power by the Constitution to 'coin money [and] regulate the value thereof[.]'"[54] Two years later, the Ninety-Fourth Congress cited the Coinage Clause in adopting House Concurrent Resolution 133, which instructed the Fed to use monetary policy to improve economic conditions nationwide.[55] A decade following passage of this resolution, a report from the Congressional Budget Office noted that Congress had the authority "to coin Money, regulate the Value thereof," but had "delegated this power in the main to the Federal Reserve."[56] In the early 1990s, the third edition of a popular textbook on interbranch budgetary politics noted that this power, "which critically affects the budget, was transferred by Congress to the Federal Reserve System in 1913[.]"[57]

This line of constitutional thought continues to prevail in the early twenty-first century, especially among students of American fiscal and monetary politics. Bob Woodward noted in his chronicle of Alan Greenspan's tenure as Fed chairman that "the power to coin money and set its value" belongs to Congress but has been "delegated to the Federal Reserve."[58] Around the same time, a study of congressional delegation in budgetary affairs suggested that "the power to coin and regulate the value of money was transferred" in 1913 by the Sixty-Third Congress "to the new Federal Reserve System."[59] Other recent scholarship fails to speak in terms of congressional delegation but nonetheless affirms that Congress exercised its power under the Coinage Clause in creating the Federal Reserve System.[60]

Perhaps the most prominent recent invocation of the Coinage Clause on behalf of the Fed came in the midst of the September 2008 stock market meltdown. Ben Bernanke, then serving as Fed chairman, was testifying before the Joint Economic Committee of the 110th Congress.[61] That committee included Representative Ron Paul (R-TX), a longtime critic of the Federal Reserve on both constitutional and policy grounds.[62] Paul's questioning of Bernanke that day began with the former invoking a Bush administration proposal—subsequently adopted by Congress and signed by the president[63]—that called for the Treasury Department to purchase up to $700 billion in illiquid mortgage-backed securities. Paul neither envisioned a program of this sort being funded through new domestic taxes nor believed that investors would purchase $700 billion in new federal bonds. He expressed concern that the Treasury Department would ultimately ask the Fed to purchase the bonds—that is, to "monetize" the new debt. In a situation like that, Paul told Bernanke, "I don't even know where you get the authority to create credit out of thin air. There is certainly no authority in the Constitution[.]"[64] When given the opportunity to respond, Bernanke denied Paul's factual premise—"[t]here is no need for the Federal Reserve to monetize any of this borrowing"—but nonetheless defended his institution's authority to purchase federal bonds: "[O]f course the Constitution gives the Congress the right to coin money and regulate the value thereof . . . [a]nd that authority has been delegated to the Federal Reserve through the Federal Reserve Act[.]"[65]

My objective here is not to criticize modern scholars and public officials for implicitly (but wrongly) treating the Court decisions on which the Federal Reserve "depend[s] for its legitimacy"[66] as resting upon the Coinage Clause alone. Rather, it is simply to appreciate the implications of doing so. Though mentioned in *Juilliard* (1884), post–Civil War defenses of the power to "coin Money, regulate the Value thereof" as a basis for congressional monetary activity really began thirteen years earlier, with Justice Strong's *Knox* (1871) opinion. There is a very good chance, in turn, that Strong's opinion drew from arguments offered in the 1816 debate over reviving the Bank of the United States. Although the constitutional line from the mid-1810s to the twenty-first century can hardly be called straight, there is reason to believe that the roots for modern claims respecting the Federal Reserve run all the way to the Early American Republic.

AMERICAN CONSTITUTIONAL DEVELOPMENT: BRINGING "ECONOMIC FACTS" BACK IN

If producing a revisionist account of the Bank controversy between 1791 and 1832 is akin to dropping a stone into the normally placid waters of early American constitutional history, then tracing the post-1832 story of the Compromise of 1816 is analogous to tracking the stone's ripple effects out toward more recent events. We can also consider how the evolution of this particular constitutional quarrel squares with broader claims about how constitutional development unfolds—in essence, to compare and contrast one stone with others that have been periodically dropped into the waters of our constitutional history. While the general developmental propositions that flow from this study are certainly worthy of appreciation (and earn it here), I will also argue that students of public law can benefit from thinking critically about why a revisionist history of the Bank drama was necessary in the first place.

Taken as a whole, my rendering of the protracted antebellum struggle over a national bank confirms anew that forces we tend to associate with the everyday vicissitudes of politics exert a powerful influence on American constitutional development. Far from periodically reproducing (as conventional wisdom would have it) a two-sided debate over the appropriate interpretation of the Necessary and Proper Clause, the struggle over the Bank's constitutional status was dynamic, and owed much of that dynamism to shifting combinations of slow-moving change in the institution (both the erosion of its industry dominance and the development of its regulatory function vis-à-vis state-chartered peers), ideological strife between moderate or nationalist Republicans and their more conservative peers, and the abrupt arrival of inflation in much of the nation during the War of 1812. In short, the constitutional controversy over a national bank not only changed over time, but it did so in large part on the basis of forces having little to do with law.

My account does more, however, than simply confirm anew the importance of ordinary politics to American constitutional development. It also helps to refine and develop more specific propositions about how the former drives the latter. Republicans in control of both Congress and the White House, for example, elected to forgo another round of debate over a national bank's constitutional necessity in the mid-1810s in favor of justifying the institution with reference to the Coinage Clause. Their employment of the power to coin money as a kind of constitutional heresthetic—a device for effectively narrowing the range of federal activity sanctioned by the national bank bill to the bank *alone*, in order to build intraparty support for it[67]—tells us that divided regimes do more than simply invite courts to resolve divisive questions; they also forge their own internal compromises.

Reconstructing the National Bank Controversy also refines our understanding of the forces at work in American constitutional development in two other ways. First, it confirms—perhaps unsurprisingly, but no less importantly on that account—that economic forces shape our constitutional politics at both crucial *and* less-than-crucial historical junctures. While conditions in (or transformations of) the American economy are understood to have influenced constitutional decision-making in several periods of cardinal importance—the Founding, Reconstruction, and the New Deal crisis—the Bank's history suggests that inflation south and west of New England led to a novel (and narrow) understanding of congressional power in the period following the War of 1812. Second, the account offered here furnishes two distinct sets of evidence suggesting that gradual change in the underlying object of constitutional controversy can alter the terms of future debate over that object. Not only did the slow erosion of the Bank's industry dominance between 1791 and 1811 lead recharter opponents to prioritize a particular argument respecting constitutional necessity in 1811, but the institution's equally slow acquisition of regulatory power during those same years laid the functional foundation for Republicans' Coinage Clause argument in 1816.

Beyond confirming the importance of ordinary politics to the development of American constitutionalism, and refining more specific propositions about the influence of those politics, this book offers one final—and hopefully rather provocative—lesson for students of public law. That lesson flows from one of the principal reasons a revisionist narrative was necessary in the first place: the failure of past students of this constitutional controversy to make and apply the basic distinction between *fiscal* and *monetary* phenomena. The Bank of the United States tends to be treated by constitutional scholars as an unchanging institution between 1791 and 1832; on this account, it was born and remained a *fiscal* auxiliary to the federal government. What this omits, as should now be clear, is both the first Bank's development of a *monetary* function and the manner in which that development facilitated the institution's postwar rebirth on novel constitutional terms. Similarly, those same scholars tend to treat the federal government's *fiscal* difficulties during the War of 1812 as the policy problem that inspired the Bank's revival. As should now be equally clear, this account confuses federal lawmakers' wartime quandary with their peacetime plight; it was the imperative to restore *monetary* order (in the form of nationwide specie payments) after February 1815 that led Republicans to both consider a national bank bill and explain its constitutionality as they did.

Writing in 1982, Kenneth Dam sought to explain the "disappear[ance]" of *Knox* and the other Legal Tender Cases from treatises and casebooks on constitutional law.[68] He argued that they had become "remote to the modern constitutional law mind simply because of a lack of knowledge of the necessary economic facts."[69] I am suggesting something analogous with respect to the controversy over the Bank of the United States: that the conventional wisdom surrounding it has endured at least in part because of a lack of knowledge of the necessary economic facts.

The question, of course, is whether ignorance of important economic facts extends *beyond* scholarship on the Bank controversy, to the broader study of constitutional development since 1789. On the one hand, I have no direct evidence that this problem afflicts other lines of work in APD-themed public law; it can only be discovered (as it was here) when a conventional narrative of constitutional development is interrogated and found wanting. On the other hand, at least one proxy for knowledge of economic facts—developmental work on the Constitution's manifestly economic provisions—invites us, I think, to approach the question with an open mind. While there is no shortage of historically oriented work on some textual provisions with obvious economic import—the Commerce Clause,[70] the (*Lochner*-era) Due Process Clause,[71] and the Contract Clause[72] immediately spring to mind—others have been given comparatively short shrift. These include a number of Congress's fiscal and monetary powers under Article I: laying and collecting taxes, borrowing money, establishing uniform bankruptcy laws, and (as already noted) coining money. While the title and subtitle of Bill White's 2014 tome—*America's Fiscal Constitution: Its Triumph and Collapse*—appear to promise a partial solution to this problem, the book is less a study of how Congress's fiscal powers have evolved and more an argument that until the dawn of the twenty-first century, the United States had an unwritten fiscal constitution that limited use of the borrowing power to specific circumstances.[73]

It is far from clear why these clauses have largely escaped the analytic gaze of scholars interested in American constitutional development. They are surely implicated in matters of substantive importance for American politics today: Obamacare was ultimately upheld as an exercise of the power to lay and collect taxes, recent debt-ceiling crises have invited debate over which branch(es) get(s) to borrow money,[74] and the Coinage Clause is trotted out whenever institutional critics inquire into the Federal Reserve's constitutional foundations. It could be—and I am only speculating here—that the study of these clauses is perceived as requiring greater and more specialized background knowledge than the study of many others; on this account, students of American constitutional development have collectively opted for paths of less resistance. Ultimately, however, the actual reason for our avoidance of certain provisions that require command of economic facts is less important than simply acknowledging this state of scholarly affairs and working to rectify it going forward.

NOTES

INTRODUCTION

1. Howard Gillman, Mark Graber, and Keith Whittington, *American Constitutionalism*, vol. 1, *Structures of Government* (New York: Oxford University Press, 2013), 122.

2. Sandra F. VanBurkleo, "'The Paws of Banks': The Origins and Significance of Kentucky's Decision to Tax Federal Bankers, 1818–1820," *Journal of the Early Republic* 9, no. 4 (Winter 1989): 457–87 at 457.

3. For scholarship that takes an interest in the production of constitutional narratives, see Pamela Brandwein, *Reconstructing Reconstruction: The Supreme Court and the Production of Historical Truth* (Durham, NC: Duke University Press, 1999).

4. For an early use of this nickname for the Necessary and Proper Clause, see Joseph M. Lynch, *Negotiating the Constitution: The Earliest Debates over Original Intent* (Ithaca, NY: Cornell University Press, 1999), 43 (quoting James Madison at the Virginia ratifying convention in June 1788).

5. Brandwein, *Reconstructing Reconstruction*, 15.

6. The helpful conceit of "central arguments" is borrowed from Emily Zackin, *Looking for Rights in All the Wrong Places: Why State Constitutions Contain America's Positive Rights* (Princeton, NJ: Princeton University Press, 2013), 11–13.

7. H. M. Collins, *Changing Order: Replication and Induction in Scientific Practice* (Chicago: University of Chicago Press, 1985), 6.

8. Bray Hammond, *Banks and Politics in America: From the Revolution to the Civil War* (Princeton, NJ: Princeton University Press, 1957), 214.

9. Charles L. Black Jr., *Structure and Relationship in Constitutional Law* (Woodbridge, CT: Ox Bow Press, 1985), 13–15.

10. *McCulloch v. Maryland*, 17 US 316 (1819), at 424.

11. An argument couched in the language of institutions, ideology, and economics is an argument in need of some preliminary term definition. By *institutions* or *institutional change*, I mean two dimensions of the national bank: its size relative to the American banking industry as a whole and its services to the federal government and the public at large. By *ideology* or *ideological conflict*, I mean both the party in

control of Congress and the degree of internal cohesion over the legitimate scope of federal power. And by *economics* or *economic stress,* I mean the year-over-year stability of prices for basic goods and services as measured in bank notes or checks (as opposed to gold or silver coin).

12. Karen Orren and Stephen Skowronek would characterize them as discrete "orders" in American politics. Orren and Skowronek, "Institutions and Intercurrence: Theory Building in the Fullness of Time," in *NOMOS 38: Political Order,* ed. Ian Shapiro and Russell Hardin (New York: New York University Press, 1996), 111–46 at 113.

13. The logic of this approach aligns generally with that recommended by Rogers M. Smith in "Political Jurisprudence, the 'New Institutionalism,' and the Future of Public Law," *American Political Science Review* 82, no. 1 (March 1988): 89–108 at 101–3.

14. The David-Solar consumer price index, with a base value of 100, stood at 106 in 1789, 110 in 1790, and 113 in 1791. See Peter H. Lindert and Richard Sutch, "Consumer Price Indexes, for All Items: 1774–2003," Table Cc1-2 in *Historical Statistics of the United States: Millennial Edition Online,* ed. Susan B. Carter et al. (Cambridge, UK: Cambridge University Press, 2006), http://hsus.cambridge.org/HSUSWeb/ HSUSEntryServlet.

15. Joseph Van Fenstermaker, *The Development of American Commercial Banking: 1782–1837* (Kent, OH: Bureau of Economic and Business Research, 1965), 136, 139, and 169; see also Hammond, *Banks and Politics in America,* 65–66.

16. Ron Chernow, *Alexander Hamilton* (New York: Penguin, 2004), 349; William Nisbet Chambers, *Political Parties in a New Nation: The American Experience, 1776–1809* (New York: Oxford University Press, 1963), 39.

17. Richard E. Ellis, *The Jeffersonian Crisis: Courts and Politics in the Young Republic* (New York: W. W. Norton, 1971), esp. at 19 ("[T]he most striking fact about the Republican party after 1800 is the rapidity with which it began to divide into factions").

18. Fenstermaker, *The Development of American Commercial Banking,* 111.

19. Donald R. Hickey, *The War of 1812: A Forgotten Conflict* (Urbana: University of Illinois Press, 1989), 225.

20. Edwin J. Perkins, *American Public Finance and Financial Services, 1700–1815* (Columbus: Ohio State University Press, 1994), 341–42.

21. Susan Hoffmann, *Politics and Banking: Ideas, Public Policy, and the Creation of Financial Institutions* (Baltimore: Johns Hopkins University Press, 2001), 41.

22. Yonatan Eyal, *The Young America Movement and the Transformation of the Democratic Party, 1828–1861* (Cambridge, UK: Cambridge University Press, 2007), 22–23.

23. Gillman, Graber, and Whittington, *American Constitutionalism,* vol. 1, 123.

24. Stephen Skowronek, *The Politics Presidents Make: Leadership from John Adams to Bill Clinton* (Cambridge, MA: Belknap Press of Harvard University Press, 1997), 197.

25. Justin J. Wert, *Habeas Corpus in America: The Politics of Individual Rights* (Lawrence: University Press of Kansas, 2011), 3. On "regime politics" generally, see Robert A. Dahl, "Decision-Making in a Democracy: The Supreme Court as a National Policy-Maker," *Journal of Public Law* 6, no. 2 (Fall 1957): 279–95; Cornell Clayton and David May, "A Political Regimes Approach to the Analysis of Legal Decisions," *Polity*

32, no. 2 (Winter 1999): 233–52; Howard Gillman, "Courts and the Politics of Partisan Coalitions," in *The Oxford Handbook of Law and Politics*, ed. Keith Whittington, R. Daniel Keleman, and Gregory Caldeira (New York: Oxford University Press, 2008), 644–62.

26. Keith Whittington, *Political Foundations of Judicial Supremacy: The Presidency, the Supreme Court, and Constitutional Leadership in U.S. History* (Princeton, NJ: Princeton University Press, 2007), 125–34, esp. at 125; Mark A. Graber, "The Nonmajoritarian Difficulty: Legislative Deference to the Judiciary," *Studies in American Political Development* 7, no. 1 (Spring 1993): 35–73, esp. at 36.

27. David Brian Robertson, *The Constitution and America's Destiny* (Cambridge, UK: Cambridge University Press, 2005), 58ff.

28. Robert G. McCloskey, *The American Supreme Court*, 5th ed., rev. Sanford Levinson (Chicago: University of Chicago Press, 2010), 296; see also Gerard N. Magliocca, *American Founding Son: John Bingham and the Invention of the Fourteenth Amendment* (New York: New York University Press, 2013), 191n1 (quoting Barry Friedman).

29. Roger L. Ransom, *Conflict and Compromise: The Political Economy of Slavery, Emancipation, and the American Civil War* (Cambridge, UK: Cambridge University Press, 1993), esp. at 9 ("Everyone concedes that slave labor was the cornerstone that supported the plantation economy of the antebellum period") and 11 ("[E]conomic interests alone cannot account for the coming of the Civil War. The politics of slavery are equally important to explain why North and South were willing to fight").

30. Howard Gillman, *The Constitution Besieged: The Rise and Demise of Lochner Era Police Powers Jurisprudence* (Durham, NC: Duke University Press, 1993), 10–11.

31. Bruce Ackerman, *We the People*, vol. 1, *Foundations* (Cambridge, MA: Belknap Press of Harvard University Press, 1991).

32. Wolfgang Streeck and Kathleen Thelen, "Introduction: Institutional Change in Advanced Political Economies," in *Beyond Continuity: Institutional Change in Advanced Political Economies*, ed. Wolfgang Streeck and Kathleen Thelen (New York: Oxford University Press, 2005), 1–39 at 1; see also James Mahoney and Kathleen Thelen, "A Theory of Gradual Institutional Change," in *Explaining Institutional Change: Ambiguity, Agency, and Power*, ed. James Mahoney and Kathleen Thelen (Cambridge, UK: Cambridge University Press, 2010), 1–37.

33. These terms are defined in Streeck and Thelen, "Introduction," 24–29.

34. Mark A. Graber, *A New Introduction to American Constitutionalism* (New York: Oxford University Press, 2013), xi.

35. Mark Kishlansky, *A Monarchy Transformed: Britain, 1603–1714* (New York: Penguin, 1996), xi.

CHAPTER ONE

1. Matthew St. Clair Clarke and David A. Hall, *Legislative and Documentary History of the Bank of the United States: Including the Original Bank of North America* (Washington, DC: Gales and Seaton, 1832), 36, 85, and 113.

2. Ibid., 86–94.

3. Ibid., 94.

4. Ibid.

5. Ibid., 95–112; David J. Cowen, *The Origins and Economic Impact of the First Bank of the United States, 1791–1797* (New York: Garland, 2000), esp. at 5ff. and 21; Ron Chernow, *Alexander Hamilton* (New York: Penguin, 2004), 352–53.

6. This was inspired by Cowen, *Origins and Economic Impact*, 21.

7. Other terms sometimes substitute for strict (e.g., *narrow*) and broad (e.g., *loose* or *liberal*), but the basic confrontation remains the same.

For invocations of this dichotomy among legal scholars and political scientists, see Sotirios A. Barber, *On What the Constitution Means* (Baltimore: Johns Hopkins University Press, 1984), 79; Murray Dry, "The Case Against Ratification: Anti-Federalist Constitutional Thought," in *The Framing and Ratification of the Constitution*, ed. Leonard W. Levy and Dennis J. Mahoney (New York: Macmillan, 1987), 271–91 at 289; Walter Dellinger and H. Jefferson Powell, "The Constitutionality of the Bank Bill: The Attorney General's First Constitutional Law Opinions," *Duke Law Journal* 44, no. 1 (October 1994): 110–33 at 112 and 119; Paul Brest, Sanford Levinson, Jack Balkin, and Akhil Reed Amar, "The Bank of the United States: A Case Study," in *Processes of Constitutional Decisionmaking: Cases and Materials*, 4th ed., ed. Brest, Levinson, Balkin, and Amar (New York: Aspen Law and Business, 2000), 7–70 at 11; Daniel A. Farber, "The Story of *McCulloch*: Banking on National Power," *Constitutional Commentary* 20, no. 3 (Winter 2003–2004): 679–714 at 687; Jesse H. Choper, Richard H. Fallon Jr., Yale Kamisar, and Steven H. Shiffrin, *Constitutional Law: Cases, Comments, Questions*, 10th ed. (St. Paul, MN: Thomson/West, 2006), 55–61 at 56; Howard Gillman, Mark Graber, and Keith Whittington, *American Constitutionalism*, vol. 1, *Structures of Government* (New York: Oxford University Press, 2013), 125; David M. O'Brien, *Constitutional Law and Politics*, vol. 1, *Struggles for Power and Governmental Accountability*, 9th ed. (New York: W. W. Norton, 2014), 546–48; Lee Epstein and Thomas G. Walker, *Constitutional Law for a Changing America: A Short Course*, 6th ed. (Thousand Oaks, CA: CQ Press, 2015), 105. I should also admit that in an early pass at the Bank controversy, I too adopted a version of the strict/broad dichotomy; see Eric Lomazoff, "Symmetry and Repetition: Patterns in the History of the Bank of the United States," in *Routledge Handbook of Major Events in Economic History*, ed. Randall E. Parker and Robert Whaples (New York: Routledge, 2013), 3–14 at 5.

Among historians, see John C. Miller, *The Federalist Era, 1789–1801* (New York: Harper & Row, 1960), 59; Kenneth R. Bowling, "The Bank Bill, the Capital City and President Washington," *Capitol Studies* 1, no. 1 (Spring 1972): 59–71 at 59; Stanley Elkins and Eric McKitrick, *The Age of Federalism: The Early American Republic, 1788–1800* (New York: Oxford University Press, 1993), 229 and 233; Jack N. Rakove, *Original Meanings: Politics and Ideas in the Making of the Constitution* (New York: Alfred A. Knopf, 1997), 355; Ron Chernow, *Alexander Hamilton* (New York: Penguin Books, 2004), 350, 352, and 353; Richard E. Ellis, *Aggressive Nationalism: McCulloch v. Maryland and the Foundation of Federal Authority in the Young Republic* (New York: Oxford University Press, 2007), 35; Gordon Wood, *Empire of Liberty: A History of the Early Republic, 1789–1815* (New York: Oxford University Press, 2009), 144; Thomas K. McCraw, *The Founders and Finance: How Hamilton, Gallatin, and Other Immigrants*

Forged a New Economy (Cambridge, MA: Belknap Press of Harvard University Press, 2012), 116 and 118.

8. For a broader critique of this dichotomy, see Walter F. Murphy, James E. Fleming, Sotirios A. Barber, and Stephen Macedo, *American Constitutional Interpretation*, 4th ed. (New York: Foundation Press, 2008), 451–52.

9. For scholarship that arguably gestures toward this variation (but certainly does not explore it at any length), see Joseph M. Lynch, *Negotiating the Constitution: The Earliest Debates over Original Intent* (Ithaca, NY: Cornell University Press, 1999), 80–82, and Gary Lawson, Geoffrey P. Miller, Robert G. Natelson, and Guy I. Seidman, *The Origins of the Necessary and Proper Clause* (Cambridge, UK: Cambridge University Press, 2010), 117–18.

10. David McCullough, *John Adams* (New York: Simon & Schuster, 2001), 404–8; see also Robert E. Wright, *One Nation under Debt: Hamilton, Jefferson, and the History of What We Owe* (New York: McGraw-Hill, 2008), 126.

11. 1 Stat. 24 (July 4, 1789): "Duties on Merchandise imported into the United States"; 1 Stat. 27 (July 20, 1789): "Duties on Tonnage."

12. "[I] flatter myself that I may confidently calculate upon the aid of the Bank of North America as one of the principal means by which I may be enabled to fulfill the public expectations." Hamilton to Thomas Willing, September 13, 1789, in *Papers of Alexander Hamilton* (hereafter *PAH*), ed. Harold Syrett et al. (New York: Columbia University Press, 1961–1987), vol. 5, 370–71 at 371.

13. Wood, *Empire of Liberty*, 95.

14. McCraw, *The Founders and Finance*, 94.

15. Ibid.; see also Cowen, *Origins and Economic Impact*, 11 (quoting Noah Webster from 1791 on the idea that "fifty millions of dollars in public paper" had recently been trading at "a sixth part of its value").

16. Alexander Hamilton, "Report on Public Credit," in *Alexander Hamilton: Writings* (hereafter *AH:W*), ed. Joanne B. Freeman (New York: Library of America, 2001), 531–74 at 533.

17. "[E]xigencies are to be expected to occur . . . in which there will be a necessity for borrowing." Ibid., 531.

18. William Bingham, a Philadelphia businessman, cautioned Hamilton in November 1789 that absent a clear congressional commitment to debt management, the federal government would face the "payment of an exorbitant Interest, whenever it is compelled to anticipate its revenue, by the Negotiation of domestic Loans." Bingham to Hamilton, November 25, 1789, reprinted in James O. Wettereau, "Letters from Two Business Men to Alexander Hamilton on Federal Fiscal Policy, November, 1789," *Journal of Economic and Business History* 3, no. 4 (August 1931): 667–86 at 674.

19. Introductory note to "Report Relative to a Provision for the Support of Public Credit," in *PAH*, vol. 6, 51–168 at 66n99.

20. Hamilton, "Report on Public Credit," 532, 537, and 540–41.

21. 1 Stat. 138 (4 August 1790): "An Act making provision for the Debt of the United States."

22. The most comprehensive accounts belong to Elkins and McKitrick, *The Age of Federalism*, 146–61; Wright, *One Nation under Debt*, 135–43; Charles A. Beard,

Economic Origins of Jeffersonian Democracy (New York: Free Press, 1915), 132–52. As Edwin J. Perkins has noted, how the impasse over the assumption of state debts was resolved—crucial Southern votes for it were acquired through a Northern promise to locate the permanent capital along the Potomac River—"ranks among the most famous backroom deals in the nation's history." Perkins, *American Public Finance and Financial Services, 1700–1815* (Columbus: Ohio State University Press, 1994), 223. For a detailed account of this episode, see Charles A. Cerami, *Dinner at Mr. Jefferson's: Three Men, Five Great Wines, and the Evening That Changed America* (New York: Wiley, 2009).

23. Hamilton, "Report on Public Credit," 534; Wright, *One Nation under Debt*, 135 and 144; Richard Sylla, Robert E. Wright, and David J. Cowen, "Alexander Hamilton, Central Banker: Crisis Management during the U.S. Financial Panic of 1792," *Business History Review* 83, special issue no. 1 (Spring 2009): 61–86 at 69–70.

24. Hamilton, "The Defence of the Funding System," July 1795, in *PAH*, vol. 19, 1–73 at 65.

25. Hamilton, "Second Report on the Further Provision Necessary for Establishing Public Credit," in *PAH*, vol. 7, 236.

26. Hamilton, "Report on a National Bank," in *AH:W*, 575=612 at 575.

27. Ibid.

28. Ibid., 604 and 608; Sylla, Wright, and Cowen, "Alexander Hamilton, Central Banker," 69.

29. Hamilton, "Report on a National Bank," 609; see also Susan Hoffmann, *Politics and Banking: Ideas, Public Policy, and the Creation of Financial Institutions* (Baltimore: Johns Hopkins University Press, 2001) at 34 ("Declaring [the federal bonds] acceptable payment for shares in the bank would strengthen [their] market further").

30. Sylla, Wright, and Cowen, "Alexander Hamilton, Central Banker," 69.

31. I emphasize the proposed institution's fiscal value here because a national bank qua *monetary* auxiliary is a major theme of subsequent chapters.

32. Richard H. Timberlake has emphasized, however, that the "*most important* [fiscal] function of the [national] bank was that of sustaining government credit." Timberlake, *Monetary Policy in the United States: An Intellectual and Institutional History* (Chicago: University of Chicago Press, 1993), 6 (emphasis added). The formal title of Hamilton's report, of course, does little to disparage this claim.

33. Hamilton, "Report on a National Bank," 575 (emphasis added).

34. Ibid., 576–80. In this vein, much of the material cited in note 7 speaks of the national bank as a fiscal auxiliary but only invokes one or more of these four functions; the institution's support of public credit goes unmentioned. For an example of this among legal scholars and political scientists, see Brest, Levinson, Balkin, and Amar, "The Bank of the United States," 8. Among historians, see Miller, *The Federalist Era*, 55.

35. Recitations of the action that escaped citation in note 7 (because they eschew the language of strict and broad interpretation) include Bray Hammond, *Banks and Politics in America: From the Revolution to the Civil War* (Princeton, NJ: Princeton University Press, 1957), 115–19; Benjamin B. Klubes, "The First Federal Congress and the First National Bank: A Case Study in Constitutional Interpretation," *Journal of the*

Early Republic 10, no. 1 (Spring 1990): 19–41; David P. Currie, *The Constitution in Congress: The Federalist Period, 1789–1801* (Chicago: University of Chicago Press, 1997), 78–80; Mark R. Killenbeck, *M'Culloch v. Maryland: Securing a Nation* (Lawrence: University Press of Kansas, 2006), 15–28.

36. For an argument that constitutional opposition in 1791 was rooted in lingering Southern anxiety respecting the location of the national capital, not sincere doubts over the scope of congressional power, see Bowling, "The Bank Bill," esp. at 59: "The emphasis on the constitutional aspects of the [bank] question has clouded our understanding of what actually happened."

37. The impending discussion of *federal* necessity should help to bring this claim into relief.

38. I use the term *federal* because antibank arguments of this sort (both in 1791 and 1811) frequently pointed to *state* alternatives to congressional action.

39. Lawson, Miller, Natelson, and Seidman, *The Origins of the Necessary and Proper Clause*, 118.

40. My ensuing review of antibank constitutional claims adopts what might be called a "compounding" assumption: If a member of the House or the executive branch separately invokes two or more standards of necessity in a single floor speech or memorandum, I use *and* as the conjunction joining those standards. In other words, I assume that bank opponents meant to make constitutional necessity as *difficult* to establish as possible.

41. The only known prior comment on the bank's constitutionality was a *private* one; the journal of Senator William Maclay of Pennsylvania included the following passage for December 24, 1790: "Yesterday [Secretary Hamilton's] report on the subject of a national bank was handed to us, and I can readily find that a bank will be the consequence . . . [t]he power of incorporating may be inquired into." Maclay, *The Journal of William Maclay: United States Senator from Pennsylvania, 1789–1791* (New York: Albert and Charles Boni, 1927), 345.

42. Clarke and Hall, *Legislative and Documentary History*, 37.

43. Ibid., 37–38. On the Bank of North America—the institution chartered in 1781—see Lawrence Lewis Jr., *A History of the Bank of North America* (Philadelphia: J. B. Lippincott, 1882) and especially George David Rappaport, *Stability and Change in Revolutionary Pennsylvania: Banking, Politics, and Social Structure* (University Park: Pennsylvania State University Press, 1996).

44. Clarke and Hall, *Legislative and Documentary History*, 39.

45. *Annals of Congress*, 1st Cong, 3rd Sess., 1944–1945.

46. Clarke and Hall, *Legislative and Documentary History*, 53. See also Theodore Sedgwick of Massachusetts, who clarified—in response to a contrary claim—that "he never conceived the authority [to charter] granted by the express words of the constitution[.]" Ibid., 70.

47. Moreover, at least three bank supporters—Hamilton, Laurance, and Fisher Ames of Massachusetts—suggested that it would facilitate the exercise of Congress's Article IV, Section 3 power "to dispose of and make all needful Rules and Regulations respecting the Territory or other Property belonging to the United States[.]" The Necessary and Proper Clause, after all, applies not simply to the seventeen "foregoing

Powers" in Article I, Section 8 but also to "all *other* Powers vested by this Constitution in the Government of the United States" (emphasis added). Hamilton's argument on this point was that "the money of the nation"—namely its tax revenue—constituted "Property belonging to the United States[,]" and a national bank was "necessary" for the management of that property. Ibid., 109.

48. Ibid., 72 (emphasis added).

49. Ibid., 71.

50. Ibid., 72. Though Giles's language here lacks precision—he did not volunteer, for example, that the means had to directly execute an enumerated power—I classify his argument as functional based in part on (1) the general tenor of the passage, but principally on (2) the utter absence of references (throughout his floor speech) to alternative means for achieving the same constitutional ends. My discussion of the next antibank interpretation should bring this point into sharper relief.

51. Dellinger and Powell, "The Constitutionality of the Bank Bill," 110.

52. Clarke and Hall, *Legislative and Documentary History*, 88.

53. Ibid., 89 (emphasis added).

54. Ibid., 42 and Alexander Hamilton, James Madison, and John Jay, *The Federalist with Letters of "Brutus,"* ed. Terence Ball (Cambridge, UK: Cambridge University Press, 2003), 227 (No. 45).

55. Ibid., 44 (emphasis added).

56. Ibid. It is likely that Madison also had in mind here the Manhattan-based Bank of New York, which had been operative (but technically unchartered) since 1784; the institution would secure a charter from the state legislature later in 1791. For histories of these banks, see N. S. B. Gras, *The Massachusetts First National Bank of Boston, 1784–1934* (Cambridge, MA: Harvard University Press, 1937); Rappaport, *Stability and Change;* Alfred Cookman Bryan, *History of State Banking in Maryland* (Baltimore: Johns Hopkins University Press, 1899); Allan Nevins, *History of the Bank of New York and Trust Company, 1784 to 1934* (New York: William E. Rudge's Sons, 1934).

57. Joseph Lynch is notably attentive to this strand of Madison's thinking: "Madison briefly advanced a second argument against the proposition that since the bank would afford a convenient depository for the government's revenues and would facilitate the payment of its debt, its establishment could be justified as a necessary and proper measure[:] . . . since state banks and individuals could offer the same depository and discounting services to the United States, the government could conduct its business without a national bank." *Negotiating the Constitution*, 82. Lynch's attention, however, is far more of an exception than the rule among scholars.

58. Clarke and Hall, *Legislative and Documentary History*, 55.

59. See note 12 and attending text.

60. Clarke and Hall, *Legislative and Documentary History*, 55. It is worth noting that Jackson's February 1 address included the statement that "there was no necessity for instituting a new bank; there is one already established in this city [Philadelphia], under the style of the Bank of North America." However, the comment *precedes* his brief discussion of the constitutional question and reads (in context) like a comment about expediency. Ibid., 37.

61. Ibid., 93.

62. Ibid.

63. Ibid., 65, 67, and 68.

64. For another example of Stone raising constitutional objections in the First Congress, this time with respect to a proposal for a national university, see George Thomas, *The Founders and the Idea of a National University: Constituting the American Mind* (Cambridge, UK: Cambridge University Press, 2014), 64.

65. This fact explains, perhaps, why the traditional narrative is really only attentive to disagreement over how to read the functional standard.

66. Clarke and Hall, *Legislative and Documentary History*, 51.

67. Ibid., 97.

68. Ibid., 47.

69. Ibid., 53.

70. For constitutional claims on behalf of the national bank, I adopt essentially the opposite assumption from the one discussed in note 40: If a House or cabinet member invokes two or more standards of necessity in a single address or memorandum, I assume that *only* satisfaction of a permissive version of the functional standard is required to establish constitutionality. Discussion of the federal and/or frequency standards is only designed to establish—as here—that a national bank could (if needed) fulfill those requirements. I assume, all told, that bank supporters meant to make constitutional necessity as *easy* to establish as possible.

71. Clarke and Hall, *Legislative and Documentary History*, 97.

72. Ibid., 50–51 (emphasis added).

73. See note 63 and attending text.

74. Clarke and Hall, *Legislative and Documentary History*, 111.

75. Ibid., 78.

76. Ibid., 85. "Madison seems to have recognized all along that there was no chance of defeating it [in the House], and he was directing his strategy [in part] toward . . . present[ing] a case to Washington in support of a veto." Elkins and McKitrick, *The Age of Federalism*, 232.

77. William Nisbet Chambers, ed., *The First Party System: Federalists and Republicans* (New York: John Wiley & Sons, 1972).

78. See, for example, James Roger Sharp, *The Deadlocked Election of 1800: Jefferson, Burr, and the Union in the Balance* (Lawrence: University Press of Kansas, 2010).

79. Stephen Skowronek employs both terms in *The Politics Presidents Make: Leadership from John Adams to Bill Clinton* (Cambridge, MA: Harvard University Press, 1997), 79 and 87.

80. Ibid., 80.

CHAPTER TWO

Portions of chapters 2 and 3 represent adaptations (and expansions) of arguments first offered in "Turning (Into) 'The Great Regulating Wheel': The Conversion of the Bank of the United States, 1791–1811," *Studies in American Political Development* 26, no. 1 (April 2012): 1–23. Copyright © 2012 Cambridge University Press; reprinted with permission. This chapter in particular benefited from the research assistance of Sara Ciccolari-Micaldi.

1. Justice Antonin Scalia during argument in *McCutcheon v. Federal Election Commission* (2014), quoted in Sam Baker, "Justices Clash over Campaign Finance Law," *The Hill*, October 9, 2013, http://thehill.com/blogs/ballot-box/fundraising/327171 -justices-clash-over-campaign-finance-law.

2. Axel Madsen, *John Jacob Astor: America's First Multimillionaire* (New York: John Wiley and Sons, 2002), 49.

3. In addition to the state banks chartered prior to February 1791 (Pennsylvania's Bank of North America, the Massachusetts Bank, and the Bank of Maryland), two institutions gained their formal leases on life in the months that followed Washington's signing of the national bank bill: the Bank of New York (March) and Rhode Island's Providence Bank (October). Henry W. Domett, *A History of the Bank of New York, 1784–1884* (New York: G. P. Putnam's Sons, 1884), 34–35; Howard Kemble Stokes, *Chartered Banking in Rhode Island, 1791–1900* (Providence, RI: Prestor & Rounds, 1902), 3. On combined state bank capital at the close of 1791, see Joseph Van Fenstermaker, *The Development of American Commercial Banking: 1782–1837* (Kent, OH: Bureau of Economic and Business Research, 1965), 111.

4. I treat the awkward birth of the Louisiana Bank in 1804 below.

5. Fenstermaker, *Development of American Commercial Banking*, 13.

6. Ibid., 111.

7. Wolfgang Streeck and Kathleen Thelen, "Introduction: Institutional Change in Advanced Political Economies," in *Beyond Continuity: Institutional Change in Advanced Political Economies*, ed. Wolfgang Streeck and Kathleen Thelen (New York: Oxford University Press, 2005), 1–39 at 24–25; see also James Mahoney and Kathleen Thelen, "A Theory of Gradual Institutional Change," in *Explaining Institutional Change: Ambiguity, Agency, and Power*, ed. James Mahoney and Kathleen Thelen (Cambridge, UK: Cambridge University Press, 2010), 1–37 at 17.

8. Years later, Nicholas Biddle—president of the reconstituted Bank between 1823 and 1836—would quip to Daniel Webster respecting a proposed charter alteration, "[i]f our purpose can be obtained without bringing on two weeks' debate upon the constitutionality of the Bank, the usurpations of the Supreme Court [in *McCulloch v. Maryland*], [and] *omni scibile & quibusdem aliis* [every knowable thing, and even certain other things], it would be a great satisfaction." Biddle to Webster, February 16, 1826, in *The Correspondence of Nicholas Biddle Dealing with National Affairs, 1807–1844*, ed. Reginald C. McGrane (Boston: J. S. Canner, 1966), 38–39 at 39.

9. Modern treatments of the subject begin with Davis R. Dewey, *State Banking Before the Civil War* (Washington, DC: National Monetary Commission, 1910), and include Bray Hammond, *Banks and Politics in America: From the Revolution to the Civil War* (Princeton, NJ: Princeton University Press, 1957): 144–71 ("Politics and the Growth of Banking"); Fenstermaker, *Development of American Commercial Banking*, 4–14 ("Commercial Bank Expansion: 1782–1818"); Benjamin J. Klebaner, *American Commercial Banking: A History* (Boston: Twayne, 1990), 4–11; Edwin J. Perkins, *American Public Finance and Financial Services, 1700–1815* (Columbus: Ohio State University

Press, 1994), 266–81 ("State Banks in the New Nation"); Warren E. Weber, "Early State Banks in the United States: How Many Were There and When Did They Exist?" *Journal of Economic History* 66, no. 6 (June 2006): 433–55 at 443.

10. See especially Joseph Stancliffe Davis, *Essays in the Earlier History of American Corporations* (Cambridge, MA: Harvard University Press, 1917), vol. 1, 202–12; Stanley Elkins and Eric McKitrick, *The Age of Federalism: The Early American Republic, 1788–1800* (New York: Oxford University Press, 1993), 242–44; Robert Sobel, *Panic on Wall Street: A History of America's Financial Disasters* (Washington, DC: Beard Books, 1999), 17–21; David J. Cowen, *The Origins and Economic Impact of the First Bank of the United States, 1791–1797* (New York: Garland, 2000), 35–43; Stuart Banner, *Anglo-American Securities Regulation: Cultural and Political Roots, 1690–1860* (Cambridge, UK: Cambridge University Press, 2002), 140–46.

11. The only detailed account appears to belong to Cowen, *Origins and Economic Impact*, 43–54.

12. Subscription books were opened at the Massachusetts Bank in Boston, the Bank of New York in Manhattan, the Bank of North America in Philadelphia, the Bank of Maryland in Baltimore, and the Chamber of Commerce in Charleston, South Carolina. Ibid., 36–37.

13. James O. Wettereau, "New Light on the First Bank of the United States," *Pennsylvania Magazine of History and Biography* 61, no. 3 (July 1937): 263–85 at 273. Subsequent accounts appear to have averaged these times and applied the result to all five sites, suggesting that all subscription books were completely filled within one hour. See Margaret Myers, *A Financial History of the United States* (New York: Columbia University Press, 1970), 68; Elkins and McKitrick, *The Age of Federalism*, 242.

14. The Bank of North America paid dividends of 6, 6.5, or 7 percent every year between 1785 and 1790. See Lawrence Lewis Jr., *A History of the Bank of North America* (Philadelphia: J. B. Lippincott, 1882), 152. The institution's reported dividends for 1782–1784 are even more impressive, but their veracity has recently been called into question; see Robert E. Wright, *Origins of Commercial Banking in America, 1750–1800* (Lanham, MD: Rowman & Littlefield, 2001), 12n21.

15. Cowen, *Origins and Economic Impact*, 39 (emphasis added).

16. For Boston, see Donald H. Stewart, *The Opposition Press of the Federalist Period* (Albany: State University of New York Press, 1969), 58 and 672n156. For New York, see Sobel, *Panic on Wall Street*, 18. For Philadelphia, see Jose R. Torre, *Political Economy of Sentiment: Paper Credit and the Scottish Enlightenment in Early Republic Boston, 1780–1820* (London: Pickering and Chatto, 2007), 214.

17. Cowen, *Origins and Economic Impact*, 39 and 41.

18. Elkins and McKitrick, *Age of Federalism*, 242.

19. Jefferson to Pendleton, July 24, 1791, in *Papers of Thomas Jefferson* (hereafter *PTJ*), ed. Julian Boyd et al. (Princeton, NJ: Princeton University Press, 1950–2016), vol. 20, 669–70 at 670.

20. Jefferson to Humphreys, August 23, 1791, in *PTJ*, vol. 22, 61–62 at 62; see also Jefferson to Gouverneur Morris, August 30, 1791, in *PTJ*, vol. 22, 104–5 at 104: "I have rarely seen a gamester cured even by the disasters of his vocation."

21. Jefferson to Rutledge, August 25, 1791, ibid., 73–75 at 74. Around the same time,

New York City merchant Seth Johnson offered a similar lament to Andrew Craigie, a land and stock trader based in Cambridge: "The best support & surest resource of a nation is in the industry & frugality of its Citizens—whatever in any way tends to lessen or destroy those useful habits must be considered as prejudicial[.] The present rage for speculation by producing in some, a sudden & great acquisition of wealth, allures others, of all ranks, from those regular habits of business thro' which, the acquirement of property tho' slow is certain[.]" Johnson to Craigie, August 20, 1791, reprinted in James O. Wettereau, *Documentary History of the First Bank of the United States* (hereafter *DHFBUS*), in James O. Wettereau Research Papers, Columbia University Rare Book and Manuscript Library, Box 27, Book "B."

22. Jefferson to Rutledge, August 25, 1791, in *PTJ*, vol. 22, 73–75 at 74.

23. Jefferson to Morris, August 30, 1791, ibid., 104–5 at 105. Even Federalists privately acknowledged the effects invoked by Jefferson. Senator Rufus King of New York, writing to Alexander Hamilton in mid-August, recounted scenes of "mechanics deserting their shops, shopkeepers sending their goods to auction, and . . . merchants neglecting their regular and profitable commerce of the city" for the chance to get rich quick. King to Hamilton, August 15, 1791, in *Papers of Alexander Hamilton* (hereafter *PAH*), ed. Harold Syrett et al. (New York: Columbia University Press, 1961–1987), vol. 9, 59–61 at 60. Similarly, Benjamin Rush wrote his wife a few days earlier that "[y]ou hear of nothing but *script* and of all the numbers between 50 and 300 at every corner. Merchants, grocers, shopkeepers, sea captains, and even prentice boys have embarked in the business." Rush to Julia Rush, August 12, 1791, in *Letters of Benjamin Rush*, ed. L. H. Butterfield (Philadelphia: American Philosophical Society, 1951), vol. 1, 602–3 at 603.

24. Cowen, *Origins and Economic Impact*, 44–46; John Thom Holdsworth, *The First Bank of the United States* (Washington, DC: National Monetary Commission, 1910), 25. On Willing, a good starting point is Burton Alva Konkle's *Thomas Willing and the First American Financial System* (Philadelphia: University of Pennsylvania Press, 1937); a more concise but richer portrait is offered in Robert E. Wright, "Thomas Willing (1731–1821): Philadelphia Financier and Forgotten Founding Father," *Pennsylvania History* 63, no. 4 (October 1996): 525–60.

25. Cowen, *Origins and Economic Impact*, 47–48.

26. Quoted in ibid., 50.

27. Alexander Hamilton, "Report on a National Bank," in *Alexander Hamilton: Writings*, ed. Joanne B. Freeman (New York: Library of America, 2001), 575–612 at 599.

28. Ibid., 600. In this vein, consider the letter that Thomas Willing—then president of the Bank of North America—sent to the founders of the Massachusetts Bank in January 1784. Reflecting on his recent experience leading the nation's first commercial bank in its earliest days, Willing wrote that "[w]hen the Bank [of North America] was first Opened here the Business was as much a Novelty to us, who undertook the management of it as it can Possibly be to you—It was a pathless wilderness . . . but little known to this Side the Atlantick, no Book then spoke of the Interior Arrangements or Rules observ'd in Europe[.]" Willing to William Phillips et al., January 6, 1784, reprinted in N. S. B. Gras, *The Massachusetts First National Bank of Boston, 1784–1934* (Cambridge, MA: Harvard University Press, 1937), 209–12 at 209–10.

29. Hamilton, "Report on a National Bank," 600. Section 15 of "An Act to Incor-

porate the Subscribers to the Bank of the United States" ultimately adopted language to this effect, stating that "[i]t shall be lawful for the directors . . . to establish offices wheresoever they shall think fit within the United States, for the purposes of discount and deposite [sic] only[.]" *Annals of Congress*, 1st Cong., 3rd Sess., 2375–81 at 2380.

A few months before the Bank's first board was elected, Hamilton solicited Wolcott's thoughts on the branch question. Wolcott argued that if the branches' revenue exceeded their operational expenses, advantages both public (dispersed access to credit) and private (stockholder profit) recommended their establishment. The original Wolcott memorandum, dated September 1791, is held with his papers at the Connecticut Historical Society but is reprinted in Wettereau, *DHFBUS*.

30. Perkins, *American Public Finance*, 243.

31. Ibid. On the 1784 episode more generally, see both Anna Schwartz, "The Beginning of Competitive Banking in Philadelphia, 1782–1809," *Journal of Political Economy* 55, no. 5 (October 1947): 417–31 and George David Rappaport, *Stability and Change in Revolutionary Pennsylvania: Banking, Politics, and Social Structure* (University Park: Pennsylvania State University Press, 1996), 159–65.

32. These opened gradually over the first half of 1792, with the Boston office commencing operations first (late March), followed by New York and Charleston (early April); Baltimore's branch did not open until late June. Cowen, *Origins and Economic Impact*, 106.

33. On this point, see Davis, *Earlier History of American Corporations*, vol. 2, 58: "State pride and local feeling were so strong . . . that a centralized system even in the mild form which Hamilton suggested could hardly have withstood a certainly hostile opinion." See also James O. Wettereau, "The Branches of the First Bank of the United States," *Journal of Economic History* 2, Supplement: The Tasks of Economic History (December 1942): 66–100 at 73.

34. Paul Pierson, *Politics in Time: History, Institutions, and Social Analysis* (Princeton, NJ: Princeton University Press, 2004), 131; see also Streeck and Thelen, "Introduction," 19.

35. Hamilton to Seton, November 25, 1791, in *PAH*, vol. 9, 538–39.

36. Davis, *Earlier History of American Corporations*, vol. 2, 57; Wettereau, "New Light," 272.

37. The discussions in this and the next two sections should not be construed as a denial that any particular state charter secured between 1791 and 1811 may ultimately represent the product of mixed motivations. My goal in these sections is to offer several historical examples of the relevant factor as at least a *partial* force in institutional formation.

38. Davis, *Earlier History of American Corporations*, vol. 2, 81–82.

39. Ibid., 82–83.

40. Ibid., 89. On New York City in mid-January 1792 as a "hot speculative environment," see Bruce Mann, *Republic of Debtors: Bankruptcy in the Age of American Independence* (Cambridge, MA: Harvard University Press, 2009), 300n6.

41. Quoted in Edwin Burrows and Mike Wallace, *Gotham: A History of New York City to 1898* (New York: Oxford University Press, 1999), 309.

42. Watson to Wadsworth, January 28, 1792, reprinted in Wettereau, *DHFBUS*.

43. The term is used by Walter Werner and Steven T. Smith in *Wall Street* (New York: Columbia University Press, 1991), 3, but that use is criticized in Perkins, *American Public Finance*, 314–15.

44. See in particular Richard Sylla, Robert E. Wright, and David J. Cowen, "Alexander Hamilton, Central Banker: Crisis Management during the U.S. Financial Panic of 1792," *Business History Review* 83, no. 1 (Spring 2009): 61–86; earlier accounts are listed by them at 62n1.

45. Perkins, *American Public Finance*, 314.

46. Howard Bodenhorn, *State Banking in Early America: A New Economic History* (New York: Oxford University Press, 2003), 12.

47. On the mania's ebbing in New York City, see both Philip Schuyler to Alexander Hamilton, January 29, 1792, in *PAH*, vol. 10, 579–81 at 580 ("The bank Mania has somewhat subsided") and Walter Rutherford to John Rutherford, January 30, 1792, in Davis, *Earlier History of American Corporations*, vol. 2, 83 ("The Bank mania subsides a little"). These are references to the consolidation of the Million, Tammany, and Merchants' projects.

48. Joel Munsell, "Notices of the Several Banks Located at Albany," *Merchants' Magazine and Commercial Review* 21, no. 5 (November 1849): 561–63 at 561 (emphasis added).

49. Davis, *Earlier History of American Corporations*, vol. 2, 80.

50. Munsell, "Notices of the Several Banks," 562.

51. Davis, *Earlier History of American Corporations*, vol. 2, 81.

52. Chester McArthur Destler, "The Union Bank of New London: Formative Years," *Connecticut Historical Society Bulletin* 24, no. 1 (January 1959): 14–26 at 14.

53. Ibid., 15–16; see esp. 15 on the degree to which the dividends paid in Boston were "known in Connecticut's chief port[.]" The Massachusetts Bank had recently paid dividends of 8.5 (1789), 10.75 (1790), and 10 percent (1791). Gras, *Massachusetts First National Bank*, 660–62.

54. Destler, "The Union Bank," 16–17 and 19.

55. Richard Sylla, John Legler, and John Wallis, "Banks and State Public Finance in the New Republic: The United States, 1790–1860," *Journal of Economic History* 47, no. 2 (June 1987): 391–403 at 402; see also Fenstermaker, *Development of American Commercial Banking*, 19.

56. On significant investment by the Commonwealth of Massachusetts in 1792 in the newly chartered Union Bank of Boston, see Hammond, *Banks and Politics in America*, 165.

57. John Thom Holdsworth, *Financing an Empire: History of Banking in Pennsylvania* (Chicago: S. J. Clarke, 1928), vol. 1, 133.

58. Belden L. Daniels, *Pennsylvania: Birthplace of Banking in America* (Harrisburg: Pennsylvania Bankers Association, 1976), 62.

59. Sylla, Legler, and Wallis, "Banks and State Public Finance," 393–99, esp. at 396.

60. Alan D. Watson, *Wilmington, North Carolina, to 1861* (Jefferson, NC: McFarland, 2003), 205; Hammond, *Banks and Politics in America*, 127; George Walton Williams, *History of Banking in South Carolina from 1712 to 1900* (Charleston, SC: Walker, Evans & Cogswell, 1903), 6.

61. Watson, *Wilmington*, 205; James H. Broussard, *The Southern Federalists, 1800–1816* (Baton Rouge: Louisiana State University Press, 1999), 341.

62. William C. C. Claiborne to James Madison, March 7, 1804, in *Official Letter Books of W. C. C. Claiborne, 1801–1816*, ed. Dunbar Rowland (Madison, WI: Democrat Printing Company, 1917), vol. 2, 21–23 at 22–23.

63. Albert Gallatin to Thomas Jefferson, April 12, 1804, in *The Writings of Albert Gallatin*, ed. Henry Adams (Philadelphia: J. B. Lippincott, 1879), vol. 1, 184–85; Hammond, *Banks and Politics in America*, 127.

64. Larry Schweikart, *Banking in the American South from the Age of Jackson to Reconstruction* (Baton Rouge: Louisiana State University Press, 1987), 57.

65. Naomi Lamoreaux, *Insider Lending: Banks, Personal Connections, and Economic Development in Industrial New England* (Cambridge, UK: Cambridge University Press, 1994).

66. Gras, *Massachusetts First National Bank*, 61. Robert E. Wright has argued that Lamoreaux's finding may be limited to her region of focus, New England. Early commercial banks in New York and Pennsylvania, he argues, tended to "eschew[] insider lending practices in favor of a more outsider-oriented model of lending." Wright, "Bank Ownership and Lending Patterns in New York and Pennsylvania, 1781–1831," *Business History Review* 73, no. 1 (Spring 1999): 40–60 at 41.

67. Lamoreaux, *Insider Lending*, 13; Gras, *Massachusetts First National Bank*, 70.

68. Oscar Handlin and Mary Flug Handlin, *Commonwealth: A Study of the Role of Government in the American Economy: Massachusetts, 1774–1861* (Cambridge, MA: Harvard University Press, 1969), 115.

69. Perkins, *American Public Finance*, 275, but cf. Wright, "Bank Ownership and Lending Patterns."

70. James Cheetham, quoted in Beatrice Reubens, "Burr, Hamilton, and the Manhattan Company: Part 1: Gaining the Charter," *Political Science Quarterly* 72, no. 4 (December 1957): 578–607 at 578–79.

71. Ibid., 579.

72. Jabez D. Hammond, *The History of Political Parties in the State of New York, from the Ratification of the Federal Constitution to December 1840* (Buffalo, NY: Phinney, 1850), vol. 1, 325.

73. Ron Chernow, *Alexander Hamilton* (New York: Penguin, 2004), 585–86.

74. Ibid., 587 (emphasis added). On the episode more generally, see Reubens, "Burr, Hamilton, and the Manhattan Company," and more recently Brian Phillips Murphy, "'A Very Convenient Instrument': The Manhattan Company, Aaron Burr, and the Election of 1800," *William and Mary Quarterly* 65, no. 2 (April 2008): 233–66.

75. Quoted in Stokes, *Chartered Banking in Rhode Island*, 2.

76. Ibid.; see also Richard Sylla, "Reversing Financial Reversals: Government and the Financial System since 1789," in *Government and the American Economy: A New History*, Price Fishback et al. (Chicago: University of Chicago Press, 2007), 115–47 at 123.

77. Hammond, *Banks and Politics in America*, 127.

78. Davis, *Earlier History of American Corporations*, vol. 2, 62n2 (emphasis added).

79. See Richard Bland Lee to Thomas Willing, November 18, 1791, reprinted in Wet-

tereau, *DHFBUS*; Lee enclosed a "memorial from the Merchants and inhabitants" of Alexandria. A renewed appeal to Willing and his colleagues in late December, ostensibly on the premise that the Bank board would consider establishing *additional* branches, is reprinted in "The Bank of the United States: Petitions of Virginia Cities and Towns for the Establishment of Branches, 1791," *Virginia Magazine of History and Biography* 8, no. 3 (January 1901): 287–95 at 288.

80. John Fitzgerald to Hamilton, November 21, 1791, reprinted in Wettereau, *DHFBUS*.

81. Both are reprinted in full in "The Bank of the United States: Petitions of Virginia Cities and Towns," 289–95; the Richmond petition notably included the signature of future Chief Justice John Marshall.

82. Hamilton to Heth, June 7, 1792, in *PAH*, vol. 11, 493–94. Three weeks later, Heth replied and recommended Richmond; see Heth to Hamilton, June 28, 1792, reprinted in Wettereau, *DHFBUS*.

83. Jefferson to Madison, July 3, 1792, reprinted in Wettereau, *DHFBUS*. "Bankmongers" is drawn from Jefferson's subsequent correspondence with John Adams; see Jefferson to Adams, January 24, 1814, quoted in A. Glenn Crothers, "Banks and Economic Development in Post-Revolutionary Northern Virginia, 1790–1812," *Business History Review* 73, no. 1 (Spring 1999): 1–39 at 13n20. On Alexander Hamilton's surprise that Richmond was chosen so quickly, see Hamilton to Edward Carrington, July 25, 1792, reprinted in Wettereau, *DHFBUS*.

84. Lee to Madison, September 10, 1792, reprinted in Wettereau, *DHFBUS*.

85. Cowen, *Origins and Economic Impact*, 56. Not until 1795 would the Bank authorize a branch in Virginia, but it was for Norfolk, not Richmond. *PAH*, vol. 12, 85n3.

86. "Many republicans believed that chartering a state bank . . . would prevent the creation of a federal branch in Virginia." Crothers, "Banks and Economic Development," 14.

87. On the charter for the Richmond bank, see John J. Walsh, *Early Banks in the District of Columbia* (Washington, DC: Catholic University of America Press, 1940), 22.

88. On the insufficiency of the subscriptions, see Duke de la Rochefoucault Liancourt, *Travels through the United States of America, the Country of the Iroquois, and Upper Canada, in the Years 1795, 1796, and 1797*, 2nd ed. (London: T. Gillet, 1800), vol. 3, 667. On the first bank in Richmond—the Bank of Virginia—see Fenstermaker, *Development of American Commercial Banking*, 183.

89. It might also be rendered, to employ the jargon of American Political Development, a kind of "institutional thickening" in a specific order of American politics. Stephen Skowronek, *The Politics Presidents Make: Leadership from John Adams to Bill Clinton* (Cambridge, MA: Belknap Press of Harvard University Press, 1997), 31.

90. I employ Fenstermaker's figures for the number of state banks (as opposed to Weber's) for two related reasons. First and foremost, only Fenstermaker offers attending data respecting the *capital* of these institutions (which makes possible a running calculation—even a rough one—of the national bank's market share). Second, even if Fenstermaker's figures are imperfect, they still capture the general phenomenon—the Bank's drift from industry dominance—of interest here. Compare Fenstermaker, *Devel-*

opment of American Commercial Banking, 13 and Weber, "Early State Banks in the United States," 442–43.

91. No modern treatment of early American banking—see note 9 for the relevant literature—includes a graphical depiction of the institutional landscape (let alone comparable depictions at different points in time).

92. This theme is explored at some length in J. Lawrence Broz, *The International Origins of the Federal Reserve System* (Ithaca, NY: Cornell University Press, 1997), 233–37.

CHAPTER THREE

1. Richard H. Timberlake, *Monetary Policy in the United States: An Intellectual and Institutional History* (Chicago: University of Chicago Press, 1993), 1.

2. Bray Hammond, *Banks and Politics in America: From the Revolution to the Civil War* (Princeton, NJ: Princeton University Press, 1957), 199. While it is certainly true—as Richard H. Timberlake has noted—that the charter granted in 1791 lacked "any imputation that [the Bank of the United States] was to control the [state] banks or regulate the monetary system in any way[,]" this fact merely reflects the broader reality that federal interference in state banking operations was never even discussed. Timberlake, "The Specie Standard and Central Banking in the United States before 1860," *Journal of Economic History* 21, no. 3 (September 1961): 318–41 at 320–21.

In this vein, it is worth noting that at least two members of the House in 1791—James Madison and Michael Jenifer Stone—expressed concern that the prospective national bank would "defeat" or "swallow up" the existing state banks. Madison claimed on February 2 that the "proposed bank would interfere, so as indirectly to defeat a State bank at the same place." Three days later, Stone invoked the same concern with more violent rhetoric; he suggested that a national bank would "swallow up the State banks." However, a concern for the *survival* of state-chartered institutions following the creation of a national bank is simply not the same thing as an understanding that the latter would *regulate* the former, or periodically restrain their lending. The statements of Madison and Stone should ultimately be construed as emblematic of the uncertainty in 1791 surrounding the question—briefly discussed in chapter 2—of whether multiple banks issuing convertible currency could coexist in a single setting (e.g., a state bank and a branch of the national bank). Matthew St. Clair Clarke and David A. Hall, *Legislative and Documentary History of the Bank of the United States: Including the Original Bank of North America* (Washington, DC: Gales and Seaton, 1832), 41 and 68.

3. Wolfgang Streeck and Kathleen Thelen, "Introduction: Institutional Change in Advanced Political Economies," in *Beyond Continuity: Institutional Change in Advanced Political Economies*, ed. Wolfgang Streeck and Kathleen Thelen (New York: Oxford University Press, 2005), 1–39 at 26; see also James Mahoney and Kathleen Thelen, "A Theory of Gradual Institutional Change," in *Explaining Institutional Change: Ambiguity, Agency, and Power*, ed. James Mahoney and Kathleen Thelen (Cambridge, UK: Cambridge University Press, 2010), 1–37 at 17–18.

4. David J. Cowen, *Origins and Economic Impact of the First Bank of the United States, 1791–1797* (New York: Garland, 2000), 142.

5. William J. Shultz and M. R. Cain, *Financial Development of the United States* (New York: Prentice Hall, 1937), 125; see also Chase Mooney, *William H. Crawford, 1772–1834* (Lexington: University Press of Kentucky, 1974), at 19–20 ("The bank played a vital role as fiscal agent of the government and acted as a . . . restraining force on state banks").

6. Stephen Mihm, *A Nation of Counterfeiters: Capitalists, Con Men, and the Making of the United States* (Cambridge, MA: Harvard University Press, 2007), 108–9. Susan Hoffmann has similarly written that the Bank "[a]s anticipated . . . provided credit and currency in the process of its lending activity." However, "the primary purpose of the national bank became more complex . . . [its] mission became regulation of the money supply[.]" Hoffmann, *Politics and Banking: Ideas, Public Policy, and the Creation of Financial Institutions* (Baltimore: Johns Hopkins University Press, 2001), 41.

7. Edwin J. Perkins, *American Public Finance and Financial Services, 1700–1815* (Columbus: Ohio State University Press, 1994), 249; see also Joseph Van Fenstermaker, *The Development of American Commercial Banking: 1782–1837* (Kent, OH: Bureau of Economic and Business Research, 1965), at 7 ("The Bank returned state bank notes which it had received on deposit, for redemption in gold and silver, and as a result tended to prevent excessive note issues by state chartered banks") and Richard Sylla, "Reversing Financial Reversals: Government and the Financial System since 1789," in *Government and the American Economy: A New History*, Price Fishback et al. (Chicago: University of Chicago Press, 2007), 115–47 at 123 ("By redeeming state banknotes and checks for base-money reserves, the federal banks could discourage the state banks from running down reserves in favor of pursuing profits").

8. See Stuart Bruchey, *Enterprise: The Dynamic Economy of a Free People* (Cambridge, MA: Harvard University Press, 1990), 171–72 and especially Cowen, *Origins and Economic Impact*, 141–43 (a portion of which supplies this chapter's opening epigram). Both Bruchey and Cowen rely on primary source material gathered by James O. Wettereau, an economic historian who was working on a single-volume history of the Bank at the time of his death in 1961. The James O. Wettereau Research Papers (hereafter JOW) are held by Columbia University's Rare Book and Manuscript Library. Included in that collection (Box 4, Folder 2) is his unfinished essay on the Bank's emergence as a monetary force, "The First Bank of the United States: Government Depository and Embryonic Central Bank, 1791–1811."

9. Thomas Willing to John Sergeant, December 19, 1815, reprinted in *Documentary History of the First Bank of the United States* (hereafter *DHFBUS*), in JOW, Box 27, Book "B."

10. Timberlake, *Monetary Policy in the United States*, 4.

11. George Cabot to Josiah Quincy, January 9, 1807, in JOW, Box 7, Folder 81. The original letter is held at the Massachusetts Historical Society.

12. Jesse Atwater, *Considerations on the Approaching Dissolution of the United States Bank* (New Haven, CT: Sidney's Press, 1810), 4.

13. Karen Orren and Stephen Skowronek, "The Study of American Political De-

velopment," in *Political Science: The State of the Discipline*, ed. Ira Katznelson and Helen V. Milner (New York: W. W Norton, 2003), 722–54 at 749.

14. As figure 2.1 indicates, the Charleston branch of the national bank, which opened in April 1792, initially had no state bank in its vicinity.

15. Orren and Skowronek, "The Study of American Political Development," 753; Orren and Skowronek, "Institutions and Intercurrence: Theory Building in the Fullness of Time," in *NOMOS 37: Political Order*, ed. Ian Shapiro and Russell Hardin (New York: New York University Press, 1996), 111–46 at 138 and 140. See also Paul Pierson, *Politics in Time: History, Institutions, and Social Analysis* (Princeton, NJ: Princeton University Press, 2004), 136.

16. Wettereau, "Government Depository and Embryonic Central Bank," 11.

17. See especially Anna Schwartz, "The Beginning of Competitive Banking in Philadelphia, 1782–1809," *Journal of Political Economy* 55, no. 5 (October 1947): 417–31 at 417.

18. Jonathan Mason to Andrew Craigie, December 17, 1791, reprinted in Wettereau, *DHFBUS*. A copy also appears in JOW, Box 7, Folder 81.

19. N. S. B. Gras, *The Massachusetts First National Bank of Boston, 1784–1934* (Cambridge, MA: Harvard University Press, 1937), 36–37; see also Fritz Redlich, *The Molding of American Banking: Men and Ideas* (New York: Johnson Reprint Corporation, 1968), vol. 1, 16.

20. William Seton to Alexander Hamilton, July 23, 1792, reprinted in Wettereau, *DHFBUS*.

21. Gras, *Massachusetts First National Bank*, 73.

22. Hammond, *Banks and Politics in America*, 198.

23. Ibid.

24. During the 1791–1811 period, the Treasury Department did (on occasion) employ state banks as depositories. For a list of local institutions being used as of January 1811, see document no. 334 in the *American State Papers on Finance* (hereafter *ASPF*) (Buffalo, NY: Hein, 1998), vol. 2, 460–63 at 463. See also Cowen, *Origins and Economic Impact*, at 138 ("The Treasury department deposited the bulk of its funds in the vaults of the First Bank and its branches").

25. John Kenneth Galbraith, *Money: Whence It Came, Where It Went* (Boston: Houghton Mifflin, 1975), 74.

26. J. Lawrence Broz, *The International Origins of the Federal Reserve System* (Ithaca, NY: Cornell University Press, 1997), 233. For other work that recognizes the role of federal deposits in generating the Bank's routine creditor status, see Timberlake, *Monetary Policy in the United States*, 10; Cowen, *Origins and Economic Impact*, 138 (citing an 1808 comment by then Treasury Secretary Albert Gallatin); Hoffmann, *Politics and Banking*, 41; Mihm, *A Nation of Counterfeiters*, 109.

27. In late September 1789, Hamilton circulated a note to federal tax collectors announcing that the paper of two institutions that had recently lent to the Treasury—the Bank of North America and the (then unincorporated) Bank of New York—"should be received in payment of the duties, as equivalent to Gold or Silver[.]" By Thanksgiving Day of that year, that privilege had been extended to paper issued by the Massachusetts Bank and collected in Boston. "Treasury Department Circular to the Collectors of the

Customs," September 22, 1789, and "Treasury Department Circular to the Collectors of the Customs in Massachusetts," November 20, 1789, both in *Papers of Alexander Hamilton*, ed. Harold Syrett et al. (New York: Columbia University Press, 1961–1987), vol. 5, 394–95 at 394 and 532–33 at 532.

28. Stuart Bruchey, "Alexander Hamilton and the State Banks, 1789–1795," *William and Mary Quarterly* 27, no. 3 (July 1970): 347–78, esp. at 362n46 (citing a Treasury memorandum, circulated to revenue collectors in different cities at different times, instructing them to "receive no notes but those of the Bank of the United States").

29. Wettereau, "Government Depository and Embryonic Central Bank," 11.

30. Willing, who served as the Bank's president between 1791 and 1807, resigned following a stroke. Lenox held the position until the institution's 1811 dissolution. JOW, Box 6, Folder 67; see also Burton Alva Konkle, *Thomas Willing and the First American Financial System* (Philadelphia: University of Pennsylvania Press, 1937), 189.

31. Albert Gallatin to David Lenox, November 5, 1808, quoted in Cowen, *Origins and Economic Impact*, 146.

32. Samuel Smith to Albert Gallatin, November 2, 1808, quoted in ibid., 145–46.

33. Thomas Jefferson to Albert Gallatin, October 7, 1802, in *Writings of Albert Gallatin*, ed. Henry Adams (Philadelphia: J. B. Lippincott, 1879), vol. 1, 101–2 at 102.

34. Timberlake, *Monetary Policy in the United States*, 10.

35. Bruchey, *Enterprise*, 171.

36. Timberlake, *Monetary Policy in the United States*, 10.

37. "Report of a Committee Appointed to Draft a Circular Letter to the Different Offices, Concerning the Present State of Bank Operations," October 27, 1795, reprinted in Wettereau, *DHFBUS*. The report is also discussed at some length in Bruchey, *Enterprise*, 171.

38. Ibid.

39. The language of "disease" and "remedy" is hardly imposed upon the board's memorandum. The directors themselves announced a disposition to "remedy the Evil" at hand. "Report of a Committee Appointed to Draft a Circular Letter."

40. Ibid.

41. Hammond, *Banks and Politics in America*, 197.

42. Timberlake, *Monetary Policy in the United States*, 10; see also Sylla, "Reversing Financial Reversals," 128, and Donald R. Adams Jr., *Finance and Enterprise in Early America: A Study of Stephen Girard's Bank, 1812–1831* (Philadelphia: University of Pennsylvania Press, 1978), 4.

43. Oliver Wolcott Jr. to Matthew Clarkson, March 25, 1795, quoted in Cowen, *Origins and Economic Impact*, 77n100.

44. With respect to internal hiring, David J. Cowen has noted that the Bank of the United States had a "logical chain of command starting with the [Philadelphia] board . . . [t]he management team was small and flexible. If possible, vacancies were filled within from existing Bank employees before conducting a search of the outside business community." Ibid., 48.

45. See especially Peter H. Lindert and Richard Sutch, "Consumer Price Indexes, for All Items: 1774–2003," Table Cc1-2 in *Historical Statistics of the United States: Millen-*

nial Edition Online, ed. Susan B. Carter et al. (Cambridge, UK: Cambridge University Press, 2006), http://hsus.cambridge.org/HSUSWeb/HSUSEntryServlet.

46. William Constable to William Rogers, July 7, 1795, quoted in Cowen, *Origins and Economic Impact,* 201.

47. Ibid.

48. Mooney, *William H. Crawford,* 20.

49. Draft letter from the Bank of the United States to its Baltimore branch, January 28, 1800, quoted in James O. Wettereau, "The Branches of the First Bank of the United States," *Journal of Economic History* 2, Supplement: The Tasks of Economic History (December 1942): 66–100 at 97n130.

50. Memorial of the Stockholders of the Bank of the United States, December 18, 1810, reprinted as document no. 328 in *ASPF,* vol. 2, 451–52 at 452.

51. Ibid.

52. George Cabot to Josiah Quincy, January 9, 1807, in JOW, Box 7, Folder 81 (emphasis added).

53. Quoted in Richard N. Rosenfeld, *American Aurora: A Democratic-Republican Returns: The Suppressed History of Our Nation's Beginnings and the Heroic Newspaper That Tried to Report It* (New York: St. Martin's Press, 1998), 904. Edward C. Carter II has suggested that in 1811—the year of Jefferson's remark—"[t]he *Aurora* was still considered by many Jeffersonians to be the Bible of Republicanism, and its influence was felt throughout America." Carter, "The Birth of a Political Economist: Matthew Carey and the Recharter Fight of 1810–1811," *Pennsylvania History* 33, no. 3 (July 1966): 274–88 at 284.

54. On Duane generally, see Allen C. Clark, *William Duane* (Washington, DC: Press of W. F. Roberts, 1905).

55. William Duane, "A Review of Certain Pamphlets on Banking [No. 1]," *Aurora General Advertiser,* December 25, 1810.

56. William Duane, "The Bank Charter—No. II," *Aurora General Advertiser,* January 10, 1811.

57. Atwater, *Considerations on the Approaching Dissolution,* 3.

58. The same solution was arguably implicit in William Duane's formulation of the problem: "[T]he deposit of the public revenue of the United States, being limited to [the national bank], all the advantages derived from the public money, go in the proportion of two thirds *out of our circulation* and to enrich *persons adverse to America.*" Duane, "Bank Business," *Aurora General Advertiser,* November 8, 1810. Duane's assertion that the Bank of the United States acted as the *sole* depository for Treasury funds was incorrect; see note 24.

With no effective counter to the claim that profits flowing from federal deposits belonged—as a matter of distributive justice—in the pockets of Americans, Bank defenders opted to highlight the instrumental value of foreign investment in this domestic venture; Matthew Carey wrote that foreigners "furnish capital—our citizens employ it, and pay interest—and the borrowers and the country are benefited." Carey, *Desultory Reflections upon the Ruinous Consequences of a Non-Renewal of the Charter of the Bank of the United States,* 3rd ed. (Philadelphia: Fry and Kammerer, 1810), 21.

59. Atwater, *Considerations on the Approaching Dissolution*, 4.

60. Lloyd Mints, *A History of Banking Theory in Great Britain and the United States* (Chicago: University of Chicago Press, 1945), 68. Bollmann's life and economic thought are discussed at length in Joseph Dorfman, *The Economic Mind in American Civilization, 1606–1865* (New York: Viking Press, 1946), 484–99.

On Bollmann's pre-1811 adventures in the Early American Republic, which led to accusations of treason against him and an ensuing role in the development of habeas corpus jurisprudence, see Justin J. Wert, *Habeas Corpus in America: The Politics of Individual Rights* (Lawrence: University Press of Kansas, 2011), 39–45.

61. Erick Bollmann, *Paragraphs on Banks*, 2nd ed. (Philadelphia: C & A Conrad, 1811), 89–90 (emphasis added).

62. See generally Carter, "The Birth of a Political Economist."

63. Mathew Carey, *Letters to Dr. Adam Seybert, Representative in Congress for the City of Philadelphia, on the Subject of the Renewal of the Charter of the Bank of the United States*, 2nd ed. (Philadelphia: published by author, 1811), 34.

64. Memorial of the President and Directors of the Bank of New York, January 8, 1811, reprinted as document no. 333 in *ASPF*, vol. 2, 460.

65. Ibid. (emphasis added).

66. Alexander Hamilton, "Report on a National Bank," in *Alexander Hamilton: Writings*, ed. Joanne B. Freeman (New York: Library of America, 2001), 575–612 at 575.

67. Eric Lomazoff, "Turning (Into) 'The Great Regulating Wheel': The Conversion of the Bank of the United States, 1791–1811," *Studies in American Political Development* 26, no. 1 (April 2012): 1–23 at 21–23.

68. Wettereau, "The First Bank of the United States: Government Depository and Embryonic Central Bank," 1; Cowen, *Origins and Economic Impact*, 165n3; Redlich, *The Molding of American Banking*, vol. 1, 96: "Professor [Friedrich von] Hayek has . . . drawn attention to the fact that the term was probably used in Europe around 1830 by Saint Simon for the depository of all wealth in a socialist community."

69. This set of functions, it should be noted, varies from one economist or economic historian to another. Compare Galbraith, *Money*, 71; Cowen, *Origins and Economic Impact*, 138–43; Timberlake, *Monetary Policy in the United States*, 4; Redlich, *The Molding of American Banking*, vol. 1, 96.

CHAPTER FOUR

1. On the corporeal metaphor with respect to the Bank, see Jesse Atwater, *Considerations on the Approaching Dissolution of the United States Bank* (New Haven, CT: Sidney's Press, 1810), esp. at 6, where Atwater notes that the institution "has had its youth, its middle age, and now comes on its old age."

2. Memorial of the Stockholders of the Bank of the United States, December 18, 1810, reprinted as document no. 328 in the *American State Papers on Finance* (hereafter *ASPF*) (Buffalo, NY: Hein, 1998), vol. 2, 451–52.

3. Matthew St. Clair Clarke and David A. Hall, *Legislative and Documentary History of the Bank of the United States: Including the Original Bank of North America* (Washington, DC: Gales and Seaton, 1832), 274 and 446.

4. See, in essence, what is *not* said in Sotirios A. Barber, *On What the Constitution Means* (Baltimore: Johns Hopkins University Press, 1984), 79; Daniel A. Farber, "The Story of *McCulloch*: Banking on National Power," *Constitutional Commentary* 20, no. 3 (Winter 2003–2004): 679–714 at 690; Jesse H. Choper, Richard H. Fallon Jr., Yale Kamisar, and Steven H. Shiffrin, *Constitutional Law: Cases, Comments, Questions*, 10th ed. (St. Paul, MN: Thomson/West, 2006), 57; Richard E. Ellis, *Aggressive Nationalism: McCulloch v. Maryland and the Foundation of Federal Authority in the Young Republic* (New York: Oxford University Press, 2007), 37; Howard Gillman, Mark Graber, and Keith Whittington, *American Constitutionalism*, vol. 1, *Structures of Government* (New York: Oxford University Press, 2013), 125; David M. O'Brien, *Constitutional Law and Politics*, vol. 1, *Struggles for Power and Governmental Accountability*, 9th ed. (New York: W. W. Norton, 2014), 548.

5. Scholarship in law and political science that offers this narrative—sometimes in greater detail, sometimes in lesser—includes Paul Brest, Sanford Levinson, Jack Balkin, and Akhil Reed Amar, "The Bank of the United States: A Case Study," in *Processes of Constitutional Decisionmaking: Cases and Materials*, 4th ed., ed. Paul Brest, Sanford Levinson, Jack Balkin, and Akhil Reed Amar (New York: Aspen Law and Business, 2000), 7–70 at 16; Susan Hoffmann, *Politics and Banking: Ideas, Public Policy, and the Creation of Financial Institutions* (Baltimore: Johns Hopkins University Press, 2001), 42–43; David P. Currie, *The Constitution in Congress: The Jeffersonians, 1801–1829* (Chicago: University of Chicago Press, 2001), 251–53; Mark R. Killenbeck, *M'Culloch v. Maryland: Securing a Nation* (Lawrence: University Press of Kansas, 2006), 45–50; Lee Epstein and Thomas G. Walker, *Constitutional Law for a Changing America: A Short Course*, 6th ed. (Thousand Oaks, CA: CQ Press, 2015), 105.

Among historians, see Bray Hammond, *Banks and Politics in America: From the Revolution to the Civil War* (Princeton, NJ: Princeton University Press, 1957), 209–26; Edwin J. Perkins, *American Public Finance and Financial Services, 1700–1815* (Columbus: Ohio State University Press, 1994), 257; Thomas K. McCraw, *The Founders and Finance: How Hamilton, Gallatin, and Other Immigrants Forged a New Economy* (Cambridge, MA: Belknap Press of Harvard University Press, 2012), 292–97.

6. George Washington never identified with the Federalists after their formal emergence in the early to mid-1790s but tended to adopt positions consistent with the party's preferences. Ralph Ketcham, *Presidents above Party: The First American Presidency, 1789–1829* (Chapel Hill: University of North Carolina Press, 1984), 92.

7. James Roger Sharp, *The Deadlocked Election of 1800: Jefferson, Burr, and the Union in the Balance* (Lawrence: University Press of Kansas, 2010), esp. at 169ff.

8. As Noble Cunningham Jr. has written, "[t]he defeat of the Federalist party in 1800 removed from the Republicans the pressure of Federalist power which had cemented them together as an opposition party." Cunningham, *The Jeffersonian Republicans in Power: Party Operations, 1801–1809* (Chapel Hill: University of North Carolina Press, 1963), 203; see also 235.

9. Ibid., 203ff. (on the "Problems of Party Unity").

10. Richard E. Ellis, *The Jeffersonian Crisis: Courts and Politics in the Young Republic* (New York: W. W. Norton, 1971), 19–22, esp. at 22.

11. In 1809, the Mississippi legislature chartered the Natchez-based Bank of the

Mississippi. Joseph Van Fenstermaker, *The Development of American Commercial Banking: 1782–1837* (Kent, OH: Bureau of Economic and Business Research, 1965), 152.

12. Governor Thomas McKean of Pennsylvania, in an August 1801 letter to President Jefferson, seems to suggest that the problem is simply endemic to partisan majorities: "When ever any party are notoriously predominant they will split . . . this is in nature; it has been the case [since] time immemorial, and will be so until mankind become wiser and better." Quoted in Cunningham, *The Jeffersonian Republicans in Power*, 203.

13. William F. Connelly Jr., *James Madison Rules America: The Constitutional Origins of Congressional Partisanship* (Lanham, MD: Rowman & Littlefield, 2010), 82.

14. William F. Connelly Jr. and John J. Pitney Jr., "The House Republicans: Lessons for Political Science," in *New Majority or Old Minority? The Impact of Republicans on Congress*, ed. Nicol C. Rae and Colton C. Campbell (Lanham, MD: Rowman & Littlefield, 1999), 173–94 at 190.

15. Ellis, *The Jeffersonian Crisis*, 19.

16. Cunningham, *The Jeffersonian Republicans in Power*, 203.

17. William Nisbet Chambers, *Political Parties in a New Nation: The American Experience, 1776–1809* (New York: Oxford University Press, 1963), 176.

18. Thomas Jefferson, "Inaugural Address," March 4, 1801, http://www.presidency .ucsb.edu/ws/index.php?pid=25803.

19. Ibid.

20. Quoted in Norman K. Risjord, *The Old Republicans: Southern Conservatism in the Age of Jefferson* (New York: Columbia University Press, 1965), 19.

21. W. Elliot Brownlee, *Federal Taxation in America: A Short History* (Cambridge, UK: Cambridge University Press, 2004), 24.

22. Chambers, *Political Parties in a New Nation*, 173; see also Dennis S. Ippolito, *Deficits, Debt, and the New Politics of Tax Policy* (Cambridge, UK: Cambridge University Press, 2012), 12.

23. Chambers, *Political Parties in a New Nation*, 173.

24. Ippolito, *Deficits, Debt, and the New Politics of Tax Policy*, 12; see also W. Elliot Brownlee, "Long-Run Fiscal Consolidations in the United States: The History at the Federal Level," in *Deficits and Debt in Industrialized Democracies*, ed. Eisaku Ide and Gene Park (New York: Routledge, 2015), 171–98 at 174 and McCraw, *The Founders and Finance*, 233.

25. Charles Sellers, *The Market Revolution: Jacksonian America, 1815–1846* (New York: Oxford University Press, 1991), 36.

26. Cunningham, *The Jeffersonian Republicans in Power*, 203–13.

27. Ellis, *The Jeffersonian Crisis*, 36ff.

28. Cunningham, *The Jeffersonian Republicans in Power*, 53–56; Chambers, *Political Parties in a New Nation*, 179–81; Risjord, *The Old Republicans*, 20–21; Lance Banning, *The Jeffersonian Persuasion: Evolution of a Party Ideology* (Ithaca, NY: Cornell University Press, 1978), 282.

29. Chambers, *Political Parties in a New Nation*, 183. On the Yazoo scandal more generally, see C. Peter Magrath, *Yazoo: Law and Politics in the New Republic: The Case of Fletcher v. Peck* (New York: W. W. Norton, 1967).

30. Risjord, *The Old Republicans*, 2–3.

31. Banning, *The Jeffersonian Persuasion*, 282. See also John Ashworth, *Slavery, Capitalism, and Politics in the Antebellum Republic*, vol. 1, *Commerce and Compromise, 1820–1850* (Cambridge, UK: Cambridge University Press, 1995), 76–77 ("These men were the heirs of the Antifederalists, deeply suspicious of government, and especially of the federal government, and profoundly hostile to banks, corporations and funding systems. They hoped that Jefferson's election would merely be the first stage in a much needed process of constitutional restoration").

32. Hammond, *Banks and Politics in America*, 211; Ellis, *The Jeffersonian Crisis*, 20.

33. Emphasis added.

34. Ellis, *The Jeffersonian Crisis*, 20.

35. Sellers, *The Market Revolution*, 40 and 46.

36. Banning, *The Jeffersonian Persuasion*, 288 (emphasis added).

37. Lawrence A. Peskin, "How the Republicans Learned to Love Manufacturing: The First Parties and the 'New Economy,'" *Journal of the Early Republic* 22, no. 2 (Summer 2002): 235–62 at 238.

38. Dice Robins Anderson, *William Branch Giles: A Study in the Politics of Virginia and the Nation from 1790 to 1830* (Menasha, WI: George Banta, 1914), 177–78; see also Hammond, *Banks and Politics in America*, 211.

39. Clarke and Hall, *Legislative and Documentary History*, 336–37 and 349.

40. Risjord, *The Old Republicans*, 112.

41. Clarke and Hall, *Legislative and Documentary History*, 226.

42. Risjord, *The Old Republicans*, 185; see also Jeanne T. Heidler and David S. Heidler, "Rhea, John," in *Encyclopedia of the War of 1812*, ed. David S. Heidler and Jeanne T. Heidler (Santa Barbara, CA: ABC-CLIO, 1997), 446.

43. Clarke and Hall, *Legislative and Documentary History*, 280 and 282.

44. Ibid., 215.

45. I borrow this term from an 1801 letter sent by Thomas Jefferson to William Duane in which the former promised to treat any law comparable to the recently expired Sedition Act of 1798 "as a nullity." Jefferson to Duane, May 23, 1801, in *The Papers of Thomas Jefferson*, ed. Julian Boyd et al. (Princeton, NJ: Princeton University Press, 1950–2013), vol. 34, 169–70 at 169.

46. James J. Horn, Jan Ellen Lewis, and Peter S. Onuf, eds., *The Revolution of 1800: Democracy, Race, and the New Republic* (Charlottesville: University of Virginia Press, 2002).

47. Clarke and Hall, *Legislative and Documentary History*, 152.

48. The Bank established its New Orleans branch the following year. Hammond, *Banks and Politics in America*, 127.

49. Clarke and Hall, *Legislative and Documentary History*, 206–7; see also Stephen Mihm, *A Nation of Counterfeiters: Capitalists, Con Men, and the Making of the United States* (Cambridge, MA: Harvard University Press, 2007), 109–10.

50. Clarke and Hall, *Legislative and Documentary History*, 342 (emphasis added).

51. Ibid., 215.

52. Ibid., 212.

53. Cf. ibid., 72.

54. Ibid., 280.

55. Ibid., 163–64.

56. Ibid., 269 (emphasis added).

57. Ibid., 177–78.

58. Paul C. Nagel, *One Nation Indivisible: The Union in American Thought, 1776–1861* (New York: Oxford University Press, 1964), 90.

59. Hammond, *Banks and Politics in America*, 211 (where the author misidentifies him as "P. B. Butler." Two pages later, the same member of the House is correctly identified as "P. B. Porter"). See also Daniel Dean Roland, "Peter Buell Porter and Self-Interest in American Politics" (PhD diss., Claremont Graduate School [History], 1990), 22.

60. As Crawford advocated a federal "protective tariff, [this] constitutional argument must have sounded a little hollow." Risjord, *The Old Republicans*, 111. On McKim's strong ties to the Baltimore merchant community, see Hammond, *Banks and Politics in America*, 211.

61. Risjord, *The Old Republicans*, 116; Hammond, *Banks and Politics in America*, 211.

62. Clarke and Hall, *Legislative and Documentary History*, 282.

63. Ibid., 269. For approving references to Porter's speech from Desha and McKim, see ibid., 181 and 219.

64. Ibid., 171 (emphasis added).

65. Ibid., 172–73.

66. Ibid., 175.

67. Ibid.

68. Peskin, "How the Republicans Learned to Love Manufacturing," 235.

69. Clarke and Hall, *Legislative and Documentary History*, 165.

70. Document no. 334 in *ASPF*, vol. 2, 460–63; see also note 24 of chapter 3.

71. Clarke and Hall, *Legislative and Documentary History*, 165.

72. Risjord, *The Old Republicans*, 111; Hammond, *Banks and Politics in America*, 211.

73. Clarke and Hall, *Legislative and Documentary History*, esp. Wright at 198–99 and 203 ("Sir, there can be no necessity for this bank. The State banks are abundantly sufficient to supply every requisition, if the United States' deposites [sic] are made in them") and Smith at 378–79 and 382–83 (arguing that far from being "necessary and all-essential," the Bank of the United States could easily be replaced by a constellation of state banks).

74. Risjord, *The Old Republicans*, 115; Hammond, *Banks and Politics in America*, 211.

75. Clarke and Hall, *Legislative and Documentary History*, 354.

76. Ibid., 356.

77. Ibid., 357 (emphasis added).

78. Risjord, *The Old Republicans*, 112 (Burwell's "whole record in Congress was conservative").

79. Clarke and Hall, *Legislative and Documentary History*, 140.

80. Ibid., 141.

81. Ibid., 142 (emphasis added).

82. The phrase was used by both supporters and critics of the two-prong interpretation. On this point, compare (1) the conclusion of the long block quote from Adam Seybert in the previous section with (2) the claim from recharter supporter David Garland, a Republican member of the House from Virginia: "[I]f it be necessary and proper, then the plain language of the constitution is satisfied, and [the Bank's status] is not made to depend on being *absolutely necessary*, as gentlemen seem to argue." Ibid., 248 (emphasis added).

83. On Findley as a moderate Republican, see Peter Gilmore and Kerby A. Miller, "Searching for 'Irish' Freedom—Settling for 'Scotch-Irish' Respectability: Southwestern Pennsylvania, 1780–1810," in *Ulster to America: The Scots-Irish Migration Experience, 1680–1830*, ed. Warren R. Hofstra (Knoxville: University of Tennessee Press, 2012), 165–210 at 195–96.

84. Clarke and Hall, *Legislative and Documentary History*, 217.

85. Ibid.

86. Ibid., 243.

87. Ibid., 308.

88. Ibid., 397, 398, and 399. For other iterations of this argument from recharter supporters, see ibid., 209 (Rep. Samuel McKee [R-KY]), 253 (Rep. Benjamin Tallmadge [F-CT]), 366 (Rep. John Pope [R-KY]), and 412 (Sen. John Taylor [R-SC]).

89. Ibid., 260.

90. Ibid., 225.

91. Or vice versa, of course.

92. Clarke and Hall, *Legislative and Documentary History*, 226.

93. Ibid., 243 (emphasis added).

94. Ibid., 309.

95. Ibid., 191.

96. Ibid., 188.

97. Ibid., 158.

98. Ibid., 290.

99. Ibid., 314.

100. See note 64 of chapter 3.

101. Clarke and Hall, *Legislative and Documentary History*, 317.

102. Ibid., 220–21.

103. Ibid., 142.

104. Ibid., 213.

105. Ibid., 355.

106. Ibid., 260–61.

107. Ibid., 187 (emphasis added).

108. Hammond, *Banks and Politics in America*, 214.

109. Hoffmann, *Politics and Banking*, 43.

CHAPTER FIVE

1. Alexander Hamilton, "Report on a National Bank," in *Alexander Hamilton: Writings*, ed. Joanne B. Freeman (New York: Library of America, 2001), 575–612 at 579.

2. The text of that bill is reprinted in Matthew St. Clair Clarke and David A. Hall, *Legislative and Documentary History of the Bank of the United States: Including the Original Bank of North America* (Washington, DC: Gales and Seaton, 1832), 585–93.

3. Ibid., 594.

4. Jesse H. Choper, Richard H. Fallon Jr., Yale Kamisar, and Steven H. Shiffrin, *Constitutional Law: Cases, Comments, Questions*, 10th ed. (St. Paul, MN: Thomson/ West, 2006), 57 (emphasis added). For a non-casebook version of the same, see Daniel A. Farber, "The Story of *McCulloch*: Banking on National Power," *Constitutional Commentary* 20, no. 3 (Winter 2003–2004): 679–714 at 690.

5. See Paul Brest, Sanford Levinson, Jack Balkin, and Akhil Reed Amar, "The Bank of the United States: A Case Study," in *Processes of Constitutional Decisionmaking: Cases and Materials*, 4th ed., ed. Paul Brest, Sanford Levinson, Jack Balkin, and Akhil Reed Amar (New York: Aspen Law and Business, 2000), 7–70 at 16–17; Howard Gillman, Mark Graber, and Keith Whittington, *American Constitutionalism*, vol. 1, *Structures of Government* (New York: Oxford University Press, 2013), 125; David M. O'Brien, *Constitutional Law and Politics*, vol. 1, *Struggles for Power and Governmental Accountability*, 9th ed. (New York: W. W. Norton, 2014), 548; Lee Epstein and Thomas G. Walker, *Constitutional Law for a Changing America: A Short Course*, 6th ed. (Thousand Oaks, CA: CQ Press, 2015), 105. Beyond these casebooks, see Sotirios A. Barber, *On What the Constitution Means* (Baltimore: Johns Hopkins University Press, 1984), 79.

6. Scholarship that speaks directly to the policy and/or constitutional themes of this alternative narrative includes Bray Hammond, *Banks and Politics in America: From the Revolution to the Civil War* (Princeton, NJ: Princeton University Press, 1957), 227–50; Edwin J. Perkins, *American Public Finance and Financial Services, 1700–1815* (Columbus: Ohio State University Press, 1994), 324–48; Susan Hoffmann, *Politics and Banking: Ideas, Public Policy, and the Creation of Financial Institutions* (Baltimore: Johns Hopkins University Press, 2001), 45–49; David P. Currie, *The Constitution in Congress: The Jeffersonians, 1801–1829* (Chicago: University of Chicago Press, 2001), 254–58; Mark R. Killenbeck, *M'Culloch v. Maryland: Securing a Nation* (Lawrence: University Press of Kansas, 2006), 53–63; Richard E. Ellis, *Aggressive Nationalism: McCulloch v. Maryland and the Foundation of Federal Authority in the Young Republic* (New York: Oxford University Press, 2007), 37–41.

7. Perkins, *American Public Finance*, 326.

8. Raymond Walters Jr., "The Origins of the Second Bank of the United States," *Journal of Political Economy* 53, no. 2 (June 1945): 115–31 at 122.

9. W. B. Lawrence, "Bank of the United States," *North American Review* 32, no. 71 (April 1831): 524–63 at 546.

10. Document no. 425 in the *American State Papers on Finance* (hereafter *ASPF*) (Buffalo, NY: Hein, 1998), vol. 2, 866–69 at 869.

11. For this understanding of the congressional action, see Keith Whittington, "Judicial Review of Congress before the Civil War," *Georgetown Law Review* 97, no. 5 (May 2009): 1257–1332 at 1295.

12. The notes and checks circulated by state banks in the South, for example, had "already depreciated from 8 to 15 per cent, and [were] constantly tending to further

depreciation[.]" "Will the Southern Banks Pay Specie Again?" *Boston Daily Advertiser*, June 15, 1815.

13. James Madison, "Seventh Annual Message," December 5, 1815, http://www .presidency.ucsb.edu/ws/?pid=29457. For Dallas's report, see Document no. 454 in *ASPF*, vol. 3, 1–32 at 18.

14. John Ashworth, *Slavery, Capitalism, and Politics in the Antebellum Republic*, vol. 1, *Commerce and Compromise, 1820–1850* (Cambridge, UK: Cambridge University Press, 1995), 77; see also Kunal M. Parker, *Common Law, History, and Democracy in America, 1790–1900: Legal Thought before Modernism* (Cambridge, UK: Cambridge University Press, 2011), 100.

15. In 1983, J. C. A. Stagg wrote that "[t]he historical literature on the War of 1812 can be divided into two broad categories[:] a lengthy and inconclusive debate on the causes of the war, and a more diffuse body of writings devoted largely to the operational histories of its various military campaigns." Stagg, *Mr. Madison's War: Politics, Diplomacy, and Warfare in the Early American Republic, 1783–1830* (Princeton, NJ: Princeton University Press, 1983), ix. On the war's causes, see Donald R. Hickey, *The War of 1812: A Forgotten Conflict* (Urbana: University of Illinois Press, 1989), 5–28, and (from the British perspective) Jon Latimer, *1812: War with America* (Cambridge, MA: Harvard University Press, 2007), 13–34.

16. See Robert S. Quimby, *The U.S. Army in the War of 1812: An Operational and Command Study*, 2 vols. (East Lansing: Michigan State University Press, 1997), and William S. Dudley and Michael J. Crawford, eds., *The Naval War of 1812: A Documentary History*, 3 vols. (Washington, DC: Naval Historical Center, 1985–2002).

17. In particular, see Walters, "The Origins of the Second Bank"; Donald H. Kagin, "Monetary Aspects of the Treasury Notes of the War of 1812," *Journal of Economic History* 44, no. 1 (March 1984): 69–88; Perkins, *American Public Finance*, 324–48; Max M. Edling, *A Hercules in the Cradle: War, Money, and the American State, 1783–1867* (Chicago: University of Chicago Press, 2014), 108–44.

18. Robert E. Cray Jr., "Remembering the USS Chesapeake: The Politics of Maritime Death and Impressment," *Journal of the Early Republic* 25, no. 3 (Fall 2005): 445–74; see also Spencer C. Tucker and Frank T. Reuter, *Injured Honor: The Chesapeake-Leopard Affair, June 22, 1807* (Annapolis, MD: Naval Institute Press, 1996).

19. Document no. 267 in *ASPF*, vol. 2, 246–55.

20. Ibid., 248.

21. Hickey, *War of 1812*, 34–35.

22. Document no. 375 in *ASPF*, vol. 2, 564–68 at 564.

23. Ibid., 565 (Statement A).

24. Ibid., 564.

25. Ibid., 568 (Statement E).

26. Ibid., 565.

27. Document no. 386 in *ASPF*, vol. 2, 600–601 at 601; document no. 380 in *ASPF*, vol. 2, 580–91 at 590 (Statement F).

28. As in May, some state banks lent "by special contract" instead of the offered Treasury terms. More specifically, $540,000 was lent for anywhere between one and five

years, with the remainder of the August funds ($2.91 million) for no less than the stipu-
lated twelve. The totals from the August sale were computed by comparing individual
and institutional investments in December 1812 with those from May 1812; compare
document no. 375 in *ASPF*, vol. 2, 564–68 at 568 (Abstract E) with document no. 380 in
the same volume, 580–91 at 590–91 (Statement F).

29. Document no. 380 in *ASPF*, vol. 2, 580–81.

30. Document no. 393 in *ASPF*, vol. 2, 622–27 at 622–23.

31. Document no. 403 in *ASPF*, vol. 2, 651–62 at 661 (Statement F).

32. Document no. 393 in *ASPF*, vol. 2, 622–27 at 624 (Statement A).

33. Max M. Edling cites this commentary but misrenders the final word ("ALONE")
and thus fails to capture its intended double meaning ("A-LONE"). Edling, "The War
of 1812 and the Modernization of American War Finance," unpublished paper on file
with the author, at 22. For reprints of the commentary, see the New York *Evening Post*,
March 18, 1813; the *Alexandria Daily Gazette*, March 23, 1813; and the Philadelphia
Tickler, November 10, 1813.

34. Document no. 393 in *ASPF*, vol. 2, 622–27 at 626 (Statement B2).

35. Furthermore, it promised *all* subscribers—even those who committed to the
Treasury's original terms in mid-March—the lowest price ultimately accepted by the
government. Ibid.

36. Document no. 399 in *ASPF*, vol. 2, 646–47 at 647 (Statements C, D, and E). On
the additional cost of Stephen Girard's investment—that the notes and checks of his
unincorporated bank in Philadelphia (operating in the former home of the Bank of the
United States) be accepted by state banks in the city—see Donald R. Adams Jr., *Finance
and Enterprise in Early America: A Study of Stephen Girard's Bank, 1812–1831* (Philadelphia: University of Pennsylvania Press, 1978), 25ff. but esp. at 30–31: "[H]e insisted
that the *quid pro quo* of his participation was recognition of his bank on an equal basis
with other Philadelphia institutions."

37. On Gallatin in England, see Henry Adams, *The Life of Albert Gallatin* (Philadelphia: J. B. Lippincott, 1880), 493ff.

38. Document no. 397 in *ASPF*, vol. 2, 644.

39. Document no. 403 in *ASPF*, vol. 2, 651–62 at 662 (Statement Ga).

40. For a list of those investors, see ibid., 661 (Statement G).

41. Hickey, *War of 1812*, 159.

42. Quoted in ibid.

43. Document no. 403 in *ASPF*, vol. 2, 651–62 at 652.

44. "Taxes," *Orange County Patriot*, January 11, 1814, reprinted from the New York
Examiner, December 5, 1813.

45. Document no. 404 in *ASPF*, vol. 2, 663. On Barker's authorship, see Robert W.
Keyes III, "The Formation of the Second Bank of the United States, 1811–1817" (PhD
diss., University of Delaware [History], 1975), 15 and 190n30.

46. Document no. 422 in *ASPF*, vol. 2, 840–53 at 841.

47. Ibid.

48. Hickey, *War of 1812*, 196–97 and 199; document no. 422 in *ASPF*, vol. 2, 840–53
at 842 and 846–47 (Statement C).

49. Carole L. Herrick, *August 24, 1814: Washington in Flames* (Falls Church, VA:

Higher Education Publications, 2005) and Anthony Pitch, *The Burning of Washington: The British Invasion of 1814* (Annapolis, MD: Naval Institute Press, 1998).

50. Campbell would later write that "there was no prospect of obtaining the money on better terms[.]" Document no. 422 in *ASPF*, vol. 2, 840–53 at 842.

51. After Campbell accepted $2.72 million in bids at $80—those who bid higher than $80 also received this price—new offers were made (and accepted) for $207,000 in additional securities at the same price. As such, $2.93 million multiplied by 0.80 yields the secured sum: $2.34 million. Ibid., 842 and 847 (Statement Cb).

52. At a price of $88, the spring sale of $5 million in securities (with the retroactive condition attached) netted $4.4 million. Adjusted downward to $80, those same securities now yielded only $4 million.

53. *Washingtonian* (Windsor, Vermont), August 29, 1814. See also the *Worcester Gazette* (also known as the *Massachusetts Spy*) from September 21 that fall: "Mr. Madison can get no money."

54. Henry Adams, *History of the United States of America during the Administrations of James Madison* (New York: Library of America, 1986), 1076.

55. James Madison, "Sixth Annual Message," September 20, 1814, http://www .presidency.ucsb.edu/ws/?pid=29456.

56. Clarke and Hall, *Legislative and Documentary History*, 481.

57. For an early claim to this effect, see John Jay Knox, *A History of Banking in the United States* (New York: Bradford Rhodes, 1900), at 485 ("During 1814 the British army directed its operations against the Middle and Southern States especially . . . [s]uch alarm was occasioned that the banks suspended and had their specie conveyed to places of safety"). More recently, see Hammond, *Banks and Politics in America*, 227 and Keyes, "The Formation of the Second Bank," 39. For competing causal accounts, see Adams, *Finance and Enterprise*, 45 (interregional specie flows in favor of northeastern banks); Daniel Elazar, "Banking and Federalism in the Early American Republic," *Huntington Library Quarterly* 28, no. 4 (August 1965): 301–20 at 310 (irresponsible lending by unregulated state banks); Richard H. Timberlake, *Monetary Policy in the United States: An Intellectual and Institutional History* (Chicago: University of Chicago Press, 1993), 14 and 17–18 (irresponsible lending by state banks that employed Treasury notes as reserves). .

58. Walters, "The Origins of the Second Bank," 121. On Campbell's poor health, see John Jacob Astor to James Monroe, September 2, 1814, reprinted in Kenneth Wiggins Porter, *John Jacob Astor: Business Man* (New York: Russell and Russell, 1966), vol. 1, 563–64. On the appointment of Dallas, see George M. Dallas, *The Life and Writings of Alexander James Dallas* (Philadelphia: J. B. Lippincott, 1871), 127–30.

59. Document no. 425 in *ASPF*, vol. 2, 866–69 at 866 (emphasis added).

60. Ralph Catterall, *The Second Bank of the United States* (Chicago: University of Chicago Press, 1903), 17 (emphasis added).

61. Document no. 425 in *ASPF*, vol. 2, 866–69 at 866.

62. Clarke and Hall, *Legislative and Documentary History*, 607–8.

63. That proposal is laid out in document no. 425 in *ASPF*, vol. 2, 866–69 at 867. With respect to ownership, Dallas suggested that "six per cent. stock, issued since the declaration of war, and treasury notes" be accepted for the purpose of purchas-

ing (up to 80 percent of) a share in the national bank. Because Federalists—the war's domestic opponents—had largely eschewed the purchase of federal securities since early 1812, the proposed rule would hardly facilitate their investment in (and profiting from) the institution. Daniel Webster, then a Federalist member of the House from New Hampshire, told his brother Ezekiel in mid-November 1814 that the Dallas plan "was calculated only for the benefit of the holders of the stock created since the War." Daniel Webster to Ezekiel Webster, November 21, 1814, in *Papers of Daniel Webster: Correspondence Series,* ed. Charles M. Wiltse (Hanover, NH: University Press of New England, 1974–1989), vol. 1, 176–77 at 176. As for management, Dallas proposed that the president of the United States (with the Senate's consent) name five of the institution's fifteen board members, with one among that group serving as national bank president. With Republicans in the executive mansion since March 1801 (and little prospect of a Federalist successor in March 1817), members of the latter party were hardly enamored with this provision.

64. Document no. 425 in *ASPF,* vol. 2, 866–69 at 867. Charles Wilkes, then cashier (but later president) of the Bank of New York, wrote Senator Rufus King [F-NY] to complain that the Dallas plan would offer little "relief to the government. It appears impossible that six millions of specie should be obtained [via purchases of national bank stock], but if they could be, they would not, by any means, secure the payment of notes of such a bank in specie for a month[.]" Wilkes to King, November 3, 1814, in *The Life and Correspondence of Rufus King,* ed. Charles R. King (New York: G. P. Putnam's Sons, 1898), vol. 5, 434–35 at 435. Similarly, Representative William Gaston [F-NC] belatedly condemned the Dallas plan in a postwar letter to his constituents; he wrote that it would have "increase[d] the already intolerable evil of a depreciated currency by pouring on the country a flood of paper, which was neither money nor the representative of money." That letter is reprinted in *Circular Letters of Congressmen to Their Constituents, 1789–1829,* ed. Noble E. Cunningham Jr. (Chapel Hill: University of North Carolina Press, 1978), vol. 2, 928–35 at 935.

65. Keyes, "The Formation of the Second Bank," 55.

66. Calhoun's "very ingenious and elaborate speech" outlining this alternative is reprinted in Clarke and Hall, *Legislative and Documentary History,* 495–96. On the subject of stock purchase rules, Calhoun proposed one that would have offered Federalists much easier access to national bank shares; "the payments of subscriptions to [the institution's] capital stock [should] be made in the proportion of one-tenth in specie . . . and the remainder in specie, or in treasury notes, to be *hereafter issued*" (emphasis added). In other words, as-yet-unissued Treasury notes—notes that Federalists could and would purchase—would be used to purchase shares. As for internal decision-making, Calhoun proposed that the federal government have no "control over [the national bank's] operations" (i.e., no seats on its board of directors).

67. On the protracted congressional debate (and the resulting efforts to craft and pass compromise legislation), see Keyes, "The Formation of the Second Bank," 61–76 and Walters, "The Origins of the Second Bank," 126–27. To a lesser extent, see Hammond, *Banks and Politics in America,* 231–32.

68. An angry Dallas wrote to Madison suggesting that "I asked for bread and . . . [Congress] gave me a stone. I asked for a Bank to serve the Government during the war,

and they gave me a commercial bank to go into operation after the war." Quoted in Walters, "The Origins of the Second Bank," 126 and Hickey, *War of 1812*, 251.

69. Document no. 425 in *ASPF*, vol. 2, 866–69 at 868.

70. Ibid., 869.

71. Clarke and Hall, *Legislative and Documentary History*, 487–88.

72. Whittington, "Judicial Review of Congress," 1295.

73. Norman K. Risjord, *The Old Republicans: Southern Conservatism in the Age of Jefferson* (New York: Columbia University Press, 1965), 111–12.

74. Clarke and Hall, *Legislative and Documentary History*, 550.

75. Walters, "The Origins of the Second Bank," 124. This bloc may have been sizable enough—when combined with Federalists—to prevent passage of the administration's bill. David Parish—a major investor in the $16 million loan authorized in February 1813—wrote of that proposed legislation in mid-November 1814 that "not a federal vote will be obtained in favor of the Bank and without some aid from that side of the house the bill will not pass as many [Republicans] are opposed to it on constitutional grounds." Parish to Stephen Girard, November 11, 1814, quoted in Adams, *Finance and Enterprise*, 48.

76. Clarke and Hall, *Legislative and Documentary History*, 494; see also the December 23 floor speech of John Clopton, 549–57.

77. Walters, "The Origins of the Second Bank," 124.

78. Clarke and Hall, *Legislative and Documentary History*, 594.

79. Ibid.

80. Gary Rosen, *American Compact: James Madison and the Problem of Founding* (Lawrence: University Press of Kansas, 1999), 173; Greg Weiner, *Madison's Metronome: The Constitution, Majority Rule, and the Tempo of American Politics* (Lawrence: University Press of Kansas, 2012), 121.

81. James Madison, "Seventh Annual Message." See also Perkins, *American Public Finance* at 346 ("The war had ended months ago; military expenditures were dwindling; and customs revenues were generating substantial income for government coffers").

82. Clarke and Hall, *Legislative and Documentary History*, 660.

83. Perkins, *American Public Finance*, 341.

84. "On Banks," *Connecticut Journal*, May 1, 1815.

85. *True American*, August 3, 1815.

86. James Madison, "Seventh Annual Message."

87. Burent Gardiner, "Current Money," *Rhode-Island American*, August 25, 1815.

88. *Baltimore Patriot*, December 16, 1815 (emphasis added).

89. "Bank Mania," *Federal Republican*, October 20, 1815.

90. Mathew Carey, *Essays on Banking* (Philadelphia: published by author, 1816), 159.

91. Gardiner, "Current Money."

92. Joseph Dorfman, *The Economic Mind in American Civilization: 1606–1865* (New York: Viking Press, 1946), 365. With respect to the House, Representative Calhoun inquired into the basic "instinct" of the state banks and then proceeded to answer his own question: "Gain, gain; nothing but gain: and they would not willingly relinquish their gain from the present state of things, acting as they did without restraint, and without hazard." Clarke and Hall, *Legislative and Documentary History*, 633.

93. Carey, *Essays on Banking*, 155.

94. Clarke and Hall, *Legislative and Documentary History*, 688.

95. Willing to Sergeant, December 19, 1815, reprinted in James O. Wettereau, *Documentary History of the First Bank of the United States*, in James O. Wettereau Research Papers, Columbia University Rare Book and Manuscript Library, Box 27, Book "B."

96. *Albany Daily Advertiser*, December 11, 1815.

97. Philadelphians (a crowd that includes the author) will recognize the bank for its initials—PSFS—which have prominently adorned the top of a Center City skyscraper since 1932.

98. Condy Raguet, *An Inquiry into the Causes of the Present State of the Circulating Medium of the United States* (Philadelphia: Moses Thomas, 1815), 37. On Raguet generally, see Zelia Sa Viana Camurea, "Condy Raguet: His Life, Work, and Education" (PhD diss., University of Pennsylvania [Anthropology], 1988).

99. James Madison, "Seventh Annual Message."

100. Document no. 454 in *ASPF*, vol. 3, 1–32 at 19.

101. The original petitions are held at the main National Archives and Records Administration (NARA) site in Washington, DC (Record Group 233, HR14A, F16.1–F16.5 [Box 38]). In this box, see especially the folder for F16.3 (Select Committee/7 Petition of inhabitant of Philadelphia on currency/December 14, 1815). Access to materials from early Congresses (including the Fourteenth) is restricted, and I thank Dr. Kenneth Kato—then of NARA's Center for Legislative Archives and now of the Office of the Historian of the House of Representatives—for permitting me to examine and photograph these submissions.

102. Roy Douglas Womack, *An Analysis of the Credit Controls of the Second Bank of the United States* (New York: Arno Press, 1978), 187.

103. Clarke and Hall, *Legislative and Documentary History*, 639 (emphasis added).

104. Quoted in Kathleen Thelen, *How Institutions Evolve: The Political Economy of Skills in Germany, Britain, the United States, and Japan* (Cambridge, UK: Cambridge University Press, 2004), 26.

105. Clarke and Hall, *Legislative and Documentary History*, 713. The bill passed by the Fourteenth Congress and signed by Madison is reprinted in Catterall, *The Second Bank*, 479–88.

The prevailing tendency among scholars has been to distinguish between the First Bank of the United States (1791–1811) and the Second Bank of the United States (1816–1836). However, the linguistic distinction is entirely historiographic because the term *First Bank* was "never actually used during the period of corporate existence of the institution from 1791 to 1811. It came into vogue posthumously . . . to differentiate the 'old' Bank of the United States from a 'new' or 'second' Bank[.]" James O. Wettereau, "The Oldest Bank Building in the United States," *Transactions of the American Philosophical Society* 43, no. 1 (1953): 70–79 at 70.

In this spirit, Bray Hammond argued over half a century ago that "the corporate distinction between the first and second federal banks has been too much emphasized and the identity of their function neglected. They were separate legal entities, to be sure, but that is less significant than their likeness and continuity, for they served the same needs in the same way for forty of the forty-five years from 1791 to 1836." Hammond, *Banks and Politics in America*, 244. More recently, Edwin Perkins suggested that the chartering of the "Second Bank" in 1816 could "perhaps more accurately [be characterized] as the belated rechartering of the First [Bank]." Perkins, *American Public Finance*, 344.

Except when quoting secondary sources that employ the term *Second Bank*, I will refer to the institution chartered in 1816 simply as the *Bank of the United States*, the *Bank*, or the *national bank*.

106. See especially Jeffrey A. Jenkins and Marc Weidenmier, "Ideology, Economic Interests, and Congressional Role-Call Voting: Partisan Instability and Bank of the United States Legislation, 1811–1816," *Public Choice* 100, no. 3–4 (September 1999): 225–43.

107. Document no. 462 in *ASPF*, vol. 3, 57–61. Though the capital proposed for the institution was far larger than its predecessor ($10 million), the divide between publicly held and privately held shares would remain the same. In 1791, the federal government purchased 20 percent of the available Bank shares ($2 million), with the remainder available to individual and institutional investors. Dallas's plan called for comparable investment from the federal government ($7 million).

108. Individual and institutional investors would be required to pay at least a quarter of the share price in specie, but could pay for the remaining 75 percent with "every species of funded stock." In other words, there would be no built-in advantage for those who purchased federal securities in or after the spring of 1812. Ibid., 58.

109. On the wartime proposal vis-à-vis institutional management, see note 63. This time around, Dallas enlarged the prospective board of directors to twenty-five seats (from fifteen) but kept the number of government-appointed directors the same (five).

110. Keyes, "The Formation of the Second Bank," 91. The bill offered by the Select Committee is reprinted in Clarke and Hall, *Legislative and Documentary History*, 621–30.

111. For debate in the House on a proposed amendment that would have deprived the federal government of any role in the national bank's management, see Clarke and Hall, *Legislative and Documentary History*, 661–66. That amendment eventually failed, 64–79.

Federalist recognition of mainstream Republicans' constitutional and policy reversal on the national bank question, and frustration at their efforts to control any new instantiation of it, were both on display in the December 7, 1815 issue of the Salem, New York, *Northern Post*: "Who were they that were opposed to the establishment of a National Bank, in 1791? *The Democrats*. Who were they that twenty years afterwards, destroyed this National Bank? *The Democrats*. Who were they, that, in a few months afterwards, wished to establish a National Bank . . . under the control of the administration? *The Democrats*."

112. In early February 1791, for example, then Representative James Madison of Virginia—in the midst of combating a claim that Congress's enumerated powers also carried implied powers—argued that "Congress have power 'to regulate the value of money,' yet it is expressly added, not left to be implied, that counterfeiters may be punished." For one of several examples from the 1811 recharter debate, see the January 23 floor speech of Representative William Crawford of Pennsylvania; he suggested that *in*

contrast to the power to charter a national bank, "[t]he sole power given to the United States, to coin money, regulate commerce, or make war, has never been questioned." Clarke and Hall, *Legislative and Documentary History*, 42 and 272.

113. Document no. 454 in *ASPF*, vol. 3, 1–32 at 17.

114. Ibid., 18.

115. Ibid., 17 and 18.

116. Alexander J. Dallas to John C. Calhoun, December 24, 1815, reprinted in Dallas, *The Life and Writings of Alexander James Dallas*, 288–99 at 292.

117. Raymond Walters Jr., *Alexander James Dallas: Lawyer, Politician, Financier: 1759–1817* (Philadelphia: University of Pennsylvania Press, 1943), 210.

118. John L. Thomas, "Introduction," in *John C. Calhoun: A Profile*, ed. John L. Thomas (New York: Hill and Wang, 1968), vii–xxi at xi.

119. Clarke and Hall, *Legislative and Documentary History*, 631.

120. Ibid., 685.

121. Ibid., 686.

122. See chapter 4.

123. On the House reporter's reliance on a subsequent speech by Clay to his constituents, see Clarke and Hall, *Legislative and Documentary History*, 669.

124. On this point, see Robert V. Remini, *Henry Clay: Statesman for the Union* (New York: W. W. Norton, 1991), 68, 141, 227, 467, 516, and 614. His about-face on the constitutional question also earned him at least one early, stern, and public rebuke from a constituent. A letter from "Pitt" that appeared in a June 1816 issue of the *Western Monitor* (Lexington, KY) admonished Clay to "speedily and explicitly" retract his claim that a national bank was constitutional. Even *if* he withdrew the claim, "Pitt" assured him that "you cannot so easily remove the [effect] this disavowal has produced: no sir, [not] all the tears that you have shed upon this subject, nor all the grog that you have drank to prove your perfect devotion to the people, can wash away the stain." This letter is reprinted in *The Papers of Henry Clay*, ed. James F. Hopkins and Mary W. M. Hargreaves (Lexington: University of Kentucky Press, 1959), vol. 1, 208–10 at 210.

125. On Clay as an "unrestrained nationalist," see Bradford Perkins, *Prologue to War: England and the United States, 1805–1812* (Berkeley: University of California Press, 1970), 343. On his subsequent support for federally sponsored internal improvements under the Necessary and Proper Clause, see Remini, *Henry Clay*, 226.

126. Clarke and Hall, *Legislative and Documentary History*, 670–71.

127. Ibid., 672.

128. Ibid., 696.

129. Frank B. Cross, *The Failed Promise of Originalism* (Stanford, CA: Stanford Law Books, 2013), esp. at 37–38.

130. Ibid.

131. Clarke and Hall, *Legislative and Documentary History*, 696.

132. For an out-of-doors expression of partisan frustration with the administration's bank bill—especially its provisions for management of the institution—see the editorial that appeared in the *Courier* (New York City) on January 12, 1816: "This very republican, and unassuming administration, takes every occasion to acquire *power*. It

must have influence and patronage wherever they can be established. Money matters we know are always best managed when left to themselves."

133. James Madison, "Eighth Annual Message," December 3, 1816, http://www .presidency.ucsb.edu/ws/index.php?pid=29458 (emphasis added).

134. James Madison to C. E. Haynes, February 25, 1831, in *The Writings of James Madison* (hereafter *WJM*), ed. Gaillard Hunt (New York: G. P. Putnam's Sons, 1900– 1910), vol. 9, 442–43 at 443.

135. James Madison to N. P. Trist, December 1831, in *WJM*, vol. 9, 471–77 at 476–77.

136. The Bonus Bill of 1817 would have set aside two streams of federal revenue for the construction of roads and canals: the $1.5 million promised to the federal government from the Bank's stockholders as a bonus for granting the institution its charter, plus any future dividends earned from publicly held shares in the same. Songho Ha, *The Rise and Fall of the American System: Nationalism and the Development of the American Economy, 1790–1837* (London: Routledge, 2009), 54.

137. Despite the fact that several Republicans had raised constitutional objections to the bill, Madison had been widely expected to sign it. John Lauritz Larson has suggested that "Madison's veto surprised the entire Washington community. The president's nationalism had risen steadily since the 1800 election." Larson, *Internal Improvement: National Public Works and the Promise of Popular Government in the Early United States* (Chapel Hill: University of North Carolina Press, 2001), 67. On this point, consider the remark made by Republican DeWitt Clinton (then the governor of New York) to Federalist Rufus King (then the state's senior US senator) in late 1817: "After swallowing the National Bank . . . it was not to be supposed that Mr. Madison would strain at Canals. But so it is[.]" Quoted in Brian Phillips Murphy, *Building the Empire State: Political Economy in the Early Republic* (Philadelphia: University of Pennsylvania Press, 2015), 271n74.

138. James Madison, "Veto Message on the Internal Improvements Bill," March 3, 1817, https://millercenter.org/the-presidency/presidential-speeches/march-3-1817-veto -message-internal-improvements-bill.

139. Weiner, *Madison's Metronome*, 121.

140. See George W. Carey, *In Defense of the Constitution*, rev. ed. (Indianapolis: Liberty Fund, 1995), 107–9; Rosen, *American Compact*, 143; Jeremy D. Bailey, *James Madison and Constitutional Imperfection* (Cambridge, UK: Cambridge University Press, 2015), 154.

141. For the beginning of an effort to close it, see Eric Lomazoff, "The Developing Mind of the Founder? James Madison and the National Bank Question, 1791–1831," unpublished paper on file with the author.

CHAPTER SIX

1. On the proper spelling of the cashier's name, see Mark R. Killenbeck, *M'Culloch v. Maryland: Securing a Nation* (Lawrence: University Press of Kansas, 2006), 90. In this chapter, I will employ the standard (if flawed) version of the case's name.

2. Robert G. McCloskey, *The American Supreme Court*, 5th ed., rev. Sanford Levinson (Chicago: University of Chicago Press, 2010), 42.

3. *McCulloch v. Maryland*, 17 US 316 (1819), at 413.

4. Compare William Brockenbrough's "Amphictyon" and Spencer Roane's "Hampden" essays with Marshall's "A Friend to the Union" and "A Friend of the Constitution" essays; all four sets are reprinted in Gerald Gunther, ed., *John Marshall's Defense of* McCulloch v. Maryland (Stanford, CA: Stanford University Press, 1969). On Brockenbrough's authorship of the "Amphictyon" essays, see Killenbeck, *M'Culloch v. Maryland*, 124.

5. For this account of state taxes on the Bank of the United States in the late 1810s, see Gunther, *John Marshall's Defense*, 3; Jean Edward Smith, *John Marshall: Definer of a Nation* (New York: Henry Holt, 1996), 441; Daniel A. Farber, "The Story of *McCulloch*: Banking on National Power," *Constitutional Commentary* 20, no. 3 (Winter 2003–2004): 679–714 at 690; Jesse H. Choper, Richard H. Fallon Jr., Yale Kamisar, and Steven H. Shiffrin, *Constitutional Law: Cases, Comments, Questions*, 10th ed. (St. Paul, MN: Thomson/West, 2006), 57; Daniel Walker Howe, *What Hath God Wrought: The Transformation of America, 1815–1848* (New York: Oxford University Press, 2007), 144; R. Kent Newmyer, *John Marshall and the Heroic Age of the Supreme Court* (Baton Rouge: Louisiana State University Press, 2007), 294.

6. Richard E. Ellis, *Aggressive Nationalism:* McCulloch v. Maryland *and the Foundation of Federal Authority in the Young Republic* (New York: Oxford University Press, 2007), esp. at 68 ("[T]he Maryland law was introduced in late 1817 and adopted in February 1818, a half year before popular opinion had turned against the [Bank] in opposition to its policy of contracting loans and demanding specie from local banks"); see also Killenbeck, *M'Culloch v. Maryland*, 68.

7. Offering the standard account of *McCulloch* are Gunther, *John Marshall's Defense*, 5–6; Smith, *John Marshall*, 443–44; Farber, "The Story of *McCulloch*," 701–4; Killenbeck, *M'Culloch v. Maryland*, 116–19; Ellis, *Aggressive Nationalism*, 95–97; McCloskey, *The American Supreme Court*, 43–44; Howard Gillman, Mark Graber, and Keith Whittington, *American Constitutionalism*, vol. 1, *Structures of Government* (New York: Oxford University Press, 2013), 130; David M. O'Brien, *Constitutional Law and Politics*, vol. 1, *Struggles for Power and Governmental Accountability*, 9th ed. (New York: W. W. Norton, 2014), 548–49. To a lesser extent, see Lee Epstein and Thomas G. Walker, *Constitutional Law for a Changing America: A Short Course*, 6th ed. (Thousand Oaks, CA: CQ Press, 2015), 111.

8. James Madison to Spencer Roane, September 2, 1819, in *Papers of James Madison: Retirement Series*, ed. David Mattern et al. (Charlottesville: University of Virginia Press, 2009–2016), vol. 1, 500–504 at 501.

9. John Marshall, "A Friend to the Union [No. 2]," in Gunther, *John Marshall's Defense*, 91–105 at 103.

10. Paul Brest, Sanford Levinson, Jack Balkin, and Akhil Reed Amar, "The Bank of the United States: A Case Study," in *Processes of Constitutional Decisionmaking: Cases and Materials*, 4th ed., ed. Paul Brest, Sanford Levinson, Jack Balkin, and Akhil Reed Amar (New York: Aspen Law and Business, 2000), 7–70 at 17–18.

11. For the curtailment order from the Bank's board of directors, see Walter Buckingham Smith, *Economic Aspects of the Second Bank of the United States* (Cambridge, MA: Harvard University Press, 1953), 107–8.

12. Killenbeck, *M'Culloch v. Maryland*, 94.

13. Ellis, *Aggressive Nationalism*, 68–69.

14. Ibid., 69.

15. Killenbeck, *M'Culloch v. Maryland*, 94–95.

16. Ellis, *Aggressive Nationalism*, 72.

17. Eric Lomazoff, "*Martin v. Hunter's Lessee* (1816)," in *American Governance*, vol. 3, ed. Stephen Schechter et al. (New York: Macmillan Reference, 2016), 251–52.

18. Killenbeck, *M'Culloch v. Maryland*, 95.

19. Ellis, *Aggressive Nationalism*, 72.

20. Ibid., 74.

21. *McCulloch v. Maryland*, 17 US 316 (1819), at 322.

22. William Pinkney to Daniel Webster, December 28, 1818, in *Papers of Daniel Webster: Correspondence Series* (hereafter *PDWC*), ed. Charles M. Wiltse (Hanover, NH: University Press of New England, 1974–1989), vol. 1, 238 (emphasis added).

23. Ellis, *Aggressive Nationalism*, 76.

24. *McCulloch v. Maryland*, 17 US 316 (1819), at 324–25.

25. Ibid., 356.

26. Ibid., 386 and 388.

27. Ibid., 331.

28. Ibid., 364–65.

29. Ibid., 374.

30. *PDWC*, vol. 1, 238–54.

31. See, for example, Ellis's discussion of the Ohio, Kentucky, and Tennessee taxes in *Aggressive Nationalism*, 65 and 68.

32. Akhil Reed Amar, *America's Unwritten Constitution: The Precedents and Principles We Live By* (New York: Basic Books, 2012), 23.

33. Ibid.

34. *McCulloch v. Maryland*, 17 US 316 (1819), 412–20. It could alternatively be construed as extending to the top of page 425.

35. Ibid., 413.

36. Ibid., 407.

37. Charles L. Black Jr., *Structure and Relationship in Constitutional Law* (Woodbridge, CT: Ox Bow Press, 1985), 14 (emphasis added).

38. Ibid., 13–15; *McCulloch v. Maryland*, 17 US 316 (1819), at 408 and 411.

39. Amar, *America's Unwritten Constitution*, 23–27, esp. at 24 and 26 (emphasis added). On "structural" argument in constitutional interpretation, which infers relationships between parts through "a fair construction of the whole instrument[,]" see Philip Bobbitt, *Constitutional Fate: Theory of the Constitution* (New York: Oxford University Press, 1982), 74ff.

40. Bray Hammond, *Banks and Politics in America: From the Revolution to the Civil War* (Princeton, NJ: Princeton University Press, 1957), 265.

41. *McCulloch v. Maryland*, 17 US 316 (1819), at 402.

42. On the distinction between "fixed" and "fluid" departmentalism, see Keith Whittington, *Political Foundations of Judicial Supremacy: The Presidency, the Supreme Court, and Constitutional Leadership in U.S. History* (Princeton, NJ: Princeton University Press, 2007), 14n41 (referencing the work of Scott E. Gant).

43. Andrew Jackson, "Veto Message," in *Jackson versus Biddle: The Struggle over the Second Bank of the United States*, ed. George Rogers Taylor (Boston: D. C. Heath, 1949), 7–20 at 12 (emphasis added).

For evidence that Marshall (even as chief justice) was not necessarily hostile to departmentalism, see John Agresto, *The Supreme Court and Constitutional Democracy* (Ithaca, NY: Cornell University Press, 1984), 135. I am grateful to Alan Gibson for pointing me to Agresto's discussion.

44. For an early argument that the Court is a majoritarian institution (at least with respect to federal law), see Robert A. Dahl, "Decision-Making in a Democracy: The Supreme Court as a National Policy-Maker," *Journal of Public Law* 6, no. 2 (Fall 1957): 279–95. On the Court as suffering from the "countermajoritarian difficulty," see Alexander M. Bickel, *The Least Dangerous Branch: The Supreme Court at the Bar of Politics* (Indianapolis: Bobbs-Merrill, 1962). On situations where the prevailing "regime" fails to hold a clear preference, see Mark A. Graber, "The Nonmajoritarian Difficulty: Legislative Deference to the Judiciary," *Studies in American Political Development* 7, no. 1 (Spring 1993): 35–73.

45. I am grateful to an anonymous reviewer of an early version of the book manuscript for distinguishing between "traditional work on the countermajoritarian difficulty" and my approach to analyzing *McCulloch*.

46. Or Bassok and Yoav Dotan, "Solving the Countermajoritarian Difficulty?" *International Journal of Constitutional Law* 11, no. 1 (January 2013): 13–33 at 15.

47. Graber, "The Nonmajoritarian Difficulty," 36. On Democrats, civil rights, and the Supreme Court after 1945, see Whittington, *Political Foundations of Judicial Supremacy*, 130ff.

48. Dahl, "Decision-Making in a Democracy," 293.

49. Mark A. Graber, "Federalist or Friends of Adams: The Marshall Court and Party Politics," *Studies in American Political Development* 12, no. 2 (Fall 1998): 229–66 at 230.

50. Ibid., 232.

51. Ibid., 233.

52. R. Kent Newmyer, "John Marshall, *McCulloch v. Maryland*, and the Southern States' Rights Tradition," *John Marshall Law Review* 33, no. 4 (2000): 875–934 at 881. Newmyer writes at 880–81 that "[l]urking in the background of *McCulloch*" was the "specific issue [of] slavery . . . little was said explicitly about the slavery issues in the initial attack on *McCulloch*, but the connection was there to see."

53. Oral argument of Paul Clement in *Department of Health and Human Services v. Florida*, No. 11-398 (one of two cases heard and decided with *NFIB v. Sebelius*), March 27, 2012. Transcript available at https://www.supremecourt.gov/oral_arguments/argument_transcripts/2011/11-398-Tuesday.pdf; see pp. 78–79 of the PDF.

54. *NFIB v. Sebelius*, 567 US 519 (2012), available at https://www.law.cornell.edu/supct/pdf/11-393.pdf; see p. 20 of the PDF.

55. Ilya Somin, "A Taxing, but Potentially Hopeful Decision," *SCOTUSblog*, June 28, 2012, http://www.scotusblog.com/2012/06/a-taxing-but-potentially-hopeful-decision/.

56. See, for example, Adam J. White's account of *Sebelius* in "Marshalling Prec-

edent: With Nod to Predecessor, Roberts Affirms Mandate," *Weekly Standard*, June 28, 2012, http://www.weeklystandard.com/marshalling-precedent-with-nod-to-predecessor -roberts-affirms-mandate/article/647945.

57. *NFIB v. Sebelius*, 567 US 519 (2012); see p. 22 of the PDF cited in note 54.

58. I use the term here in the broadest possible sense, i.e., one that allows it to en-compass *both* of the alternatives to majoritarian judicial behavior (i.e., countermajoritarianism *and* nonmajoritarianism in Graber's narrower sense of the term).

59. Jeffrey A. Segal and Harold J. Spaeth, *The Supreme Court and the Attitudinal Model Revisited* (Cambridge, UK: Cambridge University Press, 2002), 48.

60. Thomas M. Keck, "Party, Policy, or Duty? Why Does the Supreme Court Invalidate Federal Statutes?" *American Political Science Review* 101, no. 2 (May 2007): 321–38 at 321.

61. Keith E. Whittington, "The Road Not Taken: *Dred Scott*, Judicial Authority, and Political Questions," *Journal of Politics* 63, no. 2 (May 2001): 365–91, esp. at 367.

62. Graber, "The Nonmajoritarian Difficulty," 41 and 42.

63. The failure of *McCulloch*'s backstory to align with Graber's theory of non-majoritarian decision-making may also suggest (to retreat briefly to the classification problem sketched out above) that Marshall's reasoning in the case is best characterized as countermajoritarian.

64. Segal and Spaeth, *The Supreme Court and the Attitudinal Model Revisited*, 86 ("Simply put, [William] Rehnquist votes the way he does because he is extremely con-servative; [Thurgood] Marshall voted the way he did because he was extremely liberal").

65. Ibid., 321.

66. Jeffrey A. Segal, "Perceived Qualifications and Ideology of Supreme Court Nominees, 1937–2012," http://www.stonybrook.edu/commcms/polisci/jsegal/QualTable .pdf.

Two alternative measures of individual ideology are calculated from previous voting behavior as recorded in the Supreme Court Database. These include (1) Martin-Quinn scores, and (2) a measure calculated by Lee Epstein and various collaborators. The database, however, only covers the post-1946 period (though contributors hope to eventually take it "back to the Court's first reported decision, *Georgia v. Brailsford* (1792)"). See Lee Epstein, William M. Landes, and Richard A. Posner, *The Behavior of Federal Judges: A Theoretical and Empirical Study of Rational Choice* (Cambridge, MA: Harvard University Press, 2013), 107 and the Supreme Court Database, http:// supremecourtdatabase.org/about.php?s=2.

67. Ellis, *Aggressive Nationalism*. Federalist Bushrod Washington and all five of his Republican colleagues signed Chief Justice Marshall's opinion for the Court.

68. David O'Brien has demonstrated that concurring and dissenting opinions were not very common during the bulk of Marshall's tenure: The number of opinions is-sued between 1801 and 1830 did not far exceed the number of opinions for the Court. O'Brien, "Institutional Norms and Supreme Court Opinions: On Reconsidering the Rise of Individual Opinions," in *Supreme Court Decision-Making: New Institutional-ist Approaches*, ed. Cornell W. Clayton and Howard Gillman (Chicago: University of Chicago Press, 1999), 91–113 at 92 (see esp. figure 4.1).

69. It should be no wonder, then, that in September 1819, several months after the

decision in *McCulloch* was announced, former president James Madison told Spencer Roane that he "wished also that the Judges [in that case] had delivered their opinions seriatim. [*McCulloch*] was of such magnitude in the scope given to it, as to call, if any case could do so, for the views of the subject individually taken by them." Quoted in Melvin I. Urofsky, *Dissent and the Supreme Court: Its Role in the Court's History and the Nation's Constitutional Dialogue* (New York: Vintage, 2017), 49; see also p. 501 of the Madison letter cited in note 8.

70. Segal and Spaeth, *The Supreme Court and the Attitudinal Model Revisited*, 59 and 75.

71. Ibid., 295ff.; see also Howard Gillman, "What's Law Got to Do with It? Judicial Behavioralists Test the 'Legal Model' of Judicial Decision Making," *Law and Social Inquiry* 26, no. 2 (Spring 2001): 464–504 at 476ff.

72. Of course, it is also possible to argue that the Compromise of 1816 was not mentioned *because the justices simply had no knowledge of it*. There are a number of reasons to reject this claim, but I will offer just two here. First, the Court's opinion referenced both "the former proceedings of the Nation respecting" a national bank *and* the fact that the "passage of the present law" resulted from "the embarrassments to which [the institution's 1811 demise] exposed the Government[.]" *McCulloch v. Maryland*, 17 US 316 (1819), at 401–2. Given these references, it is difficult to believe that the justices neither had detailed knowledge of the postwar charter debate nor corrected for ignorance of the same via study of the legislative record.

Second, even if John Marshall and his peers failed to examine the Bank's full legislative history, it is fair to assume that they (as members of a coordinate branch) routinely read the president's annual message to Congress. As discussed in the previous chapter, President Madison's final message to that body (delivered in December 1816) recognized that the outgoing members of the Fourteenth Congress had taken measures "during the last session" to exercise the power of "creating and regulating a currency of . . . equal value, credit, and use wherever it may circulate." One way or the other, in short, we should assume judicial familiarity with the Coinage Clause argument. James Madison, "Eighth Annual Message," December 3, 1816, http://www.presidency.ucsb .edu/ws/index.php?pid=29458.

73. Segal and Spaeth, *The Supreme Court and the Attitudinal Model Revisited*, 321.

CHAPTER SEVEN

1. *Register of Debates* (hereafter *RD*), vol. 8, part 3 (22nd Cong., 1st Sess.), 3852. The *Register* as a whole is available at https://memory.loc.gov/ammem/amlaw/lwrd.html.

2. Andrew Jackson, "Veto Message, July 10, 1832," reprinted in *Jackson versus Biddle: The Struggle over the Second Bank of the United States*, ed. George Rogers Taylor (Boston: D. C. Heath, 1949), 7–20 at 12 and 13–16. The veto message is also available at http://avalon.law.yale.edu/19th_century/ajveto01.asp.

3. For the standard rendering of Jackson's Bank veto—the end point for this period—see Mark R. Killenbeck, *M'Culloch v. Maryland: Securing a Nation* (Lawrence: University Press of Kansas, 2006), 170–71; Richard E. Ellis, *Aggressive Nationalism: McCulloch v. Maryland and the Foundation of Federal Authority in the Young Repub-*

lic (New York: Oxford University Press, 2007), 211–13; Howard Gillman, Mark Graber, and Keith Whittington, *American Constitutionalism*, vol. 1, *Structures of Government* (New York: Oxford University Press, 2013), 202; David M. O'Brien, *Constitutional Law and Politics*, vol. 1, *Struggles for Power and Governmental Accountability*, 9th ed. (New York: W. W. Norton, 2014), 548–49.

4. Stuart Bruchey, *Enterprise: The Dynamic Economy of a Free People* (Cambridge, MA: Harvard University Press, 1990), 182.

5. On the beginnings of the "Bank War," see Arthur M. Schlesinger Jr., *The Age of Jackson* (Boston: Little, Brown, 1946), 74–87; Bray Hammond, *Banks and Politics in America: From the Revolution to the Civil War* (Princeton, NJ: Princeton University Press, 1957), 369–76; and (for particular attention to the December 1829 annual message to Congress) Robert V. Remini, *Andrew Jackson*, vol. 2, *The Course of American Freedom, 1822–1832* (New York: History Book Club, 1998), 222–29.

6. Andrew Jackson, "First Annual Message," December 8, 1829, http://www .presidency.ucsb.edu/ws/index.php?pid=29471.

7. Sidney M. Milkis and Jesse H. Rhodes, "The President, Party Politics, and Constitutional Development," in *The Oxford Handbook of American Political Parties and Interest Groups*, ed. L. Sandy Maisel and Jeffrey M. Berry (New York: Oxford University Press, 2010), 377–402 at 381; Sean Wilentz, *The Rise of American Democracy: Jefferson to Lincoln* (New York: W. W. Norton, 2005), 295–96 and 302.

8. Matthew St. Clair Clarke and David A. Hall, *Legislative and Documentary History of the Bank of the United States: Including the Original Bank of North America* (Washington, DC: Gales and Seaton, 1832), 740.

9. Ibid., 759.

10. Jackson, "Veto Message," 16.

11. Louis Fisher, *American Constitutional Law*, vol. 1, *Constitutional Structures: Separated Powers and Federalism* (Durham, NC: Carolina Academic Press, 2001), 26–27; Walter F. Murphy, James E. Fleming, Sotirios A. Barber, and Stephen Macedo, *American Constitutional Interpretation*, 4th ed. (New York: Foundation Press, 2008), 336–37; Gillman, Graber, and Whittington, *American Constitutionalism*, vol. 1, 202–6 at 204; O'Brien, *Constitutional Law and Politics*, vol. 1, 58–60 at 60.

12. Jackson, "Veto Message," 13.

13. Wilfred S. Lake, "The End of the Suffolk System," *Journal of Economic History* 7, no. 2 (November 1947): 183–207.

14. Warren E. Weber, "Early State Banks in the United States: How Many Were There and When Did They Exist?" *Journal of Economic History* 66, no. 6 (June 2006): 433–55, esp. at 449–50 (table 2). Weber relies on the data reported by Fenstermaker in *The Development of American Commercial Banking: 1782–1837* (Kent, OH: Bureau of Economic and Business Research, 1965), 111 (Appendix A).

15. *McCulloch v. Maryland*, 17 US 316 (1819), 424 (emphasis added).

16. On the revived Bank as the "fiscal agent of the [federal] government" in particular, see Fritz Redlich, *The Molding of American Banking: Men and Ideas* (New York: Johnson Reprint Corporation, 1968), part 1, 128.

17. Actually, the deal reached at this conference only yielded payment resumption (on February 20) in the cities that sent representatives; resumption elsewhere followed

at later points in 1817. On the "substantial concessions" to state banks, see Ralph Catterall, *The Second Bank of the United States* (Chicago: University of Chicago Press,
1902), 24; see also Leon M. Schur, "The Second Bank of the United States and the Inflation after the War of 1812," *Journal of Political Economy* 68, no. 2 (April 1960): 118–34 at
134. On the tendency of the deal reached on February 1 to produce resumption outside
of these cities, see Chase Mooney, *William H. Crawford, 1772–1834* (Lexington: University Press of Kentucky, 1974), 130.

18. Robert E. Wright, *The First Wall Street: Chestnut Street, Philadelphia, and
the Birth of American Finance* (Chicago: University of Chicago Press, 2005), 155. See
also Roy Douglas Womack, *An Analysis of the Credit Controls of the Second Bank of
the United States* (New York: Arno Press, 1978), esp. at 4–5; Bruchey, *Enterprise*, 182;
Catterall, *The Second Bank*, 436–37; Redlich, *The Molding of American Banking*, part 1
at 128.

19. On Biddle generally, see Thomas Payne Govan, *Nicholas Biddle: Nationalist
and Public Banker, 1786–1844* (Chicago: University of Chicago Press, 1959).

20. Reginald C. McGrane, ed., *The Correspondence of Nicholas Biddle Dealing
with National Affairs, 1807–1844* (Boston: J. S. Canner, 1966).

21. The Letterbooks are part of the Nicholas Biddle Papers, held by the Library of
Congress (finding aid available at http://lccn.loc.gov/mm78012690). They encompass
five microfilm reels (Shelf No. MSS 13, 201; Reels 42–46) and include (by my count)
3,150 letters. In cataloging the collection, I began by assigning each letter a unique identifying number (1–3,150). A spreadsheet with basic data on each letter (unique identifying number, reel number, page number on reel, recipient, position of recipient, and date
authored) is on file with the author. When citing a letter from this collection, I refer first
to its unique identifying number.

On George W. Fairman (who is referenced as "G. W. Fairman" or simply "GWF" in
the Letterbooks) as Biddle's secretary, see No. 1543, Biddle to Morris Robinson, July 29,
1831.

22. No. 221, Biddle to John Cumming, January 12, 1825 (emphasis added).

23. No. 1006, Biddle to Joseph Hemphill, February 1, 1830 (emphasis added).

24. *RD*, vol. 6, part A (21st Cong., 1st Sess.), 103.

25. I count 308 letters (out of 3,150 in all) to members of the main board of directors.

26. No. 38, Biddle to Charles Nicholas, July 16, 1823.

27. No. 272, Biddle to Isaac Lawrence, April 22, 1825; on this point, see also no. 1810,
Biddle to Horace Binney, February 18, 1832: "So long as the Bank of the United States
issues its notes freely[,] the State Banks have the means of exchanging with it on equal
terms the notes of the Bank for their own. But if the [national] Bank issues are small,
the Public revenue will be mainly collected in State Bank paper [and] the business
of the Bank is done mainly upon the notes of the State Banks, which then accumulate
in the Bank of the U.S. while the State Banks have no means of defense against payment
of their notes by exchanging them for notes of the Bank of the U.S."

28. No. 38, Biddle to Charles Nicholas, July 16, 1823.

29. Catterall, *The Second Bank of the United States*, 171.

30. Samuel Ingham to Nicholas Biddle, July 11, 1829; reprinted in "Bank of the
United States," H.R. 460, 22nd Cong., 1st Sess. (April 1832): 438–39 at 439. A PDF ver-

sion of this report is freely available on the Internet, but can be rather difficult to locate. I work here from the file available at https://books.google.com/books/reader?id=xvG -jNQ_B-gC&printsec=frontcover&output=reader&pg=GBS.PR5.

31. This aptly named party was composed of many former nationalist or moderate members of the fallen Republican regime. G. Edward White, *Law in American History*, vol. 1, *From the Colonial Years through the Civil War* (New York: Oxford University Press: 2012), 307.

32. John McLean to Nicholas Biddle, January 5, 1829, reprinted in McGrane, *The Correspondence of Nicholas Biddle*, 63–65.

33. Hammond, *Banks and Politics in America*, 369.

34. No. 783, Nicholas Biddle to John McLean, January 11, 1829. This letter also appears in McGrane, *The Correspondence of Nicholas Biddle*, 69–71.

35. Samuel Ingham to Nicholas Biddle, July 11, 1829; reprinted in "Bank of the United States," H.R. 460, at 438.

36. Nicholas Biddle to Samuel Ingham, July 18, 1829, reprinted in ibid. at 444 (emphasis added).

37. For the entire Ingham-Biddle exchange between July and October 1829, see ibid. at 437–69.

38. On Biddle's self-described "intractable spirit" (and its role in inspiring Jacksonian hostility), see No. 1878, Biddle to John Watmough, May 11, 1832; see also No. 2265, Biddle to John S. Barbour, April 16, 1833 ("From that time [late 1829] they resolved, that as they could not bend [the Bank] they would break it") and No. 2775, Biddle to Silas Stilwell, October 30, 1834 ("It was the refusal to become partisans of the present set in power which has made [the institution] its [enemy]").

39. Jackson, "First Annual Message." On the drafting of this section of Jackson's message, see Remini, *Andrew Jackson*, vol. 2, 222–24.

40. Clarke and Hall, *Legislative and Documentary History*, 739.

41. Ibid.

42. Ibid., 740 (emphasis added).

43. No. 1187, Biddle to Albert Gallatin, June 28, 1830.

44. Nicholas Dungan, *Gallatin: America's Swiss Founding Father* (New York: New York University Press, 2010), 154.

45. Albert Gallatin, *Considerations on the Currency and Banking System of the United States* (Philadelphia: Carey and Lea, 1831), 77–78.

46. Ibid., 78–80 (emphasis added).

47. William B. Lawrence, "Bank of the United States," *North American Review* 32, no. 71 (April 1831): 524–63. Nicholas Biddle had contact with Lawrence prior to the publication of this article; see No. 1466, Biddle to Lawrence, March 24, 1831 (in which the former commented on the latter's page proofs). After publication, Biddle requested several thousand reprints of the piece for further dissemination; see No. 1481, Biddle to Lawrence, April 18, 1831.

48. Lawrence, "Bank of the United States," 525.

49. Ibid., 561.

50. On the timing of the Bank's request, especially vis-à-vis the 1832 election, see Hammond, *Banks and Politics in America*, 385–86.

51. On National Republican and Democratic support for the 1832 Bank bill (with the former being broader than the latter), see Jean Alexander Wilburn, *Biddle's Bank: The Crucial Years* (New York: Columbia University Press, 1967), 121.

52. Clarke and Hall, *Legislative and Documentary History*, 378–79 and 382–83.

53. *RD*, vol. 8, part 1 (22nd Cong., 1st Sess.), 1039.

54. Ibid., 949 (emphasis added).

55. Ibid., 957.

56. Schlesinger, *Age of Jackson*, 90.

57. Remini, *Andrew Jackson*, vol. 2, 369; Ellis, *Aggressive Nationalism*, 205.

58. On this point, see especially Keith Whittington, *Political Foundations of Judicial Supremacy: The Presidency, the Supreme Court, and Constitutional Leadership in U.S. History* (Princeton, NJ: Princeton University Press, 2007), 59–61. For two casebooks that place the veto message in a chapter on interpretive authority, see Murphy, Fleming, Barber, and Macedo, *American Constitutional Interpretation*, 336–37 and O'Brien, *Constitutional Law and Politics*, vol. 1, 58–60.

59. Jackson, "Veto Message," 12; Gerard Magliocca, *Andrew Jackson and the Constitution: The Rise and Fall of Generational Regimes* (Lawrence: University Press of Kansas, 2007), 55–56.

60. See note 11 and attending text.

61. Jackson, "Veto Message," 12.

62. Ibid., 13. This passage affirms that *McCulloch* was understood (at least in the nineteenth century) as anchoring the national bank to a specific constitutional provision.

63. Ibid.

64. Ibid. (emphasis added).

65. For evidence that President John Tyler read *McCulloch* in a similar manner when vetoing an 1841 national bank bill on constitutional grounds, see Whittington, *Political Foundations of Judicial Supremacy*, 178. David P. Currie's understanding of Jackson's veto message mirrors my own; see *The Constitution in Congress: Democrats and Whigs, 1829–1861* (Chicago: University of Chicago Press, 2005), 62–63.

66. Jackson, "Veto Message," 13–16. For a brief review of Jackson's assault, see Currie, *The Constitution in Congress: Democrats and Whigs*, 61.

67. Jackson, "Veto Message," 16.

68. Ibid.

69. *J. W. Hampton, Jr. & Co. v. United States*, 276 US 394 (1928), at 409.

70. I am grateful to an anonymous reader of an early version of the chapter for drawing my attention to this implication of Jackson's Coinage Clause commentary.

71. *Youngstown Sheet & Tube Co. v. Sawyer*, 343 US 579 (1952).

72. Sharyn O'Halloran, *Politics, Process, and American Trade Policy* (Ann Arbor: University of Michigan Press, 1994), 82–83.

73. Jerry L. Mashaw, *Creating the Administrative Constitution: The Lost One Hundred Years of American Administrative Law* (New Haven, CT: Yale University Press, 2012), 5.

74. Ibid., 156.

75. Whittington, *Political Foundations of Judicial Supremacy*, 60.

CONCLUSION

1. Richard Sylla, "Reversing Financial Reversals: Government and the Financial System since 1789," in *Government and the American Economy: A New History*, Price Fishback et al. (Chicago: University of Chicago Press, 2007), 115–47 at 137; see also Sylla, "Experimental Federalism: The Economics of American Government, 1789–1914," in *The Cambridge Economic History of the United States*, vol. 2, *The Long Nineteenth Century*, ed. Stanley L. Engerman and Robert E. Gallman (Cambridge, UK: Cambridge University Press, 2000), 483–542 at 532 and Kevin Phillips, *Wealth and Democracy: A Political History of the American Rich* (New York: Broadway Books, 2002), 227.

2. Roger Lowenstein, *America's Bank: The Epic Struggle to Create the Federal Reserve* (New York: Penguin Press, 2015).

3. "New Legislation Aims to 'Organize Our Peace,' He Says," *New York Times*, December 24, 1913, 1; see also John Milton Cooper, *Woodrow Wilson: A Biography* (New York: Random House, 2011), 225.

4. John Thom Holdsworth, *The First Bank of the United States* (Washington, DC: Government Printing Office, 1910); Davis R. Dewey, *The Second United States Bank* (Washington, DC: Government Printing Office, 1910).

5. *Knox v. Lee*, 79 US 457 (1871), at 547.

6. Readers interested less in post-1789 development and more in how the founding generation understood matters pertaining to coinage (and money more broadly) should consult James Bradley Thayer, "Legal Tender," *Harvard Law Review* 1, no. 2 (May 1887): 73–97 at 73–78; James Willard Hurst, *A Legal History of Money in the United States, 1774–1970* (Lincoln: University of Nebraska Press, 1973), 8–18; Bernard H. Siegan, *The Supreme Court's Constitution: An Inquiry into Judicial Review and Its Impact on Society* (New Brunswick, NJ: Transaction Books, 1987), 21–28; Robert G. Natelson, "Paper Money and the Original Understanding of the Coinage Clause," *Harvard Journal of Law and Public Policy* 31, no. 3 (Summer 2008): 1017–81. Primary sources that speak to this question are collected in Philip B. Kurland and Ralph Lerner, eds., *The Founders' Constitution*, vol. 3, *Article I, Section 8, Clause 5 through Article 2, Section 1* (Indianapolis: Liberty Fund, 2000), 1–12.

7. Thayer, "Legal Tender," 78ff.; Hurst, *A Legal History of Money*, 145; David R. Smith and Robert Jefferson Dillard, "The Powers to Regulate Money, Weights, and Measures and to Punish Counterfeiting," in *The Powers of the U.S. Congress: Where Constitutional Authority Begins and Ends*, ed. Brien Hallett (Santa Barbara, CA: ABC-CLIO, 2016), 69–79, esp. at 77.

8. Thomas Wilson, *The Power "to Coin" Money: The Exercise of Monetary Powers by the Congress* (Armonk, NY: M. E. Sharpe, 1992), esp. at 106; Richard H. Timberlake, *Constitutional Money: A Review of the Supreme Court's Monetary Decisions* (Cambridge, UK: Cambridge University Press, 2013), esp. at 18.

9. Richard R. John, "American Political Development and Political History," in *The Oxford Handbook of American Political Development*, ed. Richard M. Valelly, Suzanne Mettler, and Robert C. Lieberman (New York: Oxford University Press, 2016), 185–206 at 188.

10. Karen Orren and Stephen Skowronek, *The Search for American Political Development* (Cambridge, UK: Cambridge University Press, 2004), 191.

11. Article I, Section 8, Clause 17. Tyler's August 16 rejection of a bill to charter the Fiscal Bank of the United States, with headquarters in Washington, DC, but authority to establish branches in the states, offered little in terms of detailed constitutional commentary. The president

> deem[ed] it entirely unnecessary at this time to enter upon the reasons which have brought my mind to the convictions I feel and entertain on this subject . . . I will [only] say that in looking to the powers of this Government to collect, safely keep, and disburse the public revenue, and incidentally to regulate the commerce and exchanges, I have not been able to satisfy myself that the establishment by this Government of a bank of discount in the ordinary acceptation of that term was a necessary means or one demanded by propriety to execute those powers.

Tyler, "Veto Message," August 16, 1841, http://www.presidency.ucsb.edu/ws/?pid=67557.

The Twenty-Seventh Congress responded to Tyler's implicit claim—that a national bank was not "necessary" for exercising the federal government's fiscal powers—by attempting (yet again) to avoid debate over the meaning of the Sweeping Clause. In early September, it passed a bill that strongly resembled its August output (a "Fiscal Corporation" with headquarters in the District of Columbia, but authority to open offices elsewhere) under the penultimate clause of Article I, Section 8; this gave Congress power to "exercise exclusive Legislation in all Cases whatsoever" in the national capital. Several days later, Tyler vetoed the bill and suggested that Congress could not use this provision to charter a *national* bank:

> [T]he amount of its capital, the manner in which its stock is to be subscribed for and held, the persons and bodies, corporate and politic, by whom its stock may be held, the appointment of its directors and their powers and duties, its fundamental articles, especially that to establish agencies in any part of the Union, the corporate powers and business of such agencies, the prohibition of Congress to establish any other corporation with similar powers for twenty years, with express reservation in the same clause to modify or create any bank for the District of Columbia, so that the aggregate capital shall not exceed five millions, without enumerating other features which are equally distinctive and characteristic, clearly show that it can not be regarded as other than a bank *of the United States*, with powers seemingly more limited than have heretofore been granted to such an institution. It operates per se over the Union by virtue of the unaided and, in my view, assumed authority of Congress as a national legislature, as distinguishable from a bank created by Congress for the District of Columbia as the local legislature of the District.

Tyler, "Veto Message on the Creation of a Fiscal Corporation," September 9, 1841, https://millercenter.org/the-presidency/presidential-speeches/september-9-1841-veto-message-creation-fiscal-corporation.

12. Max M. Edling, *A Hercules in the Cradle: War, Money, and the American State, 1783–1867* (Chicago: University of Chicago Press, 2014), 188.

13. Richard H. Timberlake, *Monetary Policy in the United States: An Intellectual and Institutional History* (Chicago: University of Chicago Press, 1993), 131.

14. Elbridge G. Spaulding, *History of the Legal Tender Paper Money Issued during the Great Rebellion* (Buffalo, NY: Express Printing, 1869), 14.

15. Brian McGinty, *Lincoln and the Court* (Cambridge, MA: Harvard University Press, 2008), 278; Timberlake, *Constitutional Money*, 89.

16. Kenneth W. Dam, "The Legal Tender Cases," in *The Supreme Court Review: 1981*, ed. Philip B. Kurland, Gerhard Casper, and Dennis J. Hutchinson (Chicago: University of Chicago Press, 1982), 367–412 at 371.

17. *Hepburn v. Griswold*, 75 US 603 (1869), at 625.

18. Justice Robert Grier's preference was to resolve the case in Griswold's favor on statutory grounds. If forced to work with his colleagues' construction of the statute, however (which led directly to the constitutional question), Grier would have joined Chase's opinion. Ibid., 626.

19. Ibid., 616.

20. Ibid., 621.

21. *McCulloch v. Maryland*, 17 US 316 (1819), 421, paraphrased in ibid., 622.

22. US Constitution, Article I, Section 10.

23. *Hepburn v. Griswold*, 75 US 603 (1869), at 623 (emphasis added).

24. See, e.g., *Barron v. Baltimore*, 32 US 243 (1833).

25. *Hepburn v. Griswold*, 75 US 603 (1869), at 624.

26. For rival interpretations of this legislation, compare Charles Warren, *The Supreme Court in United States History*, vol. 3, *1856–1918* (Boston: Little, Brown, 1923), 143ff. with Justin Crowe, *Building the Judiciary: Law, Courts, and the Politics of Institutional Development* (Princeton, NJ: Princeton University Press, 2012), 153–56.

27. Warren, *The Supreme Court in United States History*, vol. 3, 145.

28. For competing accounts of this latter Judiciary Act, compare ibid., 223, with Crowe, *Building the Judiciary*, 156–59.

29. On Grant's failed nomination of Attorney General Ebenezer Hoar in December 1869, see Donald Grier Stephenson Jr., "The Waite Court," in *The Supreme Court: Controversies, Cases, and Characters from John Jay to John Roberts*, ed. Paul Finkelman (Santa Barbara, CA: ABC-CLIO, 2014), 309–405 at 318.

30. Ibid.

31. Stephen M. Engel, *American Politicians Confront the Court: Opposition Politics and Changing Responses to Judicial Power* (Cambridge, UK: Cambridge University Press, 2011), 216.

32. Jerre S. Williams, *The Supreme Court Speaks* (Freeport, NY: Books for Libraries Press, 1970), 115.

33. Ibid.

34. Quoted in Seth Lipsky, *The Citizen's Constitution: An Annotated Guide* (New York: Basic Books, 2011), 85.

35. Charles Fairman, *Reconstruction and Reunion, 1864–88, Part 1* (New York: Macmillan, 1971), 754n194.

36. Gerard N. Magliocca, "A New Approach to Congressional Power: Revisiting the *Legal Tender Cases*," *Georgetown Law Journal* 95, no. 1 (November 2006): 119–70 at 145.

37. *Knox v. Lee*, 79 US 457 (1871), at 553.

38. Ibid., 547. On this point, see also Dam, "The Legal Tender Cases," 391 ("[N]o member of the *Legal Tender* Courts was willing to go [so] far" as to rest upon the Coinage Clause).

39. *Knox v. Lee*, 79 US 457 (1871), at 544.

40. Ibid., 545.

41. Matthew St. Clair Clarke and David A. Hall, *Legislative and Documentary History of the Bank of the United States: Including the Original Bank of North America* (Washington, DC: Gales and Seaton, 1832), 631.

42. Ibid., 672.

43. Ibid., 671.

44. In this vein, see Wilson, *The Power "to Coin" Money*, 117–39.

45. Timberlake, *Constitutional Money*, 18 (emphasis added).

46. *Knox v. Lee*, 79 US 457 (1871), at 547.

47. *Norman v. Baltimore & Ohio Railroad Co.*, 294 US 240 (1935), at 303 (emphasis added).

48. *Knox v. Lee*, 79 US 457 (1871), at 532–33.

49. Ibid., 532 and 536.

50. *Juilliard v. Greenman*, 110 US 421 (1884).

51. Wright Patman, "The Federal Reserve System: A Brief for Legal Reform," *Saint Louis University Law Journal* 10, no. 3 (Spring 1966): 299–326 at 299; Richard A. Epstein, *The Classical Liberal Constitution: The Uncertain Quest for Limited Government* (Cambridge, MA: Harvard University Press, 2014), 221; Timberlake, *Constitutional Money*, 226. On this point, to be clear, Epstein and Timberlake are referencing the views of federal judges in the early twentieth century (rather than stating their own).

52. *Juilliard v. Greenman*, 110 US 421 (1884), at 447–48.

53. Sherman J. Maisel, *Managing the Dollar* (New York: W. W. Norton, 1973), 24; see also Sewell Chan, "Sherman J. Maisel, Former Fed Governor, Dies at 92," *New York Times*, October 7, 2010.

54. Paul Meek, quoted in Wilson, *The Power "to Coin" Money*, 202–3n1.

55. Allan H. Meltzer, *A History of the Federal Reserve: Volume 2, Book 2, 1970–1986* (Chicago: University of Chicago Press, 2010), 985–86.

56. Roy T. Meyers, *The Budgetary Status of the Federal Reserve System* (Washington, DC: Congressional Budget Office, 1985), 3.

57. Howard E. Shuman, *Politics and the Budget: The Struggle between the President and the Congress*, 3rd ed. (Englewood Cliffs, NJ: Prentice Hall, 1992), 18.

58. Bob Woodward, *Maestro: Greenspan's Fed and the American Boom* (New York: Simon & Schuster, 2001), 236.

59. Jasmine Farrier, *Passing the Buck: Congress, the Budget, and Deficits* (Lexington: University Press of Kentucky, 2001), 30.

60. See both John H. Wood, "Monetary Policy," in *The Oxford Companion to American Politics*, vol. 2, ed. David Coates (New York: Oxford University Press, 2012), 133–35, esp. at 134 (The Constitution "gives Congress the power 'to coin Money [and] regulate the Value thereof.' In 1913, Congress chose to exercise this power by creating

the Federal Reserve System") and Kathryn C. Lavelle, *Money and Banks in the American Political System* (Cambridge, UK: Cambridge University Press, 2013), 13 ("Article I, Section 8 of the Constitution gives Congress—not the executive branch or the courts—the power to coin money; hence, the Federal Reserve System is a creation of one of the three branches").

61. For a full transcript, see "The Economic Outlook: Hearing Before the Joint Economic Committee," 110th Cong., 2nd Sess., S. Hrg. 110-845, September 24, 2008, http://www.gpo.gov/fdsys/pkg/CHRG-110shrg46552/pdf/CHRG-110shrg46552.pdf.

62. See, for example, Ron Paul, *End the Fed* (New York: Grand Central, 2009).

63. The Emergency Economic Stabilization Act of 2008, Pub. L. No. 110-343, Division A, 122 Stat. 3765.

64. "The Economic Outlook," 32.

65. Ibid., 32–33.

66. Timberlake, *Constitutional Money*, 226.

67. See William H. Riker, *The Art of Political Manipulation* (New Haven, CT: Yale University Press, 1986) at 34 (where he discusses the "redefinition of [a] political situation so that formerly unsympathetic" individuals now wish to support someone or something).

68. Dam, "The Legal Tender Cases," 367.

69. Ibid., 369.

70. On the Commerce Clause during and after the mid-1930s, for example, see much of the scholarship cited at the conclusion of Herbert A. Johnson's bibliographic essay in *Gibbons v. Ogden: John Marshall, Steamboats, and the Commerce Clause* (Lawrence: University Press of Kansas, 2010).

71. For attention to (and an elaborate critique of) the conventional understanding of the Court's work here, see Howard Gillman, *The Constitution Besieged: The Rise and Demise of Lochner Era Police Powers Jurisprudence* (Durham, NC: Duke University Press, 1993).

72. James W. Ely Jr., *The Contract Clause: A Constitutional History* (Lawrence: University Press of Kansas, 2016).

73. Bill White, *America's Fiscal Constitution: Its Triumph and Collapse* (New York: PublicAffairs, 2014).

74. Compare Elizabeth Price Foley, "Only Congress Can Raise the Debt Ceiling," *New York Times*, January 29, 2014, with Eric Posner's op-ed in the same issue, "Emergency Powers Let the President Borrow beyond the Debt Limit."

BIBLIOGRAPHY

SUPREME COURT CASES

Barron v. Baltimore, 32 US 243 (1833)

Hepburn v. Griswold, 75 US 603 (1869)

Juilliard v. Greenman, 110 US 421 (1884)

J. W. Hampton, Jr. & Co. v. United States, 276 US 394 (1928)

Knox v. Lee, 79 US 457 (1871)

McCulloch v. Maryland, 17 US 316 (1819)

McCutcheon v. Federal Election Commission, 572 US ___ (2014)

NFIB v. Sebelius, 567 US 519 (2012)

Norman v. Baltimore & Ohio Railroad Co., 294 US 240 (1935)

Youngstown Sheet & Tube Co. v. Sawyer, 343 US 579 (1952)

NEWSPAPERS

Albany Daily Advertiser (1815)

Alexandria Daily Gazette (1813)

Aurora General Advertiser [Philadelphia] (1810–1811)

Baltimore Patriot (1815)

Boston Daily Advertiser (1815)

Connecticut Journal [New Haven] (1815)

Courier [New York City] (1816)

Evening Post [New York City] (1813)

Federal Republican [Georgetown, DC] (1815)

Northern Post [Salem, NY] (1815)

Orange County Patriot [Goshen, NY] (1814)

Rhode-Island American [Providence] (1815)

Tickler [Philadelphia] (1813)

True American [Trenton] (1815)

Washingtonian [Windsor, VT] (1814)

Worcester Gazette or *Massachusetts Spy* (1814)

COLLECTIONS

American State Papers on Finance. 5 vols. Buffalo, NY: Hein, 1998.

Annals of Congress. https://memory.loc.gov/ammem/amlaw/lwac.html.

Circular Letters of Congressmen to Their Constituents, 1789–1829, edited by Noble E. Cunningham Jr. 3 vols. Chapel Hill: University of North Carolina Press, 1978.

James O. Wettereau Research Papers. Columbia University Rare Book and Manuscript Library.

Letters of Benjamin Rush, edited by L. H. Butterfield. 2 vols. Philadelphia: American Philosophical Society, 1951.

The Life and Correspondence of Rufus King, edited by Charles R. King. 6 vols. New York: G. P. Putnam's Sons, 1898.

National Archives and Records Administration, Record Group 33 (Washington, DC, site).

Nicholas Biddle Papers. Library of Congress. Finding aid available at http://lccn.loc.gov/mm78012690.

Official Letter Books of W. C. C. Claiborne, 1801–1816, edited by Dunbar Rowland. 6 vols. Madison, WI: Democrat Printing Company, 1917.

Papers of Alexander Hamilton, edited by Harold Syrett et al. 27 vols. New York: Columbia University Press, 1961–1987.

Papers of Daniel Webster: Correspondence Series, edited by Charles M. Wiltse. 7 vols. Hanover, NH: University Press of New England, 1974–1989.

Papers of Henry Clay, edited by James F. Hopkins and Mary W. M. Hargreaves. 10 vols. Lexington: University of Kentucky Press, 1959.

Papers of James Madison: Retirement Series, edited by David Mattern et al. 3 vols. Charlottesville: University of Virginia Press, 2009–2016.

Papers of Thomas Jefferson, edited by Julian Boyd et al. 42 vols. Princeton, NJ: Princeton University Press, 1950–2016.

Register of Debates. https://memory.loc.gov/ammem/amlaw/lwrd.html.

Supreme Court Database. http://supremecourtdatabase.org/about.php?s=2.

The Writings of Albert Gallatin, edited by Henry Adams. 3 vols. Philadelphia: J. B. Lippincott, 1879.

The Writings of James Madison, edited by Gaillard Hunt. 9 vols. New York: G. P. Putnam's Sons, 1900–1910.

BOOKS AND ARTICLES

Ackerman, Bruce. *We the People.* Vol. 1, *Foundations.* Cambridge, MA: Belknap Press of Harvard University Press, 1991.

Adams, Donald R. Jr. *Finance and Enterprise in Early America: A Study of Stephen Girard's Bank, 1812–1831.* Philadelphia: University of Pennsylvania Press, 1978.

Adams, Henry. *History of the United States of America during the Administrations of James Madison.* New York: Library of America, 1986.

———. *The Life of Albert Gallatin.* Philadelphia: J. B. Lippincott, 1880.

Agresto, John. *The Supreme Court and Constitutional Democracy.* Ithaca, NY: Cornell University Press, 1984.

Amar, Akhil Reed. *America's Unwritten Constitution: The Precedents and Principles We Live By.* New York: Basic Books, 2012.

Anderson, Dice Robins. *William Branch Giles: A Study in the Politics of Virginia and the Nation from 1790 to 1830.* Menasha, WI: George Banta, 1914.

Ashworth, John. *Slavery, Capitalism, and Politics in the Antebellum Republic.* Vol. 1, *Commerce and Compromise, 1820–1850.* Cambridge, UK: Cambridge University Press, 1995.

Atwater, Jesse. *Considerations on the Approaching Dissolution of the United States Bank.* New Haven, CT: Sidney's Press, 1810.

Bailey, Jeremy D. *James Madison and Constitutional Imperfection.* Cambridge, UK: Cambridge University Press, 2015.

Baker, Sam. "Justices Clash over Campaign Finance Law." *The Hill,* October 9, 2013. http://thehill.com/blogs/ballot-box/fundraising/327171-justices-clash-over -campaign-finance-law.

"Bank Mania." *Federal Republican,* October 20, 1815.

"Bank of the United States." H.R. 460, 22nd Cong., 1st Sess., April 1832. https://books .google.com/books/reader?id=xvG-jNQ_B-gC&printsec=frontcover&output=reader &pg=GBS.PR5.

"The Bank of the United States: Petitions of Virginia Cities and Towns for the Establishment of Branches, 1791." *Virginia Magazine of History and Biography* 8, no. 3 (January 1901): 287–95.

Banner, Stuart. *Anglo-American Securities Regulation: Cultural and Political Roots, 1690–1860.* Cambridge, UK: Cambridge University Press, 2002.

Banning, Lance. *The Jeffersonian Persuasion: Evolution of a Party Ideology.* Ithaca, NY: Cornell University Press, 1978.

Barber, Sotirios A. *On What the Constitution Means.* Baltimore: Johns Hopkins University Press, 1984.

Bassok, Or, and Yoav Dotan. "Solving the Countermajoritarian Difficulty?" *International Journal of Constitutional Law* 11, no. 1 (January 2013): 13–33.

Beard, Charles A. *Economic Origins of Jeffersonian Democracy.* New York: Free Press, 1915.

Bickel, Alexander M. *The Least Dangerous Branch: The Supreme Court at the Bar of Politics.* Indianapolis: Bobbs-Merrill, 1962.

Black, Charles L. Jr. *Structure and Relationship in Constitutional Law.* Woodbridge, CT: Ox Bow Press, 1985.

Bobbitt, Philip. *Constitutional Fate: Theory of the Constitution.* New York: Oxford University Press, 1982.

Bodenhorn, Howard. *State Banking in Early America: A New Economic History.* New York: Oxford University Press, 2003.

Bollmann, Erick. *Paragraphs on Banks.* 2nd ed. Philadelphia: C & A Conrad, 1811.

Bowling, Kenneth R. "The Bank Bill, the Capital City and President Washington." *Capitol Studies* 1, no. 1 (Spring 1972): 59–71.

Brandwein, Pamela. *Reconstructing Reconstruction: The Supreme Court and the Production of Historical Truth.* Durham, NC: Duke University Press, 1999.

Brest, Paul, Sanford Levinson, Jack Balkin, and Akhil Reed Amar. "The Bank of the United States: A Case Study." In *Processes of Constitutional Decisionmaking: Cases and Materials,* 4th ed., edited by Paul Brest, Sanford Levinson, Jack Balkin, and Akhil Reed Amar, 7–70. New York: Aspen Law and Business, 2000.

Broussard, James H. *The Southern Federalists, 1800–1816.* Baton Rouge: Louisiana State University Press, 1999.

Brownlee, W. Elliot. *Federal Taxation in America: A Short History.* Cambridge, UK: Cambridge University Press, 2004.

———. "Long-Run Fiscal Consolidations in the United States: The History at the Federal Level." In *Deficits and Debt in Industrialized Democracies,* edited by Eisaku Ide and Gene Park, 171–98. New York: Routledge, 2015.

Broz, J. Lawrence. *The International Origins of the Federal Reserve System.* Ithaca, NY: Cornell University Press, 1997.

Bruchey, Stuart. "Alexander Hamilton and the State Banks, 1789–1795." *William and Mary Quarterly* 27, no. 3 (July 1970): 347–78.

———. *Enterprise: The Dynamic Economy of a Free People.* Cambridge, MA: Harvard University Press, 1990.

Bryan, Alfred Cookman. *History of State Banking in Maryland.* Baltimore: Johns Hopkins University Press, 1899.

Burkleo, Sandra F. "'The Paws of Banks': The Origins and Significance of Kentucky's Decision to Tax Federal Bankers, 1818–1820." *Journal of the Early Republic* 9, no. 4 (Winter 1989): 457–87.

Burrows, Edwin, and Mike Wallace. *Gotham: A History of New York City to 1898.* New York: Oxford University Press, 1999.

Camurea, Zelia Sa Viana. "Condy Raguet: His Life, Work, and Education." PhD diss., University of Pennsylvania (Anthropology), 1988.

Carey, George W. *In Defense of the Constitution,* rev. ed. Indianapolis: Liberty Fund, 1995.

Carey, Matthew. *Desultory Reflections upon the Ruinous Consequences of a Non-Renewal of the Charter of the Bank of the United States.* 3rd ed. Philadelphia: Fry and Kammerer, 1810.

———. *Essays on Banking.* Philadelphia: published by author, 1816.

———. *Letters to Dr. Adam Seybert, Representative in Congress for the City of Philadelphia, on the Subject of the Renewal of the Charter of the Bank of the United States.* 2nd ed. Philadelphia: published by author, 1811.

Carter, Edward C. II. "The Birth of a Political Economist: Matthew Carey and the Recharter Fight of 1810–1811." *Pennsylvania History* 33, no. 3 (July 1966): 274–88.

Catterall, Ralph. *The Second Bank of the United States.* Chicago: University of Chicago Press, 1903.

Cerami, Charles A. *Dinner at Mr. Jefferson's: Three Men, Five Great Wines, and the Evening That Changed America.* New York: Wiley, 2009.

Chambers, William Nisbet, ed. *The First Party System: Federalists and Republicans.* New York: John Wiley, 1972.

———. *Political Parties in a New Nation: The American Experience, 1776–1809*. New York: Oxford University Press, 1963.

Chan, Sewell. "Sherman J. Maisel, Former Fed Governor, Dies at 92." *New York Times*, October 7, 2010.

Chernow, Ron. *Alexander Hamilton*. New York: Penguin, 2004.

Choper, Jesse H., Richard H. Fallon Jr., Yale Kamisar, and Steven H. Shiffrin. *Constitutional Law: Cases, Comments, Questions*. 10th ed. St. Paul, MN: Thomson/West, 2006.

Clark, Allen C. *William Duane*. Washington, DC: Press of W. F. Roberts, 1905.

Clarke, Matthew St. Clair, and David A. Hall. *Legislative and Documentary History of the Bank of the United States: Including the Original Bank of North America*. Washington, DC: Gales and Seaton, 1832.

Clayton, Cornell, and David May. "A Political Regimes Approach to the Analysis of Legal Decisions." *Polity* 32, no. 2 (Winter 1999): 233–52.

Collins, H. M. *Changing Order: Replication and Induction in Scientific Practice*. Chicago: University of Chicago Press, 1985.

Connelly, William F. Jr. *James Madison Rules America: The Constitutional Origins of Congressional Partisanship*. Lanham, MD: Rowman & Littlefield, 2010.

Connelly, William F. Jr., and John J. Pitney Jr. "The House Republicans: Lessons for Political Science." In *New Majority or Old Minority? The Impact of Republicans on Congress*, edited by Nicol C. Rae and Colton C. Campbell, 173–94. Lanham, MD: Rowman & Littlefield, 1999.

Cooper, John Milton. *Woodrow Wilson: A Biography*. New York: Random House, 2011.

Cowen, David J. *The Origins and Economic Impact of the First Bank of the United States, 1791–1797*. New York: Garland, 2000.

Cray, Robert E. Jr. "Remembering the USS Chesapeake: The Politics of Maritime Death and Impressment." *Journal of the Early Republic* 25, no. 3 (Fall 2005): 445–74.

Cross, Frank B. *The Failed Promise of Originalism*. Stanford, CA: Stanford Law Books, 2013.

Crothers, A. Glenn. "Banks and Economic Development in Post-Revolutionary Northern Virginia, 1790–1812." *Business History Review* 73, no. 1 (Spring 1999): 1–39.

Crowe, Justin. *Building the Judiciary: Law, Courts, and the Politics of Institutional Development*. Princeton, NJ: Princeton University Press, 2012.

Cunningham, Noble Jr. *The Jeffersonian Republicans in Power: Party Operations, 1801–1809*. Chapel Hill: University of North Carolina Press, 1963.

Currie, David P. *The Constitution in Congress: The Federalist Period, 1789–1801*. Chicago: University of Chicago Press, 1997.

———. *The Constitution in Congress: The Jeffersonians, 1801–1829*. Chicago: University of Chicago Press, 2001.

———. *The Constitution in Congress: Democrats and Whigs, 1829–1861*. Chicago: University of Chicago Press, 2005.

Dahl, Robert A. "Decision-Making in a Democracy: The Supreme Court as a National Policy-Maker." *Journal of Public Law* 6, no. 2 (Fall 1957): 279–95.

Dallas, George M. *The Life and Writings of Alexander James Dallas*. Philadelphia: J. B. Lippincott, 1871.

Dam, Kenneth W. "The Legal Tender Cases." In *The Supreme Court Review: 1981,* edited by Philip B. Kurland, Gerhard Casper, and Dennis J. Hutchinson, 367–412. Chicago: University of Chicago Press, 1982.

Daniels, Belden L. *Pennsylvania: Birthplace of Banking in America.* Harrisburg: Pennsylvania Bankers Association, 1976.

Davis, Joseph Stancliffe. *Essays in the Earlier History of American Corporations.* Cambridge, MA: Harvard University Press, 1917.

Dellinger, Walter, and H. Jefferson Powell. "The Constitutionality of the Bank Bill: The Attorney General's First Constitutional Law Opinions." *Duke Law Journal* 44, no. 1 (October 1994): 110–33.

Destler, Chester McArthur. "The Union Bank of New London: Formative Years." *Connecticut Historical Society Bulletin* 24, no. 1 (January 1959): 14–26.

Dewey, Davis R. *The Second United States Bank.* Washington, DC: Government Printing Office, 1910.

———. *State Banking before the Civil War.* Washington, DC: National Monetary Commission, 1910.

Domett, Henry W. *A History of the Bank of New York, 1784–1884.* New York: G. P. Putnam's Sons, 1884.

Dorfman, Joseph. *The Economic Mind in American Civilization, 1606–1865.* New York: Viking Press, 1946.

Dry, Murray. "The Case against Ratification: Anti-Federalist Constitutional Thought." In *The Framing and Ratification of the Constitution,* edited by Leonard W. Levy and Dennis J. Mahoney, 271–91. New York: Macmillan, 1987.

Duane, William. "Bank Business," *Aurora General Advertiser,* November 8, 1810.

———. "The Bank Charter—No. II." *Aurora General Advertiser,* January 10, 1811.

———. "A Review of Certain Pamphlets on Banking [No. 1]." *Aurora General Advertiser,* December 25, 1810.

Dudley, William S., and Michael J. Crawford, eds. *The Naval War of 1812: A Documentary History.* 3 vols. Washington, DC: Naval Historical Center, 1985–2002.

Dungan, Nicholas. *Gallatin: America's Swiss Founding Father.* New York: New York University Press, 2010.

"The Economic Outlook: Hearing Before the Joint Economic Committee." 110th Cong., 2nd Sess., S. Hrg. 110-845, September 24, 2008. http://www.gpo.gov/fdsys/pkg/CHRG-110shrg46552/pdf/CHRG-110shrg46552.pdf.

Edling, Max M. *A Hercules in the Cradle: War, Money, and the American State, 1783–1867.* Chicago: University of Chicago Press, 2014.

———. "The War of 1812 and the Modernization of American War Finance." Unpublished paper on file with the author.

Elazar, Daniel. "Banking and Federalism in the Early American Republic." *Huntington Library Quarterly* 28, no. 4 (August 1965): 301–20.

Elkins, Stanley, and Eric McKitrick. *The Age of Federalism: The Early American Republic, 1788–1800.* New York: Oxford University Press, 1993.

Ellis, Richard E. *Aggressive Nationalism: McCulloch v. Maryland and the Foundation of Federal Authority in the Young Republic.* New York: Oxford University Press, 2007.

———. *The Jeffersonian Crisis: Courts and Politics in the Young Republic.* New York: W. W. Norton, 1971.

Ely, James W. Jr. *The Contract Clause: A Constitutional History.* Lawrence: University Press of Kansas, 2016.

Engel, Stephen M. *American Politicians Confront the Court: Opposition Politics and Changing Responses to Judicial Power.* Cambridge, UK: Cambridge University Press, 2011.

Epstein, Lee, William M. Landes, and Richard A. Posner. *The Behavior of Federal Judges: A Theoretical and Empirical Study of Rational Choice.* Cambridge, MA: Harvard University Press, 2013.

Epstein, Lee, and Thomas G. Walker. *Constitutional Law for a Changing America: A Short Course.* 6th ed. Thousand Oaks, CA: CQ Press, 2015.

Epstein, Richard A. *The Classical Liberal Constitution: The Uncertain Quest for Limited Government.* Cambridge, MA: Harvard University Press, 2014.

Eyal, Yonatan. *The Young America Movement and the Transformation of the Democratic Party, 1828–1861.* Cambridge, UK: Cambridge University Press, 2007.

Fairman, Charles. *Reconstruction and Reunion, 1864–88, Part One.* New York: Macmillan, 1971.

Farber, Daniel A. "The Story of *McCulloch*: Banking on National Power." *Constitutional Commentary* 20, no. 3 (Winter 2003–2004): 679–714.

Farrier, Jasmine. *Passing the Buck: Congress, the Budget, and Deficits.* Lexington: University Press of Kentucky, 2001.

Fenstermaker, Joseph Van. *The Development of American Commercial Banking: 1782–1837.* Kent, OH: Bureau of Economic and Business Research, 1965.

Fisher, Louis. *American Constitutional Law.* Vol. 1, *Constitutional Structures: Separated Powers and Federalism.* Durham, NC: Carolina Academic Press, 2001.

Foley, Elizabeth Price. "Only Congress Can Raise the Debt Ceiling." *New York Times,* January 29, 2014.

Freeman, Joanne B., ed. *Alexander Hamilton: Writings.* New York: Library of America, 2001.

Galbraith, John Kenneth. *Money: Whence It Came, Where It Went.* Boston: Houghton Mifflin, 1975.

Gallatin, Albert. *Considerations on the Currency and Banking System of the United States.* Philadelphia: Carey and Lea, 1831.

Gardiner, Burent. "Current Money." *Rhode-Island American,* August 25, 1815.

Gillman, Howard. *The Constitution Besieged: The Rise and Demise of Lochner Era Police Powers Jurisprudence.* Durham, NC: Duke University Press, 1993.

———. "Courts and the Politics of Partisan Coalitions." In *The Oxford Handbook of Laws and Politics,* edited by Keith Whittington, R. Daniel Keleman, and Gregory Caldeira, 644–62. New York: Oxford University Press.

———. "What's Law Got to Do with It? Judicial Behavioralists Test the 'Legal Model' of Judicial Decision Making." *Law and Social Inquiry* 26, no. 2 (Spring 2001): 464–504.

Gillman, Howard, Mark A. Graber, and Keith E. Whittington. *American Constitutionalism.* Vol. 1, *Structures of Government.* New York: Oxford University Press, 2013.

Gilmore, Peter, and Kerby A. Miller. "Searching for 'Irish' Freedom—Settling for

'Scotch-Irish' Respectability: Southwestern Pennsylvania, 1780–1810." In *Ulster to America: The Scots-Irish Migration Experience, 1680–1830*, edited by Warren R. Hofstra, 165–210. Knoxville: University of Tennessee Press, 2012.

Govan, Thomas Payne. *Nicholas Biddle: Nationalist and Public Banker, 1786–1844*. Chicago: University of Chicago Press, 1959.

Graber, Mark A. "Federalist or Friends of Adams: The Marshall Court and Party Politics." *Studies in American Political Development* 12, no. 2 (Fall 1998): 229–66.

———. *A New Introduction to American Constitutionalism*. New York: Oxford University Press, 2013.

———. "The Nonmajoritarian Difficulty: Legislative Deference to the Judiciary." *Studies in American Political Development* 7, no. 1 (Spring 1993): 35–73.

Gras, N. S. B. *The Massachusetts First National Bank of Boston, 1784–1934*. Cambridge, MA: Harvard University Press, 1937.

Gunther, Gerald, ed. *John Marshall's Defense of* McCulloch v. Maryland. Stanford, CA: Stanford University Press, 1969.

Ha, Songho. *The Rise and Fall of the American System: Nationalism and the Development of the American Economy, 1790–1837*. London: Routledge, 2009.

Hamilton, Alexander. "Report on a National Bank." In *Alexander Hamilton: Writings*, edited by Joanne B. Freeman, 575–612. New York: Library of America, 2001.

———. "Report on Public Credit." In *Alexander Hamilton: Writings*, edited by Joanne B. Freeman, 531–74. New York: Library of America, 2001.

Hamilton, Alexander, James Madison, and John Jay. *The Federalist with Letters of "Brutus,"* edited by Terence Ball. Cambridge, UK: Cambridge University Press, 2003.

Hammond, Bray. *Banks and Politics in America: From the Revolution to the Civil War*. Princeton, NJ: Princeton University Press, 1957.

Hammond, Jabez D. *The History of Political Parties in the State of New York, from the Ratification of the Federal Constitution to December 1840*. Buffalo, NY: Phinney, 1850.

Handlin, Oscar, and Mary Flug Handlin. *Commonwealth: A Study of the Role of Government in the American Economy: Massachusetts, 1774–1861*. Cambridge, MA: Harvard University Press, 1969.

Heidler, Jeanne T., and David S. Heidler. "Rhea, John." In *Encyclopedia of the War of 1812*, edited by David S. Heidler and Jeanne T. Heidler, 446. Santa Barbara, CA: ABC-CLIO, 1997.

Herrick, Carole L. *August 24, 1814: Washington in Flames*. Falls Church, VA: Higher Education Publications, 2005.

Hickey, Donald R. *The War of 1812: A Forgotten Conflict*. Urbana: University of Illinois Press, 1989.

Hoffmann, Susan. *Politics and Banking: Ideas, Public Policy, and the Creation of Financial Institutions*. Baltimore: Johns Hopkins University Press, 2001.

Holdsworth, John Thom. *Financing an Empire: History of Banking in Pennsylvania*. Chicago: S. J. Clarke, 1928.

———. *The First Bank of the United States*. Washington, DC: National Monetary Commission, 1910.

Horn, James J., Jan Ellen Lewis, and Peter S. Onuf, eds. *The Revolution of 1800: Democ-*

racy, Race, and the New Republic. Charlottesville: University of Virginia Press, 2002.

Howe, Daniel Walker. *What Hath God Wrought: The Transformation of America, 1815–1848.* New York: Oxford University Press, 2007.

Hurst, James Willard. *A Legal History of Money in the United States, 1774–1970.* Lincoln: University of Nebraska Press, 1973.

Ippolito, Dennis S. *Deficits, Debt, and the New Politics of Tax Policy.* Cambridge, UK: Cambridge University Press, 2012.

Jackson, Andrew. "First Annual Message." December 8, 1829. http://www.presidency .ucsb.edu/ws/index.php?pid=29471.

———. "Veto Message." In *Jackson versus Biddle: The Struggle over the Second Bank of the United States,* edited by George Rogers Taylor, 7–20. Boston: D. C. Heath, 1949.

Jefferson, Thomas. "Inaugural Address." March 4, 1801. http://www.presidency.ucsb .edu/ws/index.php?pid=25803.

Jenkins, Jeffrey A., and Marc Weidenmier. "Ideology, Economic Interests, and Congressional Role-Call Voting: Partisan Instability and Bank of the United States Legislation, 1811–1816." *Public Choice* 100, no. 3–4 (September 1999): 225–43.

John, Richard R. "American Political Development and Political History." In *The Oxford Handbook of American Political Development,* edited by Richard M. Valelly, Suzanne Mettler, and Robert C. Lieberman, 185–206. New York: Oxford University Press, 2016.

Johnson, Herbert A. *Gibbons v. Ogden: John Marshall, Steamboats, and the Commerce Clause.* Lawrence: University Press of Kansas, 2010.

Kagin, Donald H. "Monetary Aspects of the Treasury Notes of the War of 1812." *Journal of Economic History* 44, no. 1 (March 1984): 69–88.

Keck, Thomas M. "Party, Policy, or Duty? Why Does the Supreme Court Invalidate Federal Statutes?" *American Political Science Review* 101, no. 2 (May 2007): 321–38.

Ketcham, Ralph. *Presidents above Party: The First American Presidency, 1789–1829.* Chapel Hill: University of North Carolina Press, 1984.

Keyes, Robert W. III. "The Formation of the Second Bank of the United States, 1811–1817." PhD diss., University of Delaware (History), 1975.

Killenbeck, Mark R. *M'Culloch v. Maryland: Securing a Nation.* Lawrence: University Press of Kansas, 2006.

Kishlansky, Mark. *A Monarchy Transformed: Britain, 1603–1714.* New York: Penguin, 1996.

Klebaner, Benjamin J. *American Commercial Banking: A History.* Boston: Twayne, 1990.

Klubes, Benjamin B. "The First Federal Congress and the First National Bank: A Case Study in Constitutional Interpretation." *Journal of the Early Republic* 10, no. 1 (Spring 1990): 19–41.

Knox, John Jay. *A History of Banking in the United States.* New York: Bradford Rhodes, 1900.

Konkle, Burton Alva. *Thomas Willing and the First American Financial System.* Philadelphia: University of Pennsylvania Press, 1937.

Kurland, Philip B., and Ralph Lerner, eds. *The Founders' Constitution*. Vol. 3, *Article I, Section 8, Clause 5 through Article 2, Section 1*. Indianapolis: Liberty Fund, 2000.

Lake, Wilfred S. "The End of the Suffolk System." *Journal of Economic History* 7, no. 2 (November 1947): 183–207.

Lamoreaux, Naomi. *Insider Lending: Banks, Personal Connections, and Economic Development in Industrial New England*. Cambridge, UK: Cambridge University Press, 1994.

Larson, John Lauritz. *Internal Improvement: National Public Works and the Promise of Popular Government in the Early United States*. Chapel Hill: University of North Carolina Press, 2001.

Latimer, Jon. *1812: War with America*. Cambridge, MA: Harvard University Press, 2007.

Lavelle, Kathryn C. *Money and Banks in the American Political System*. Cambridge, UK: Cambridge University Press, 2013.

Lawrence, William B. "Bank of the United States." *North American Review* 32, no. 71 (April 1831): 524–63.

Lawson, Gary, Geoffrey P. Miller, Robert G. Natelson, and Guy I. Seidman. *The Origins of the Necessary and Proper Clause*. Cambridge, UK: Cambridge University Press, 2010.

Lewis, Lawrence Jr. *A History of the Bank of North America*. Philadelphia: J. B. Lippincott, 1882.

Liancourt, Duke de la Rochefoucault. *Travels through the United States of America, the Country of the Iroquois, and Upper Canada, in the Years 1795, 1796, and 1797*. 2nd ed. London: T. Gillet, 1800.

Lindert, Peter H., and Richard Sutch. "Consumer Price Indexes, for All Items: 1774–2003." Table Cc1-2 in *Historical Statistics of the United States: Millennial Edition Online*, edited by Susan Carter et al. http://hsus.cambridge.org/HSUSWeb/ HSUSEntryServlet. Cambridge, UK: Cambridge University Press, 2006.

Lipsky, Seth. *The Citizen's Constitution: An Annotated Guide*. New York: Basic Books, 2011.

Lomazoff, Eric. "The Developing Mind of the Founder? James Madison and the National Bank Question, 1791–1831." Unpublished paper on file with the author.

———. "*Martin v. Hunter's Lessee* (1816)." In *American Governance*, vol. 3, edited by Stephen Schechter et al., 251–52. New York: Macmillan Reference, 2016.

———. "Symmetry and Repetition: Patterns in the History of the Bank of the United States." In *Routledge Handbook of Major Events in Economic History*, edited by Randall E. Parker and Robert Whaples, 3–14. New York: Routledge.

———. "Turning (Into) 'The Great Regulating Wheel': The Conversion of the Bank of the United States, 1791–1811." *Studies in American Political Development* 26, no. 1 (April 2012): 1–23.

Lowenstein, Roger. *America's Bank: The Epic Struggle to Create the Federal Reserve*. New York: Penguin Press, 2015.

Lynch, Joseph M. *Negotiating the Constitution: The Earliest Debates over Original Intent*. Ithaca, NY: Cornell University Press, 1999.

Maclay, William. *The Journal of William Maclay: United States Senator from Pennsylvania, 1789–1791*. New York: Albert and Charles Boni, 1927.

Madison, James. "Sixth Annual Message." September 20, 1814. http://www.presidency
.ucsb.edu/ws/?pid=29456.

———. "Seventh Annual Message." December 5, 1815. http://www.presidency.ucsb.edu/
ws/?pid=29457.

———. "Eighth Annual Message." December 3, 1816. http://www.presidency.ucsb.edu/
ws/index.php?pid=29458.

———. "Veto Message on the Internal Improvements Bill." March 3, 1817. https://
millercenter.org/the-presidency/presidential-speeches/march-3-1817-veto-message
-internal-improvements-bill.

Madsen, Axel. *John Jacob Astor: America's First Multimillionaire.* New York: John
Wiley, 2002.

Magliocca, Gerard N. *American Founding Son: John Bingham and the Invention of the
Fourteenth Amendment.* New York: New York University Press, 2013.

———. *Andrew Jackson and the Constitution: The Rise and Fall of Generational Regimes.* Lawrence: University Press of Kansas, 2007.

———. "A New Approach to Congressional Power: Revisiting the *Legal Tender Cases.*"
Georgetown Law Journal 95, no. 1 (November 2006): 119–70.

Magrath, C. Peter. *Yazoo: Law and Politics in the New Republic: The Case of* Fletcher v.
Peck. New York: W. W. Norton, 1967.

Mahoney, James, and Kathleen Thelen. "A Theory of Gradual Institutional Change." In
Explaining Institutional Change: Ambiguity, Agency, and Power, edited by James
Mahoney and Kathleen Thelen, 1–37. Cambridge, UK: Cambridge University Press,
2010.

Maisel, Sherman J. *Managing the Dollar.* New York: W. W. Norton, 1973.

Mann, Bruce. *Republic of Debtors: Bankruptcy in the Age of American Independence.*
Cambridge, MA: Harvard University Press, 2009.

Mashaw, Jerry L. *Creating the Administrative Constitution: The Lost One Hundred
Years of American Administrative Law.* New Haven, CT: Yale University Press,
2012.

McCloskey, Robert G. *The American Supreme Court.* 5th ed., revised by Sanford Levinson. Chicago: University of Chicago Press, 2010.

McCraw, Thomas K. *The Founders and Finance: How Hamilton, Gallatin, and Other
Immigrants Forged a New Economy.* Cambridge, MA: Belknap Press of Harvard
University Press, 2012.

McCullough, David. *John Adams.* New York: Simon & Schuster, 2001.

McGinty, Brian. *Lincoln and the Court.* Cambridge, MA: Harvard University Press,
2008.

McGrane, Reginald C., ed. *The Correspondence of Nicholas Biddle Dealing with National Affairs, 1807–1844.* Boston: J. S. Canner, 1966.

Meltzer, Allan H. *A History of the Federal Reserve: Volume 2, Book 2, 1970–1986.* Chicago: University of Chicago Press, 2010.

Meyers, Roy T. *The Budgetary Status of the Federal Reserve System.* Washington, DC:
Congressional Budget Office, 1985.

Mihm, Stephen. *A Nation of Counterfeiters: Capitalists, Con Men, and the Making of
the United States.* Cambridge, MA: Harvard University Press, 2007.

Milkis, Sidney M., and Jesse H. Rhodes. "The President, Party Politics, and Consti-
    tutional Development." In *The Oxford Handbook of American Political Parties
    and Interest Groups*, edited by L. Sandy Maisel and Jeffrey M. Berry, 377–402. New
    York: Oxford University Press, 2010.

Miller, John C. *The Federalist Era, 1789–1801*. New York: Harper & Row, 1960.

Mints, Lloyd. *A History of Banking Theory in Great Britain and the United States*.
    Chicago: University of Chicago Press, 1945.

Mooney, Chase. *William H. Crawford, 1772–1834*. Lexington: University Press of
    Kentucky, 1974.

Munsell, Joel. "Notices of the Several Banks Located at Albany." *Merchants' Magazine
    and Commercial Review* 21, no. 5 (November 1849): 561–63.

Murphy, Brian Phillips. *Building the Empire State: Political Economy in the Early
    Republic*. Philadelphia: University of Pennsylvania Press, 2015.

———. "'A Very Convenient Instrument': The Manhattan Company, Aaron Burr, and
    the Election of 1800." *William and Mary Quarterly* 65, no. 2 (April 2008): 233–66.

Murphy, Walter F., James E. Fleming, Sotirios A. Barber, and Stephen Macedo. *Ameri-
    can Constitutional Interpretation*. 4th ed. New York: Foundation Press, 2008.

Myers, Margaret. *A Financial History of the United States*. New York: Columbia Uni-
    versity Press, 1970.

Nagel, Paul C. *One Nation Indivisible: The Union in American Thought, 1776–1861*.
    New York: Oxford University Press, 1964.

Natelson, Robert G. "Paper Money and the Original Understanding of the Coin-
    age Clause." *Harvard Journal of Law and Public Policy* 31, no. 3 (Summer 2008):
    1017–81.

Nevins, Allan. *History of the Bank of New York and Trust Company, 1784 to 1934*.
    New York: William E. Rudge's Sons, 1934.

"New Legislation Aims to 'Organize Our Peace,' He Says." *New York Times*, December
    24, 1913.

Newmyer, R. Kent. *John Marshall and the Heroic Age of the Supreme Court*. Baton
    Rouge: Louisiana State University Press, 2007.

———. "John Marshall, *McCulloch v. Maryland*, and the Southern States' Rights Tradi-
    tion." *John Marshall Law Review* 33, no. 4 (2000): 875–934.

O'Brien, David M. *Constitutional Law and Politics*. Vol. 1, *Struggles for Power and
    Governmental Accountability*. 9th ed. New York: W. W. Norton, 2014.

———. "Institutional Norms and Supreme Court Opinions: On Reconsidering the Rise
    of Individual Opinions." In *Supreme Court Decision-Making: New Institutionalist
    Approaches*, edited by Cornell W. Clayton and Howard Gillman, 91–113. Chicago:
    University of Chicago Press, 1999.

O'Halloran, Sharyn. *Politics, Process, and American Trade Policy*. Ann Arbor: Univer-
    sity of Michigan Press, 1994.

"On Banks." *Connecticut Journal*, May 1, 1815.

Orren, Karen, and Stephen Skowronek. "Institutions and Intercurrence: Theory Build-
    ing in the Fullness of Time." In *NOMOS 38: Political Order*, edited by Ian Shapiro
    and Russell Hardin, 111–46. New York: New York University Press.

———. *The Search for American Political Development.* Cambridge, UK: Cambridge University Press, 2004.

———. "The Study of American Political Development." In *Political Science: The State of the Discipline,* edited by Ira Katznelson and Helen V. Milner, 722–54. New York: W. W. Norton, 2003.

Parker, Kunal M. *Common Law, History, and Democracy in America, 1790–1900: Legal Thought before Modernism.* Cambridge, UK: Cambridge University Press, 2011.

Patman, Wright. "The Federal Reserve System: A Brief for Legal Reform." *Saint Louis University Law Journal* 10, no. 3 (Spring 1966): 299–326.

Paul, Ron. *End the Fed.* New York: Grand Central, 2009.

Perkins, Bradford. *Prologue to War: England and the United States, 1805–1812.* Berkeley: University of California Press, 1970.

Perkins, Edwin J. *American Public Finance and Financial Services, 1700–1815.* Columbus: Ohio State University Press, 1994.

Peskin, Lawrence A. "How the Republicans Learned to Love Manufacturing: The First Parties and the 'New Economy.'" *Journal of the Early Republic* 22, no. 2 (Summer 2002): 235–62.

Phillips, Kevin. *Wealth and Democracy: A Political History of the American Rich.* New York: Broadway Books, 2002.

Pierson, Paul. *Politics in Time: History, Institutions, and Social Analysis.* Princeton, NJ: Princeton University Press, 2004.

Pitch, Anthony. *The Burning of Washington: The British Invasion of 1814.* Annapolis, MD: Naval Institute Press, 1998.

Porter, Kenneth Wiggins. *John Jacob Astor: Business Man.* 2 vols. New York: Russell and Russell, 1966.

Posner, Eric. "Emergency Powers Let the President Borrow beyond the Debt Limit." *New York Times,* January 29, 2014.

Quimby, Robert S. *The U.S. Army in the War of 1812: An Operational and Command Study.* 2 vols. East Lansing: Michigan State University Press, 1997.

Raguet, Condy. *An Inquiry into the Causes of the Present State of the Circulating Medium of the United States.* Philadelphia: Moses Thomas, 1815.

Rakove, Jack N. *Original Meanings: Politics and Ideas in the Making of the Constitution.* New York: Alfred A. Knopf, 1997.

Ransom, Roger L. *Conflict and Compromise: The Political Economy of Slavery, Emancipation, and the American Civil War.* Cambridge, UK: Cambridge University Press, 1993.

Rappaport, George David. *Stability and Change in Revolutionary Pennsylvania: Banking, Politics, and Social Structure.* University Park: Pennsylvania State University Press, 1996.

Redlich, Fritz. *The Molding of American Banking: Men and Ideas.* New York: Johnson Reprint, 1968.

Remini, Robert V. *Andrew Jackson.* Vol. 2, *The Course of American Freedom, 1822–1832.* New York: History Book Club, 1998.

———. *Henry Clay: Statesman for the Union.* New York: W. W. Norton, 1991.

Reubens, Beatrice. "Burr, Hamilton, and the Manhattan Company: Part I: Gaining the Charter." *Political Science Quarterly* 72, no. 4 (December 1957): 578–607.

Riker, William H. *The Art of Political Manipulation.* New Haven, CT: Yale University Press, 1986.

Risjord, Norman K. *The Old Republicans: Southern Conservatism in the Age of Jefferson.* New York: Columbia University Press, 1965.

Robertson, David Brian. *The Constitution and America's Destiny.* Cambridge, UK: Cambridge University Press, 2005.

Roland, Daniel Dean. "Peter Buell Porter and Self-Interest in American Politics." PhD diss., Claremont Graduate School (History), 1990.

Rosen, Gary. *American Compact: James Madison and the Problem of Founding.* Lawrence: University Press of Kansas, 1999.

Rosenfeld, Richard N. *American Aurora: A Democratic-Republican Returns: The Suppressed History of Our Nation's Beginnings and the Heroic Newspaper That Tried to Report It.* New York: St. Martin's Press, 1998.

Schlesinger, Arthur Jr. *The Age of Jackson.* Boston: Little, Brown, 1946.

Schuman, Howard E. *Politics and the Budget: The Struggle between the President and the Congress.* 3rd ed. Englewood Cliffs, NJ: Prentice Hall, 1992.

Schur, Leon M. "The Second Bank of the United States and the Inflation after the War of 1812." *Journal of Political Economy* 68, no. 2 (April 1960): 118–34.

Schwartz, Anna. "The Beginning of Competitive Banking in Philadelphia, 1782–1809." *Journal of Political Economy* 55, no. 5 (October 1947): 417–31.

Schweikart, Larry. *Banking in the American South from the Age of Jackson to Reconstruction.* Baton Rouge: Louisiana State University Press, 1987.

Segal, Jeffrey A. "Perceived Qualifications and Ideology of Supreme Court Nominees, 1937–2012." http://www.stonybrook.edu/commcms/polisci/jsegal/QualTable.pdf.

Segal, Jeffrey A., and Harold J. Spaeth. *The Supreme Court and the Attitudinal Model Revisited.* Cambridge, UK: Cambridge University Press, 2002.

Sellers, Charles. *The Market Revolution: Jacksonian America, 1815–1846.* New York: Oxford University Press, 1991.

Sharp, James Roger. *The Deadlocked Election of 1800: Jefferson, Burr, and the Union in the Balance.* Lawrence: University Press of Kansas, 2010.

Shultz, William J., and M. R. Cain. *Financial Development of the United States.* New York: Prentice Hall, 1937.

Siegan, Bernard H. *The Supreme Court's Constitution: An Inquiry into Judicial Review and Its Impact on Society.* New Brunswick, NJ: Transaction Books, 1987.

Skowronek, Stephen. *The Politics Presidents Make: Leadership from John Adams to Bill Clinton.* Cambridge, MA: Belknap Press of Harvard University Press, 1997.

Smith, David R., and Robert Jefferson Dillard. "The Powers to Regulate Money, Weights, and Measures and to Punish Counterfeiting." In *The Powers of the U.S. Congress: Where Constitutional Authority Begins and Ends,* edited by Brien Hallett, 69–79. Santa Barbara, CA: ABC-CLIO, 2016.

Smith, Jean Edward. *John Marshall: Definer of a Nation.* New York: Henry Holt, 1996.

Smith, Rogers M. "Political Jurisprudence, the 'New Institutionalism,' and the Future of Public Law." *American Political Science Review* 82, no. 1 (March 1988): 89–108.

Smith, Walter Buckingham. *Economic Aspects of the Second Bank of the United States*. Cambridge, MA: Harvard University Press, 1953.

Sobel, Robert. *Panic on Wall Street: A History of America's Financial Disasters*. Washington, DC: Beard Books, 1999.

Somin, Ilya. "A Taxing, but Potentially Hopeful Decision." *SCOTUSblog*, June 28, 2012. http://www.scotusblog.com/2012/06/a-taxing-but-potentially-hopeful-decision/.

Spaulding, Elbridge G. *History of the Legal Tender Paper Money Issued during the Great Rebellion*. Buffalo, NY: Express Printing, 1869.

Stagg, J. C. A. *Mr. Madison's War: Politics, Diplomacy, and Warfare in the Early American Republic, 1783–1830*. Princeton, NJ: Princeton University Press, 1983.

Stephenson, Donald Grier Jr. "The Waite Court." In *The Supreme Court: Controversies, Cases, and Characters from John Jay to John Roberts*, edited by Paul Finkelman, 309–405. Santa Barbara, CA: ABC-CLIO, 2014.

Stewart, Donald H. *The Opposition Press of the Federalist Period*. Albany: State University of New York Press, 1969.

Stokes, Howard Kemble. *Chartered Banking in Rhode Island, 1791–1900*. Providence, RI: Prestor & Rounds, 1902.

Streeck, Wolfgang, and Kathleen Thelen. "Introduction: Institutional Change in Advanced Political Economies." In *Beyond Continuity: Institutional Change in Advanced Political Economies*, edited by Wolfgang Streeck and Kathleen Thelen, 1–39. New York: Oxford University Press, 2005.

Sylla, Richard. "Experimental Federalism: The Economics of American Government, 1789–1914." In *The Cambridge Economic History of the United States*, vol. 2, *The Long Nineteenth Century*, edited by Stanley L. Engerman and Robert E. Gallman, 483–542. Cambridge, UK: Cambridge University Press, 2000.

———. "Reversing Financial Reversals: Government and the Financial System since 1789." In *Government and the American Economy: A New History*, by Price Fishback et al., 115–47. Chicago: University of Chicago Press, 2007.

Sylla, Richard, John Legler, and John Wallis. "Banks and State Public Finance in the New Republic: The United States, 1790–1860." *Journal of Economic History* 47, no. 2 (June 1987): 391–403.

Sylla, Richard, Robert E. Wright, and David J. Cowen. "Alexander Hamilton, Central Banker: Crisis Management during the U.S. Financial Panic of 1792." *Business History Review* 83, special issue no. 1 (Spring 2009): 61–86.

"Taxes." *Orange County Patriot*, January 11, 1814.

Thayer, James Bradley. "Legal Tender." *Harvard Law Review* 1, no. 2 (May 1887): 73–97.

Thelen, Kathleen. *How Institutions Evolve: The Political Economy of Skills in Germany, Britain, the United States, and Japan*. Cambridge, UK: Cambridge University Press, 2004.

Thomas, George. *The Founders and the Idea of a National University: Constituting the American Mind*. Cambridge, UK: Cambridge University Press, 2014.

Thomas, John L. "Introduction." In *John C. Calhoun: A Profile*, edited by John L. Thomas, vii–xxi. New York: Hill and Wang, 1968.

Timberlake, Richard H. *Constitutional Money: A Review of the Supreme Court's Monetary Decisions*. Cambridge, UK: Cambridge University Press, 2013.

———. *Monetary Policy in the United States: An Intellectual and Institutional History.* Chicago: University of Chicago Press, 1993.

———. "The Specie Standard and Central Banking in the United States before 1860." *Journal of Economic History* 21, no. 3 (September 1961): 318–41.

Torre, Jose R. *Political Economy of Sentiment: Paper Credit and the Scottish Enlightenment in Early Republic Boston, 1780–1820.* London: Pickering and Chatto, 2007.

Tucker, Spencer C., and Frank T. Reuter. *Injured Honor: The* Chesapeake-Leopard *Affair, June 22, 1807.* Annapolis, MD: Naval Institute Press, 1996.

Tyler, John. "Veto Message." August 16, 1841. http://www.presidency.ucsb.edu/ws/?pid =67557.

———. "Veto Message on the Creation of a Fiscal Corporation." September 9, 1841. https://millercenter.org/the-presidency/presidential-speeches/september-9-1841 -veto-message-creation-fiscal-corporation.

Urofsky, Melvin I. *Dissent and the Supreme Court: Its Role in the Court's History and the Nation's Constitutional Dialogue.* New York: Vintage, 2017.

Walsh, John J. *Early Banks in the District of Columbia.* Washington, DC: Catholic University of America Press, 1940.

Walters, Raymond Jr. *Alexander James Dallas: Lawyer, Politician, Financier: 1759– 1817.* Philadelphia: University of Pennsylvania Press, 1943.

———. "The Origins of the Second Bank of the United States." *Journal of Political Economy* 53, no. 2 (June 1945): 115–31.

Warren, Charles. *The Supreme Court in United States History.* Vol. 3, *1856–1918.* Boston: Little, Brown, 1923.

Watson, Alan D. *Wilmington, North Carolina, to 1861.* Jefferson, NC: McFarland, 2003.

Weber, Warren E. "Early State Banks in the United States: How Many Were There and When Did They Exist?" *Journal of Economic History* 66, no. 6 (June 2006): 433–55.

Weiner, Greg. *Madison's Metronome: The Constitution, Majority Rule, and the Tempo of American Politics.* Lawrence: University Press of Kansas, 2012.

Werner, Walter, and Steven T. Smith. *Wall Street.* New York: Columbia University Press, 1991.

Wert, Justin J. *Habeas Corpus in America: The Politics of Individual Rights.* Lawrence: University Press of Kansas, 2011.

Wettereau, James O. "The Branches of the First Bank of the United States." *Journal of Economic History* 2, Supplement: The Tasks of Economic History (December 1942): 66–100.

———. *Documentary History of the First Bank of the United States.* In James O. Wettereau Research Papers, Box 27, Book "B."

———. "The First Bank of the United States: Government Depository and Embryonic Central Bank, 1791–1811." In James O. Wettereau Research Papers, Box 4, Folder 2.

———. "Letters from Two Business Men to Alexander Hamilton on Federal Fiscal Policy, November, 1789." *Journal of Economic and Business History* 3, no. 4 (August 1931): 667–86.

———. "New Light on the First Bank of the United States." *Pennsylvania Magazine of History and Biography* 61, no. 3 (July 1937): 263–85.

———. "The Oldest Bank Building in the United States." *Transactions of the American Philosophical Society* 43, no. 1 (1953): 70–79.

White, Adam J. "Marshalling Precedent: With Nod to Predecessor, Roberts Affirms Mandate." *The Weekly Standard*, June 28, 2012. http://www.weeklystandard.com/marshalling-precedent-with-nod-to-predecessor-roberts-affirms-mandate/article/647945.

White, Bill. *America's Fiscal Constitution: Its Triumph and Collapse.* New York: PublicAffairs, 2014.

White, G. Edward. *Law in American History.* Vol. 1, *From the Colonial Years through the Civil War.* New York: Oxford University Press: 2012.

Whittington, Keith. "Judicial Review of Congress before the Civil War." *Georgetown Law Review* 97, no. 5 (May 2009): 1257–1332.

———. *Political Foundations of Judicial Supremacy: The Presidency, the Supreme Court, and Constitutional Leadership in U.S. History.* Princeton, NJ: Princeton University Press, 2007.

———. "The Road Not Taken: *Dred Scott*, Judicial Authority, and Political Questions." *Journal of Politics* 63, no. 2 (May 2001): 365–91.

Wilburn, Jean Alexander. *Biddle's Bank: The Crucial Years.* New York: Columbia University Press, 1967.

Wilentz, Sean. *The Rise of American Democracy: Jefferson to Lincoln.* New York: W. W. Norton, 2005.

Williams, George Walton. *History of Banking in South Carolina from 1712 to 1900.* Charleston, SC: Walker, Evans & Cogswell, 1903.

Williams, Jerre S. *The Supreme Court Speaks.* Freeport, NY: Books for Libraries Press, 1970.

"Will the Southern Banks Pay Specie Again?" *Boston Daily Advertiser*, June 15, 1815.

Wilson, Thomas. *The Power "to Coin" Money: The Exercise of Monetary Powers by the Congress.* Armonk, NY: M. E. Sharpe, 1992.

Womack, Roy Douglas. *An Analysis of the Credit Controls of the Second Bank of the United States.* New York: Arno Press, 1978.

Wood, Gordon. *Empire of Liberty: A History of the Early Republic, 1789–1815.* New York: Oxford University Press, 2009.

Wood, John H. "Monetary Policy." In *The Oxford Companion to American Politics*, vol. 2, edited by David Coates, 133–35. New York: Oxford University Press, 2012.

Woodward, Bob. *Maestro: Greenspan's Fed and the American Boom.* New York: Simon & Schuster, 2001.

Wright, Robert E. "Bank Ownership and Lending Patterns in New York and Pennsylvania, 1781–1831." *Business History Review* 73, no. 1 (Spring 1999): 40–60.

———. *The First Wall Street: Chestnut Street, Philadelphia, and the Birth of American Finance.* Chicago: University of Chicago Press, 2005.

———. *One Nation under Debt: Hamilton, Jefferson, and the History of What We Owe.* New York: McGraw-Hill, 2008.

———. *Origins of Commercial Banking in America, 1750–1800.* Lanham, MD: Rowman & Littlefield, 2001.

―――. "Thomas Willing (1731–1821): Philadelphia Financier and Forgotten Founding Father." *Pennsylvania History* 63, no. 4 (October 1996): 525–60.

Zackin, Emily. *Looking for Rights in All the Wrong Places: Why State Constitutions Contain America's Positive Rights.* Princeton, NJ: Princeton University Press, 2013.

INDEX

Adams, John, 74, 132, 135, 188n83
Adams, John Quincy, 146
agriculture, 10, 35, 43, 46
Albany Bank, 40
Albany Daily Advertiser, 110
Alston, Willis, 89
Amar, Akhil Reed, 129
American Enterprise Institute, 51
American Political Development (APD), 158–59, 170, 188n89
American Quarterly Review, 149
America's Fiscal Constitution (White), 170
Ames, Fisher, 27–28, 179n47
Article I, Section 8 (US Constitution), 2, 29, 68, 81, 83, 91, 112–13, 121, 126–27, 129, 132, 141, 151, 159, 179n47, 220n11, 222n60. *See also specific clauses*
Article I, Section 10 (US Constitution), 113, 161, 170. *See also* Contract Clause
Article VI (US Constitution), 8, 130
Astor, John Jacob, 31, 100
Atwater, Jesse, 65–66, 194n1
Aurora General Advertiser, 65

Baltimore Patriot, 109
banco mania, 39–40, 186n47
"bank-mongers," 46, 188n83
Bank of Alexandria, 45–46, 48
Bank of Cape Fear, 41–42
Bank of Maryland, 24, 56, 121, 182n3, 183n12
Bank of New York, 37, 39–40, 43, 56–57, 63, 67, 90, 180n56, 182n3, 183n12, 191n27, 204n64

Bank of North America: constitutional interpretation and, 24, 180n60; institutional conversion and, 56–58, 191n27; institutional drift and, 34, 36–37, 41, 182n3, 183n12, 183n14, 184n28
Bank of Pennsylvania, 41
Bank of the United States: attracting/repelling branches of, 44–47; Baltimore branch of, 55–56, 58–59, 63, 121, 136, 185n32, 193n49, 213–14; banco mania and, 39–40, 186n47; Biddle and, 144–50, 182n8, 216n19, 216n21, 217n38, 217n47; Boston branch of, 54–57, 65, 185n32; branch issues and, 12, 28, 33–38; capital of, 31–32; Charleston branch of, 37, 60, 191n14; charter extension for, 4, 8, 12, 49, 60, 64, 66, 72, 140, 151; Compromise of 1816 and, 94–97, 103–5, 110–13, 117, 119; constitutional interpretation and, 13–15, 21, 30; dissolution of, 65–66, 70, 106, 111; distinction between first and second, 206n105; federal deposits and, 57, 65–66, 191n26, 193n58; incorporation and, 13, 21, 30, 40, 55, 67, 76, 79, 81, 87, 94, 102, 125, 148, 152, 179n41; institutional conversion and, 51–68; institutional drift and, 31–49; *McCulloch v. Maryland* and, 121–39; monetary power of, 51, 54, 61, 65, 145; New York branch and, 39, 43, 55–57, 67; objective of sound money and, 141; ordinary politics and, 5–9; organization of, 33–38; recharter and, 69–72, 76–80, 83–92, 95, 98, 105, 110, 118, 127, 142,